Dear Sarah,

I wish you a blessed time during christmas in unusual times!

I like this book because it draws us closer the the root of our faith —

— The God of Israel —

Enjoy reading and discovering

Yours Antje

Dec. 2020

BREAKING THE VEIL OF
SILENCE

JOBST BITTNER

BREAKING THE VEIL OF
SILENCE

JOBST BITTNER

TOS Publishing · Tübingen

Jobst Bittner, Breaking the Veil of Silence
Copyright © 2013 TOS Publishing (TOS GmbH), Tübingen, Germany
ISBN 978-3-9812441-8-2
All rights reserved.

Copyright of the German Original © 2011 TOS Verlag (TOS GmbH), Tübingen, Germany
Original Title: Die Decke des Schweigens; ISBN 978-3-9812441-7-5
All rights reserved.

Printed in U.S.A.
Translation: Tina Pompe
Layout: Stefan Gaertner
Cover Design: Christian Niklas
Cover Photograph: Yessica Baur

I dedicate this book to my wife, friend,
co-laborer and called in the Kingdom of God.

"Now the threat to my country cannot be overstated. Those who dismiss it are sticking their heads in the sand. Less than seven decades after six million Jews were murdered, Iran's leaders deny the Holocaust of the Jewish people, while calling for the annihilation of the Jewish state.

Leaders who spew such venom, should be banned from every respectable forum on the planet. But there is something that makes the outrage even greater: The lack of outrage. In much of the international community, the calls for our destruction are met with utter silence."

Benjamin Netanyahu
in his address to the U.S. Congress on May 24, 2011

ACKNOWLEDGEMENTS

There are a lot of people that I owe thanks to. First of all my family, who stepped back patiently; then my friends in the church, who released me time and time again without complaining.

My thanks also go to the entire TOS church, who always stood behind me with their support. You are the coolest gang on earth! Tina Pompe did the translation, Lynn McNally and Florian Kubsch the proofreading, Christian Niklas designed the powerful cover, and Stefan Gärtner was responsible for publishing. To all of you, a big "thank you" – you are great!

Last, but not least, I have to mention my friend Ted Pearce here, without whose encouragement I would surely never have written this book. Here it is, Ted – so you don't have to write it now.

Jobst Bittner

CONTENTS

FOREWORD

This is a book that could only have been written by a German pastor and activist with a solid theological background, a deep devotion to the Holy Spirit, and a lifelong commitment to Israel. Jobst Bittner is such a man.

He studied under the late, heralded professor Martin Hengel, famous for his work on Judaism and Hellenism, and so Jobst has a thorough understanding of the Jewish roots of the Christian faith, a subject of foundational importance to this book. And as a pastor who believes in taking the gospel to the streets, he both speaks and acts, putting legs to his faith and bringing a living and public demonstration. He knows that only the power of the Holy Spirit can truly deliver the captives and make the brokenhearted whole. Finally, as a man devoted to Israel and the salvation of the Jewish people, he can assess the painful legacy of the German church, but always with a hopeful eye that looks forward.

Other German Christian leaders have addressed the veil of silence that hung over the church during the fateful years of the Holocaust, among whom was Basilea (formerly Dr. Klara) Schlink, founder of the Evangelical Sisterhood of Mary.

With anguish of heart she wrote in 1958:
"We Germans were Satan's henchmen. In the midst of our people this hell was created... We are personally to blame. We all have to admit that if we, the entire Christian community, had stood up as

one man and if, after the burning of the synagogues [on Kristall-nacht], we had gone out on the streets and voiced our disapproval, rung the church bells, and somehow boycotted the actions of the S.S., the devil's vassals would probably not have been at such liberty to pursue their evil schemes. But we lacked the ardor of love – love that is never passive, love that cannot bear it when its fellow men are in misery, particularly when they are subjected to such appalling treatment and tortured to death. Indeed, if we had loved God, we would not have endured seeing those houses of God set ablaze; and holy, divine wrath would have filled our souls."

(Israel, My Chosen People: A German Confession Before God and the Jews (Eng. trans., Old Tappan, NJ: Chosen, 1987), 39, 42-43)

But this is 2011, not 1958, and Pastor Jobst contends that the veil of silence – a multifaceted veil of silence – remains over the older and younger generations, and this veil must be torn down by iden-tificational repentance and a positive, public witness.

In response, a sincere critic might ask, "Are we to endlessly repent of the sins of past generations? And is it even our place to do so?" Those are certainly worthy questions, and in my opinion, this kind of repentance is called for when: 1) The wounds of the past sins remain, which is certainly the case with regard to the subject matter of this book; and 2) The seeds of the past sins remain, and this too cannot be denied today.

And yet this is certainly not just another book about German Christians and the Holocaust. Certainly not. It is a call to dig deeper, to uproot every destructive and hurtful remnant that remains, and to move forward into wholeness, freedom, and life. And it brings a very specific call to a very literal March of Life, exalting Jesus and displaying what it really means to be one of His disciples.

As a Jewish follower of Jesus, myself indebted to Gentile Christians who introduced me to Israel's Messiah and Lord forty years ago, I commend this book to you.

Dr. Michael L. Brown

PREFACE

The development of this book is the result of a process of several years. The more I started thinking about the "Veil of Silence", the more I discovered how deeply every area of our lives is affected by it. More experience and revelation kept coming. Now I am able to present the finished book, and hope it will be helpful to you in coming to terms with this topic. The "Veil of Silence" probably concerns you more than you would have thought at first.

We are living under a veil of silence without even realizing it. It is passed on from generation to generation, preventing reconciliation, healing and restoration. Is the war generation's silence concerning the Holocaust something we still carry deep within ourselves today? Unfortunately, the annihilation of the European Jews never really had a place in German family memory. It was only in the early '80s that the long-term consequences of the war on the following generations were discovered in Germany. Most families in Germany today still live in the shadow of the past.

I would like to describe a phenomenon that may have different backgrounds and reasons, but that still goes for both the successive generations of the German war generation, as well as the generation of Holocaust survivors. The descendants of both groups started discovering only very slowly how much they have been weighed down by the burden of their family history. Step by step they are learning to speak about it and bring their family story into the light, so it can be worked through. The descendants of both generations only discovered slowly how much they have suffered under the burden of their respective family histories. Many Christians in German churches and congregations would like to finally close the book on the past of National Socialism, and to avoid it coming back into view over and over again; unfortunately, this does not conform to reality. Both the victims and the perpetrators still suffer from the heritage of their past, and they will only be able to experience healing and restoration once they perceive one another, forgive, and come together in reconciliation. This cannot happen unless the veil of silence over them is broken. I will try to present a biblical-theological perspective, a church history perspective, and a psychological perspective on where the veil of silence comes from, and how it can be broken. Let's start with our own biographical experience here in Tübingen, a university town that used to be one of the ideological centers during the Nazi era which produced executors and mass murderers.

The Family Level

In this book I will deal with the veil of silence on different levels. The level that probably concerns us most personally is the family level. More than three quarters of German families live under the veil of silence. They are children and grandchildren of the war generation, and still carry the burdens of guilt or trauma, as well as the experiences of flight and expulsion. Their common mark is silence. Many of them are going through endless deserts without ever seeing any hope of change. They have learned to put up with emotional disorders, fears, blockages, bonding disorders, and inner rigidity, without ever really finding the cause or truly getting to know the liberating power of the cross.

Once the generational silence is broken and the untold stories are shared, this opens completely new possibilities to find inner peace, security and healing.

Many Christians are missing out on a very important development that has long since become "trendy" in society. They are convinced that all the working through that is necessary has already taken place. It is about time, they say, to leave behind the old guilt complex and to look ahead. But it is amazing to see that the working through of the Nazi period in the general public has actually intensified. Genealogy, the research of family history, has been booming for years. Ancestry research is no longer just a quirky pastime for aristocrats and retirees. Dealing with one's roots has become trendy, and is considered a symbol of an increased need for identity. The basis for any change is the honest facing of the past. Personally, I had been struggling with this for years, and had to give up my own inner resistance. This happened during a service when I had the privilege of speaking before numerous Holocaust survivors. I experienced a completely different reality there. My speaking German stirred painful memories in many, and the ghosts of the past rose again. After a time of healing and reconciliation, they started sharing the fears and traumas they had inherited from their parents and grandparents. Millions of the second and third generation of Holocaust survivors are still suffering from the effects. Strangely enough, they are still captive under a speechlessness similar to the descendants of the perpetrators. For as long as the generation of victims and perpetrators are still suffering under the heritage of the past, Christians can never think of their responsibility as over.

The Historical Level

Another level of the veil of silence is the historical level. With the rebuilding process of Germany after 1945 came the tedious process of working through the past. Nazi perpetrators attempted to go into hiding; and they were largely successful. Followers and accessories took refuge in the silence of everyday life and tried

23

to repress the past. Only 20 years later, the veil of silence slowly started cracking. In the face of six million Jews brutally murdered during the Holocaust, and the strategic mass murder, meticulously implemented, of 30 million people in Eastern Europe, you cannot help but wonder whether it is permissible for Germans to hide behind the guilt of fanatic individuals at all. Hidden behind the silence was a collective moral guilt, the responsibility of a silent majority who had been watching the murderous proceedings and had not done anything. During recent decades, Germany has seen an unparalleled working through of the time of National Socialism. Germany's past was the topic of countless conferences with much repentance. With the fall of the Berlin Wall in 1989 and the reunification, the Lord visibly healed our land. And still today, there hardly is a day without reports, educational programs, and discussions about the Holocaust and other war crimes. Holocaust denial is a punishable offense. Yearly government consultations between Israel and Germany testify to this new solidarity. There are a great number of churches who are in lively contact with Israel.

The Level of Church History

But still, this veil of silence has not yet disappeared. There is an anti-Semitism that is deeply rooted in us, and that reaches back far beyond the time of National Socialism. This kind of anti-Semitism is like a negative seed that is deeply hidden in our Western culture and embedded in our thinking, so it can break out again and again.

Whether it is in the form of downplaying the Holocaust, a denial of Israel's right to exist, or anti-Jewish attitudes – the common mark of this negative seed is silence. It is the same silence as at the time of the silent majority during the Nazi era. In the guise of indifference and passivity, it has found its way deep into our churches. Both are hallmarks of the "genetic defect" that Christianity has been carrying ever since it separated from its Jewish roots. In order to prove this assumption, we will take a closer look at the church history dimension of the veil of silence. Here our main question will be why the church in the Western world has lost its authority. Despite resistance in the mainly Hellenistic Mediterranean, the early church was able to spread very rapidly. At the cost of losing its Hebrew roots, it exchanged its spiritual power for secular authority, and finally became the source of centuries of suffering for the Jewish people. Another important question asked in this book will be why we can only regain the authority of the church through openly confessing the guilt of the Christians toward the Jewish people, and through publicly standing by our Hebrew heritage. This leads us to consider what it is that the church has to face, and what means to use. Before we fall into old patterns of thought, we should actually think again about the central part of "identificational repentance" and the controversial issue of "spiritual warfare".

The Supernatural Level

I am also using the term "Veil of Silence" as a synonym for the struggle with the invisible world. The Bible speaks about darkness that covers the land. It keeps pointing out that sin can darken a nation, and cover the earth like a dark cloud (Is 60:2). What this cloud is made up of actually seems irrelevant to me. What is crucial is to see that the sin of cities and nations will not be blown over, and so will not automatically become less or obsolete. It still affects people and their descendants, preventing healing and restoration. We found that despite years of earnest efforts in prayer, we were not able to overcome this darkness. The harder we tried and added more commitment to our efforts, the thicker and more impenetrable this veil seemed to become. I will tell you in this book how the ground was pulled from underneath darkness, and how it broke. Part of this is the testimony of our city, where I have been living with my wife for the past 30 years now. With our own eyes we were able to see the spiritual situation in the city change completely.

The National Level

Part of our city's history is the March of Life movement, which by 2012 has reached and stirred hundreds of thousands in 80 cities and 12 different nations. The backdrop to this movement are the so-called death marches that are part of the darkest chapter in German history. Just before the end of WWII, the traces of the concentrations camps were supposed to be eliminated. The emaciated inmates were forced to march along the roads of Germany for weeks. 250,000 people, at least a quarter of the total number of victims of the concentration camps, perished during the last five months of the war on such death marches, right before the very eyes of the civilian population. No civilian could have missed this mass murder. It was the time when ordinary people became murderers. The death marches in Germany stand for a "veil of silence". Tens of thousands were involved, either directly as helpers, or indirectly as onlookers. These marches took place in broad daylight – "on our doorstep" – and they were the final, brutal culmination of the Holocaust, in plain sight of the German population. The "March of Life" sums up everything included in "Breaking the Veil of Silence". So in the final chapter of this book I will tell you more about this. It presents what can happen when people take a stand to break the veil of silence – personally, in their families and in their cities and nations. Many of them will get to share their personal stories and testify to darkness leaving their lives, and healing taking place. The March of Life is a living sign that curse can be transformed into blessing, and darkness into light. Its confession is like an unmistakable signal that Christians have overcome the genetic defect of silence concerning Israel and the Jewish people.

For Zion's sake I will not keep silent, for Jerusalem's sake I will not remain quiet, till her vindication shines out like the dawn, her salvation like a blazing torch. (Isa. 62:1)

There is a proverb that says, "Speech is silver, silence is golden." For some people, this is a good reason to think of silence as something very positive. Someone who can keep silent is thought to be highly principled and strong. In light of the Bible, however, we see a completely different picture. The highest expression of God's love to mankind is the ability of direct communication.

The Biblical-Theological Level

We will also take the biblical approach to the phenomenon of silence, taking a look at what the Bible has to say about this topic. I actually do not want to let the proverb "Speech is silver, silence is golden" pass unchallenged. A child who does not learn how to express itself and how to communicate with its environment is in serious trouble, and needs help urgently. Married couples who no longer communicate have closed their hearts to one another and are in serious danger of jeopardizing their marriage. A church or congregation has lost its life once silence has come upon them. How much pain, trauma, and things not dealt with in the past can be hidden behind a person's silence? And how much healing, restoration, and change can happen when somebody manages to break the silence!

After presenting the different levels of the veil of silence to you, I will begin the book as I had initially intended to. As I mentioned in the beginning, the work on this subject has taken me several years, and in the course of time, many things can change, also the preface to a book.

"In the beginning God created the heavens and the earth. It was formless and empty" – this is what we read right at the beginning of Genesis – "and darkness was upon the face of the deep." (Gen. 1:1-3). The darkness was shrouded in silence until it was broken by the voice of God. When He lifted His voice, He broke the silence and said, "Let there be light", darkness lost its power, and there was light. This was the start of creation, and the beginning of God's story with mankind. The battle against darkness has never changed. Whenever we raise our voices and break the silence, darkness loses its foundation. To this very day, marriages, families, cities, and nations are covered by a veil of silence. Fathers remain silent toward their children, and the following generations do not have the strength to break their forefathers' veil of silence. However, we find this same veil of silence also in churches and congregations whenever hearts have become closed to one another. But this is only an outward sign of a much deeper truth. The veil of silence represents the spirit of this age. The Body of Christ is completely helpless before it, to the point where it has taken away their voice completely. As the German nation, we know what it means to be covered by darkness and to lie captive in the dark. I call it the veil of silence. The majority of Germans stood by watching the atrocities of the Nazis; they were called the "silent majority". Without them, the Holocaust would never have taken place. We will have to decide whether we want to be part of the "silent majority" or not.

CHAPTER 1

THE STORY OF A FORMER NAZI CITY

The small university town of Tübingen is situated in Southern Germany, about 30 minutes from Stuttgart. It is a typical German town with old, medieval houses and a river slowly winding its way along the picturesque house fronts. On warm summer days the students sit along the river walls, watching the long punts go by, stoked along by long poles like the gondolas in Venice. Actually, Tübingen is the typical image of a German idyll. Hardly any of the many tourists have any notion that this pretty town has such an ugly and dark history of anti-Semitism, and used to belong to the ideological trailblazers during the Nazi era.

I want to reinforce this with a few facts, so you can get a better idea of what this means. Jews lived in the city, probably starting in the mid 13th century. Their settlement was centered around the "Judengasse" (Jew Alley), which still exists under this name today. In 1348-49, the Black Plague broke out in Germany. The population of entire cities and regions was wiped out. It will remain guess-work whether the persecution and expulsion of Jews in Tübingen first started then. But in any case, the full fury of the rage of the population was directed against the Jews, who were suspected of poisoning the town's well, causing the "Black Death". It is very likely that this was the first time for Jews to be expelled and killed in Tübingen. In the course of more than 1,000 years of history, up to the deportations of 1942, there has only ever been a period of 180 years that Jews were allowed to live in the city. Their life of suffering was marked by persecution, pogroms[1] and repeated expulsions. By 1471, Jews had settled in the city again; but they were expelled again from the city, and the entire region, for the next 400 years by the founder of the university, Duke Eberhard the Bearded. A few years later, the plague broke out again. This time, it killed both the father and grandfather of the founder of the university, along with a third of the population of Tübingen. Perhaps the only bright spot during that time was the important philosopher and humanist Johannes Reuchlin (1455–1522). He was the first significant scholar of Hebrew as a non-Jew to learn the Hebrew language and script. He studied, lived, and taught in Tübingen, and became advisor to Duke Eberhard the Bearded. In later years, he publicly advocated the cause of the Jews, despite all opposition.[2]

It was only in the mid-eighteen hundreds that the Jews slowly started returning to the city. They built a beautiful synagogue, which later was demolished and burnt down by SA and SS thugs during Kristallnacht. When Hitler took over on January 30th, 1933, it was a very quiet thing in Tübingen. This hardly comes as a surprise, as the racial policy of the Nazis fell on very fertile ground, well-prepared by centuries of hidden anti-Semitism that had become part of the "cultural codex" of the middle class. The old and beautifully painted city hall became a voluntary spearhead of the racial ideology of the Nazis.[3] Of his own free will, the mayor of Tübingen supported anti-Jewish decisions, and terminated all business contracts to Jewish companies. He chaired the town council that earned Tübingen sad fame by making it one of the first cities in German territory to have implemented the isolation and discrimination of Jews by banning "Jews and foreigners" from the public open-air bath as early as 1933. Less than three months after Hitler's takeover, democracy was abolished, the hardly existent opposition done away with and silenced, and the dictatorship was established.[4]

In front of the city hall of Tübingen there is the old market square which saw a memorable mass demonstration on April 1, 1933. The NSDAP had established a "Committee against Jewish Atrocity Propaganda" in Tübingen that had called for this demonstration. The basic principles of anti-Semitic propaganda used at this Nazi event have not changed to this day, and are still used in the modern shape of Western anti-Israeli attitudes. Therefore, I want to go into this a little deeper now, and expose you to a passage taken from one of the speeches at this demonstration: "We had to oppose this renewed Jewish inflammatory propaganda. Nobody ever dreamt of starting a boycott. We were forced into it. ... Because it is about Germany, nobody must stay behind in this defensive battle."[5] As the party carried "moral legitimacy", at least in the speaker's eye, it was justified in going to war against the Jews, and winning. The true victims, the Jews, are made out to be the aggressors, and the perpetrators become victims. And what is more, the NSDAP appear to be protecting the country from the alleged danger. So this actually reverses the pangs of conscience, and the Nazis' own aggression is projected onto the Jews, which helps to legitimize and morally justify their counter-attack. This way, the aggressor is portrayed as the legitimate authority and seen as the apparent deliverer from alleged evil. This reversal and deception permitted the national socialists the sense of acting righteously, and caused the disappearance of all inhibitions to make the aggressive persecution and silent complicity of an anti-Semitic bourgeois middle class possible in the first place.[6] We need to learn from history and take a careful look whenever anyone on the political scene or in the media points the finger at Israel with moralizing remarks.

Perhaps it is due to the basic anti-Jewish attitude of the founder of Tübingen University that it was this university that paved the ideological way for the "final solution of the Jewish question".

31

But certainly, the adaptation, as well as the unresisting acceptance, on the part of the citizens of Tübingen in the time prior to 1933 provided the ideal environment for it. Already in the 1920s, radical anti-Semitism flourished at the university, and there were only very few Jews among the professors. After 1929, there were none at all. So the "Jewish question" did not even arise at all for the University of Tübingen, as "Tübingen had always known how to keep Jewish professors away without losing many words about it."[7] Professors from Tübingen used the "Tübingen Society for Racial Hygiene" founded in 1924 to spread their ideas of a healthy, "racially pure" people. After the university was the first in Germany to proudly announce that it was now "free of Jews", it established a new institute for the "Research of the Jewish Question" that was devoted to scientific combat against Judaism and anything Jewish in Germany. The local press praised the new figurehead frantically. The research of the scientists was able to prove at last, so they said, that "anti-Semitism is not a matter of mayhem, but rather of serious scientific insight".[8] Eugenics and Racial Science had become the new leading sciences for the scientific legitimization of National Socialist ideology.[9]

After 1938, Tübingen evolved into a center of both theoretical and practical racial research. The history of the Anatomical Institute in Tübingen after 1933 can serve as an example of how unreservedly some members of the university accepted the criminal structures of the Nazi state. The city cemetery has one section, simply called "Burial Ground X". Here the remains of the corpses that were used in the Anatomical Institute of Tübingen for research and training purposes for future medical doctors were buried. For this purpose, they used the victims of the Nazi regime – executed Jews, gypsies, Poles, Russians, as well as those who had died as an inhumane consequence of so-called medical experiments. There is no question the anatomists made use of the plentiful supply of corpses from execution sites, correction camps and prisoner-of-war camps. The university provided special career opportunities to bio-scientists who offered themselves directly for the implementation of the Nazi ideology. One of these was the senior physician for the Psychiatric Clinic in Tübingen, Robert Ritter (1901–1951), a leading racial theoretician and head of the newly formed Institute for Racial Hygiene. The results of his research and surveys were supposed to provide medical proof for the idea of racial superiority, and were used as scientific arguments for the systematic murder of gypsies. The Race Theory developed in Tübingen attempted to provide the Nazi regime with definitions for the term "Jew" in order to make their annihilation more efficient. Hans Fleischhacker, assistant at the Institute for Racial Biology, examined the fingerprints of Jews in a ghetto for his qualification as a professor. In June 1943, Fleischhacker went to the concentration camp at Auschwitz to develop marks for racial selection there. In this extermination camp, the scientist selected Jews according to racial marks, and had them step forward during the morning roll call. He then took them to a separate barrack where he measured head, face and other prominent features. After he had sufficiently surveyed the 86 people, he sent them to the concentration camp of Natzweiler–Struthof, where they were murdered in several groups in a provisional gas chamber. Subsequently, the corpses were supposed to be taken to Strasbourg to be preserved and prepared for Fleischhacker's scientific analysis. The fact that this did not happen is owed to the advancing Allied forces, who liberated Strasbourg before the necessary preparations were completed. After the war, Fleischhacker was put on trial and classified as a "conformist". But he was directly involved in the murder of 86 people under the pretext of science. Because of his activities, thousands of Jews were deported, sterilized and murdered.

The University of Tübingen provided the ideological foundation for the Holocaust. It produced many, if not most, of the fanatical masterminds and most efficient mass murderers who stood in the first flight of the SS Sonderkommandos (death squads) and Reichssicherheitsdienst (security service) to participate in the

so-called final solution.[10] They are called the Tübingen Executors of the Final Solution. The vanguard of the murder of the
Jews mainly came from a middle class background, or even the
upper third of society. About 80% had graduated from university; about half of them even had a doctorate. So they were not
common criminals, but they acted out of conviction to ultimately
implement the Führer's racial ideology for the Third Reich. They
became murderers for a doctrinal goal, and not for personal
profit. The fact that the city's anti-Semitic "DNA" was so interwoven with the university is one important reason why so many
of the mass murderers for the final solution came from Tübingen.
Another reason is mentioned in a scientific research paper by
Horst Junginger at the University of Tübingen: The mixture of
anti-Semitic prejudices and a secularized image of God had led
the Tübingen executors to their murderous disposition. Many of
them came from a Christian background that was increasingly put
aside in the face of theologically justified hatred of the Jews.
Obviously, it was not sufficient in their eyes to proclaim judgment to the Jews. They felt called to personally execute this
judgment with fire and sword.[11] I would like to pause briefly here
and ask you to think about something. Should we not be shocked
by the fact that a secularized image of God that is completely
estranged from the Word of God, combined with anti-Semitic prejudices set on a theological foundation, led to such a murderous
attitude that finally produced the Holocaust? Don't we realize the
same deadly mixture at work even today? Is it not high time to
return to the God of the Bible and do away with the false anti-Semitic attitudes legitimized by theology, and correct them?

Only a short time after Hitler came to power, two well-known
theologians in Tübingen created quite a stir by their anti-
Semitic publications. The Catholic Professor for Dogmatics, Karl
Adam (1876–1966) was among the most renowned theologians in
Germany. He declared, "To a large degree, the goals of Christianity
and national socialist anti-Semitism are identical." The Protestant

New Testament theologian Gerhard Kittel (1888–1948) was one
of the leading proponents of the final solution. In his essay "The
Jewish Question", he suggested excluding the Jews from German
society and, if the racial segregation should prove unsuccessful,
resorting to killing all the Jews as a last resource.[12] Kittel's Translation of the New Testament, the Novum Testamentum Graecae,
and the Theological Dictionary of the New Testament of which
he was one of the editors, are still found in every pastor's and
theologian's study today. Kittel's assistant, Walter Grundmann
(1906–1976) contributed 20 articles to the dictionary. Grundmann joined the NSDAP (Nazi Party) in Tübingen, and was one
of the most radical advocates for the "German Christians" who
chose the Wartburg of all places, which is otherwise known for
Martin Luther's translation of the Bible, to establish an institute to research and eradicate Jewish influence in the church.
The institute's location was supposed to confirm Martin Luther's
anti-Semitism, who had argued for the burning of synagogues,
the destruction of prayer books and the Talmud, and the expulsion of the Jews.[13] Grundmann became head of the institute, and
advanced to become one of the most well-known theologians
among the "German Christians". This harmless name disguised a
neo-pagan movement working toward a Germanic faith, rejecting
Christianity, and intending to replace it with pagan ceremo-
nies, Nazi ideology and the glorification of Hitler. The institute
developed the idea of an Aryan Jesus with whom the Nazis could
identify.[14] For this purpose, he had to be completely carved out of
his Jewish context. So Jesus became a mythical Teutonic savior,
whose resurrection was supposed to demonstrate the Aryans' final
victory over the Jews. Grundmann had provided the religious
legitimization for the annihilation of the Jews. His example helps
us to make an extraordinary observation which is still valid today
for any kind of totalitarianism: Even though they vary greatly
in their form, they all share anti-Semitism as a common mark.
When we see the Christian faith being purposely severed from its

historic Jewish context, we need to take a very good look and pay close attention to the goal behind that.

Exactly how many from Tübingen University found their way to the murderous death squads is impossible to prove today. The only thing that is certain is that it was an exceptionally large number. At this point, I would like to give you a few names of people who began their sinister "career" in Nazi Tübingen as examples, to give you a better understanding of this situation.

The founder of the "German Faith Movement" was the Tübingen orientalist and indologist Jakob Wilhelm Hauer (1881–1962). Hauer, who came from a strict Pietist home, first became a missionary. In India, he came into close contact with Hinduism and Buddhism, which gave his life a completely new direction. From 1927 to 1945, he taught as a professor at Tübingen University. In June 1934, Hauer was personally initiated into the SS by Heinrich Himmler and Reinhard Heydrich, the real organizer of the Holocaust. He had excellent connections to both of them.[15] Hauer became head of the newly established Aryan Institute in 1935. He put his private secretary Paul Zapp[16] in touch with the Waffen SS and made him national executive director of the "German Faith Movement". Paul Zapp is one of those mass murderers who were responsible for the mass execution of hundreds of thousands of Jews. Zapp headed the Sonderkommando (special commando) 11a in Einsatzgruppe D (special operations unit), whose trail of blood ran across Eastern Romania, the Southern Ukraine and right up to Russia.

Eugen Steimle was also from a very religious background. He was one of the Nazi activists among the students in Tübingen.[17] He was involved in the pogroms in Württemberg, and headed the Sonderkommando 7a of Einsatzgruppe B in 1941. In 1942, he took over the Sonderkommando 4a of Einsatzgruppe C in the Ukraine. He is responsible for the deaths of at least 500 Jews, for which he was sentenced to death on April 10, 1948. In 1951, however, the death sentence was revoked, and he was released from prison in 1954. He died in Ravensburg in 1987. Politicians and clergy had protested his imprisonment. Up until 2003, his name was still found on a memorial plaque honoring returning war veterans that the city had installed at a central position on one of the supporting walls at the foot of the central church in Tübingen in 1951.

Martin Sandberger was from a well-known pastor's family in Württemberg, and besides numerous massacres, he was responsible for the pogroms in Kaunas, Lithuania. After the invasion of Russia, Sandberger took over the Sonderkommando 1a of Einsatzgruppe A. Along with another jurist from Tübingen, Walter Stahlecker, he was the main perpetrator for the genocide in the Baltic countries. Sandberger was sentenced to death in April 1948, but because of a long list of people who intervened on his behalf, ten years later he was released from prison.[18] After his release, he quickly established himself in society again and for decades lived an undisturbed life in Germany. Just before his death at the age of 98, a journalist tracked him down in an old people's home in Stuttgart. He was one of the last leading war criminals of the SS murder machinery. This encounter resulted in the following report in one of the leading German magazines:[19] Where had Sandberger been during the past five decades? Does he still see pictures from the days of war? The advance eastward in the rear of the Heeresgruppe Nord (Northern Army)? The years spent between the Baltic States and Russia? Himself in an assault boat on Lake Peipus, the Jews kneeling in front of recently dug pits? Sandberger closes his eyes, almost falling asleep any moment. "He was doing fine just now," says the woman who keeps him company this afternoon. A passing moment of weakness, most likely. "Just keep asking." Sandberger opens his eyes again. In a high-pitched voice and broad Swabian dialect he declares, "What I remember is absolutely insignificant." Historians describe... Sandberger as the spearhead of the genocide. "You were not just a cog in the works of an anonymous extermination machinery, but you developed the concept, constructed and implemented the apparatus that made the murder of millions possible." Sandberger was the last surviving leader of the Sonderkommandos in Himmler's murder machinery. In the days of old, whether in Tallinn or Verona, he would appear as a demigod clad in the gray military cloth of the SS. During just the first year of Nazi rule, there were a total of 5,643 executions under his command on Estonian ground. At the peak of his power borrowed from the Führer, just a few strokes of Sandberger's pen would be sufficient behind the lines of the Eastern front to have a "subject totally worthless to the national community" executed – in his own words.... Once in the Christian old people's home in Stuttgart, however, the retired Sandberger claimed compassion for himself.... Unfortunately, Sandberger "remembers very little" of those years, during his first and only interview. His memory is more reliable talking about the time before and after the war. This is an excerpt from his last interview. Three months later, Sandberger was dead. He had never asked for forgiveness for his crimes, or lifted the veil of his silence.

Walter Stahlecker (1900–1942) had received his PhD in Tübingen, and then started a career with the police of Württemberg. His father was a Lutheran pastor. Stahlecker headed Einsatzgruppe A, which was responsible for the mass executions during the campaign in Poland and Russia. He has to be perceived as one of the greatest criminals in the Third Reich. His cold-blooded determination to kill makes him stand out among all the other violent criminals. His last preserved report adds the number of people killed under his orders to an unimaginable 240,410. Resistance fighters finally managed to assassinate him in 1942.

The Chief Mayor of Tübingen, Ernst Weinmann, was nick-named "executioner of Belgrade". He was in office from 1939 to 1945. During the war, he spent the majority of his time in office as SS Sturmbannführer (SS rank within the Storm Troops, equivalent to Major) in Yugoslavia, where he was instrumental in abducting

Slovenes and deporting Jews. After the end of the war, he was sentenced to death in Yugoslavia for his crimes, and hanged.

His brother Erwin Weinmann (1909-?) was born close to Tübingen, and already worked for the NSDAP while he was still at school. He qualified as a medical doctor in Tübingen, and worked as junior doctor at Tübingen Polyclinic. He found his way into politics and was recruited for the Sicherheitsdienst (intelligence arm of the SS). During the summer of 1942, he was made head of the Sonderkommando 4a and was responsible for mass executions in the Ukraine. As commander of the security police in Prague, he was said to have fallen during the battle for Prague. Even though he was pronounced dead, the rumors never stopped that he had managed to escape via the so-called "rat line" from Italy via Spain to Egypt. According to the research by the Association of Persecuted Jews, he was an active adviser to the police there for many years.[20]

Yet another mass murderer who had studied in Tübingen was Adolf Rapp (1908-?). In the political climate of Tübingen, he advanced to SS Sturmbannführer. Rapp was head of the Sonderkommando 7a of Einsatzgruppe B and with a special commando of 100 men, he was responsible for mass executions among Ukrainians and Russians. He disappeared after 1945 and was sentenced to life in 1965.

One of Rapp's fellow students was Rudolf Bilfinger (1903–1998). After receiving his PhD in Tübingen, he worked as a lawyer before making his way via the Stuttgart police into the Reichssicherheitshauptamt ("SS subsidiary organization made up of 7 main departments including the intelligence & security forces and secret police forces for Germany and occupied territories; also oversaw the Einsatzgruppen"[21]). There he exercised high administrative powers and was personally involved in the implementation of the "final solution to the Jewish question". Following the Wannsee Conference in January 1942, Bilfinger took part in several consultations to organize the Holocaust. Bilfinger was sentenced to eight years in prison by a French military court, but very soon he was deported to Germany and subsequently released. Afterward, he was employed in civil service again; he died in Hechingen, a small town only about 15 miles away from Tübingen.[22]

Theodor Dannecker (1913–1945) was one of the organizers of the Holocaust, and he was among Eichmann's closest aides. He had grown up in the heart of Tübingen. A failure as a tradesman, he slowly emerged as an expert in "Jewish questions", and later organized the deportation of Jews from France, Bulgaria, Hungary and Italy to the extermination camps.[23]

According to conservative estimates, at least 600,000 Jews perished due to the racial hatred of the executors from Tübingen.

While writing these lines, I am filled with deep pain. But unless you understand why I am speaking about a cloud of darkness that covered us, I cannot tell you about our city. And also, this is the only way to help you realize the miracle of change that we have seen in our city in the course of the past few years.

See, darkness covers the earth
and thick darkness is over the peoples,
but the LORD rises upon you and his glory appears over you.
(Isa. 60:2)

When my wife and I moved to Tübingen 28 years ago, it was simply a pretty and quiet university town where we intended to study. At the same time, we knew for sure that the Lord had led us to this city. Our Baptist elders had sent us out with the laying on of hands, which could not be taken for granted. We started praying for our city with a few other couples, and we were stunned by the resistance we met.

40

This surely also had to do with the tedious working through of the city's Nazi past, which had only just begun in the early '80s. In my description of the individual perpetrators, I have mentioned again and again how quickly and easily they were able to escape prosecution and their just punishment. In Germany after the war, people were easily classified as perpetrators and conformists. Nonetheless, even convicted war criminals tended to receive so much backing from the highest political ranks that many times they were released prematurely from prison, re-socialized and even reintegrated into social life again. There were hardly any clear confessions or admissions of guilt. All who managed to be classified as conformists were rehabilitated. And so a heavy, dark curtain was drawn over the sin of the past.

The working through of the past and the denazification process at the university turned out to be a total disaster. Eighty-five percent of the professors who were either dismissed or suspended for an extended period of time ended up achieving their rehabilitation within the first ten years, and the majority returned to the university. I would like to add at this point that this occurrence was an all-German fiasco for the universities. At any rate, it is hardly surprising that the dark chapter of Tübingen's Nazi past remained untouched. For almost 30 years, all had remained silent, or even lied. The generation who had become guilty had largely managed to cover up all shameful, or even criminal, occurrences. Also in this respect, we can see the close connection between city and university. After 1945, everything connected to the Nazi time was subjected to silence, repression and a disgraceful haggling over Jewish possessions misappropriated by the tax authorities.[24] Hans Gmelin was a former SA Standartenführer (equivalent to Colonel) and Nazi diplomat who had been involved in the deportation of 59,000 Jews in Slovakia as mayor, yet he won almost 55% of the votes in 1954, despite his past. He remained in office for many years and was even made an honorary citizen. Naturally this was not exactly helpful for working through the city's Nazi past. Obviously, for the majority of the voters, his Nazi past was more of a recommendation than a reproach. Gmelin remained in office for 20 years, and by virtue of his office, decisively formed the way that the past was dealt with. In Tübingen he became a key figure of repression and political silence.

It was only three years after my wife and I came to Tübingen in 1982 that a memorial plaque was set up "In Memory of the Persecution and Murder of Jewish Fellow Citizens". For decades, only the remains of an old garden fence had commemorated the former synagogue. It was only in 2000 that a memorial was established at the site of the synagogue to honor the Jews from Tübingen as a "Place Against Forgetting".[25]

While strolling through Tübingen one day, we came across a memorial plaque in the city center commemorating the returning war veterans of WWII. Among those honored, as I mentioned previously, were two lawfully convicted war criminals who had been responsible for the deportation and death of thousands of Jews. Only 21 years later, in 2003, was this memorial plaque removed.[26]

Right next to the Theological Institute in Tübingen is the city cemetery. Philosophers, theologians and political figures are buried there. As a student, this place seemed ideal to take a walk. There I came across the "Burial Ground X", the place where remains from the Anatomical Institute were buried and which had sunk into oblivion after 1945. The city's dealings with the burial ground exemplify the length of time that Tübingen lived under the veil of silence, before it finally accepted the truth about the Nazi crimes as its own history. Up until 1987, medical students were still trained with preparations taken from victims of the Nazis. Only after increasing international pressure on the university leadership were the human remains of the victims of the Nazi regime removed from the university and buried in the city cemetery in 1990. The following week, the newly set up memorial plaques on Burial Ground X were devastated by right-wing radicals, and covered with graffiti and swastika.

In the mid-'60s, critical students at the university sparked a process of working through its past that was slowly advanced through a series of lectures, essays and books. With the recent publication of a detailed, 1,200 page anthology[27] by a team of scientists from Tübingen University on "Tübingen University During National Socialism" the university has comprehensively worked through its history. This publication is a visible sign of the many changes that have taken place. At last, the Nazi filth nobody wanted to look at, and the filthy ones nobody wanted to mention are finally called by name. The veil of silence has been torn.

When we started praying for the city, it was different. The resistance was like an impenetrable wall of darkness. We prayed much – very much. There were regular nights of prayer, and repeated prayer chains of 40 days. We would get up very early in the morning to stand in the gap for our city, almost every day of the week. We would walk through the entire city praying, over and over again – but nothing changed. When we would proclaim the gospel on the market square, people would just walk by scornfully, or laughing. Others disturbed the meeting through deafening noise or by pouring out water over us. Allow me to fast-forward a few years. By then we had seen the first fruits of our labors, and had started a church in Tübingen in the early '90s. We never relented in our prayers, but still the resistance did not decrease. We had a shop for evangelism in the city center which was smeared with excrement; absolute strangers would approach us in the city and curse us. After somebody stole our prayer notes, we found them published in the daily paper. We were struggling against a veil of darkness, and we had no key on how to break it open. In the meantime, we saw our ministry grow and spread all over Germany and other nations. But what about our own city? Why did we not have authority over the power structures of darkness? The veil of silence weighed heavily on us like a stifling blanket. Why did we not have the authority to break this veil of darkness over us? We were desperate, until the Lord took us to a point when we had to break the veil of silence in our own lives first. But before I tell you more about this, we should think about the question of where such a veil of silence comes from, and how it is produced.

There is no darkness that cannot be overcome by the power of God. My city is a living testimony to this. So if we, with our history, can experience something like this, then the same can happen in any other place in the world! In the next few chapters of this book, we will take a closer look at how this happened for us and what is the spiritual dimension behind it.

CHAPTER 2

WHERE DOES THE VEIL OF SILENCE COME FROM?

The best example to study on how to break a veil is found in the history of the early church. This is the common beginning for all Christians, irrespective of which nation or culture they belong to today. For me, it is one of the greatest miracles in history, how a small band of believers succeeded in such rapid growth and managed to gain such influence as to be able to penetrate the entire Mediterranean region. If there ever was a time when a veil of darkness covered the nations, it was then.

I would have wished an easier start for the early church, because everything was set against them. The Roman occupying power saw the first believers as one of the many cults, eyeing them suspiciously. They were threatened by libel, persecution, and the deaths of the first martyrs; but they still had to combat a much greater problem, which often was not so easy for them to recognize. The society of the Roman Empire in the entire Mediterranean was permeated by fascinating philosophical ideas and a Greek-Hellenistic lifestyle. Self-proclaimed redeemers managed to throw the first believers into confusion with their teachings, causing them to go astray. We have to realize that at the time of the first believers, the Roman Empire was largely Hellenized and governed by Greek thinking. To put it differently: It was hip to be Greek.[28] We can read in Paul's epistles about his own struggle with the spirit of that age.[29] Astrology, belief in fate, idolatry, and emperor worship determined the religious mindset of that time. Everyone was free to determine who and what they worshiped and what they believed, as long as their god did not claim any exclusive right for himself. The pantheon of the Roman Empire overflowed and offered a god for every personal whim and desire. You may be right in saying that everybody was free to believe, worship, and find his own salvation, as long as they kept the laws of the Roman Empire. This leads us to a surprising observation: Most of the ideas that we come across in the modern Western world were already around during the Hellenized time of the first believers. This makes me wonder what made the early church so successful in effectively permeating the pluralistic society of its time. What was the true substance of its unique authority and power? Was it the outpouring of the Holy Spirit in the upper room in Jerusalem? There is no doubt that without the equipping of the Holy Spirit, the testimony of the Gospel and the growth of the church would have been impossible. After Pentecost, the Gospel started spreading rapidly. Even though the New Testament only reports details of Paul's missionary journeys, the other apostles also traveled extensively, preaching and planting churches, spreading the Gospel. But as momentous as this event was for the early church, there was still another contributing factor for their tremendous authority in a Hellenistic world that is usually overlooked. It was their Jewish roots. Sometimes I put it this way: The power of the Holy Spirit was poured into a Jewish vessel, and made the church the most effective instrument of its time. To help you to understand the significance of this question, let us take a closer look at the correlation between the early church's Jewish roots, and their authority.

For a long time, to me the Jewish nature of the early church had been more of a theological question that did not really have anything to do with our here and now situation. I knew the church had been birthed in a Jewish setting, but I did not think this terribly significant. My theological teacher had been an expert in the field of "Judaism and Hellenism". But I still did not understand why the Jewish roots of the Christian faith are of such fundamental importance today, until I discovered one thing: The more the early church broke away from its Jewish heritage, the more it exchanged its spiritual influence for worldly influence and political power, and had nothing to counteract the pagan spirits of its time. Despite increasing influence in politics and society, it strangely lost its testimony and spiritual power. How was it possible for this church that had spread so powerfully, to increasingly lose its voice? What was the reason for this veil of silence? Do we stand at a similar crossroads today? To find out what really happened, we should try to discover the source of the early church's authority.

Let's go on a time journey and take an inside look at the early church. Obviously, it was extremely attractive and exceptionally effective.[30] The authority of the church was not limited by anything, so wherever it took root, it saw exponential growth. Signs and wonders were commonplace among the believers. They healed the sick, cast out demons, and raised the dead. That church was so attractive that more and more people were added, and young believers quickly became mature disciples of Jesus. By the end of the day, a small group of 120 people who were together in Jerusalem for Pentecost had grown to a congregation of 3,000 people. Within one year, the congregation tripled in size, and increased to more than ten thousand people.[31] Some church historians estimate that by the time Stephen was martyred (Acts 7:60) the church had more than 20,000 members. Of course the religious leaders tried to combat this phenomenon; but still the church kept growing continuously. It is possible that at the peak of the movement, half of the inhabitants of Jerusalem were saved and part of the church.[32] The model for church growth from Jerusalem worked wherever new congregations were planted. Even though they had to struggle with an often hostile, Greek environment marked by idolatry, syncretism and philosophical mindsets, nothing was able to prevent them from transforming entire cities and regions. Of course, in the early church there were normal people with the same problems that we have today – but they still carried a spiritual authority that the world was not able to resist. It was like a blueprint that contained everything we would dream of for today's church. This church was no theological fiction; it really existed, which is proven by a great number of historical reports. It lived in constant revival. Apparently, it was so attractive not only for other people, but also for the Holy Spirit, that the presence of God never left it. Many simply call it the New Testament Church. If we want to describe it, it was a Jewish-Christian congregation that I would rather call a "church with the spirit of the sons of Zion".

Many of the congregations had grown to more than 50,000 by the end of the first century. Ephesus is a good example; Paul reports in Acts that he lived in Ephesus for two years to plant the congregation there. Obviously he had a permanent evangelistic campaign there, as he had daily discussions in the lecture hall of Tyrannus (Acts 19:9). That time was sufficient for him to evangelize the entire city with its 200,000 inhabitants and to permeate it with the Gospel. The congregation in Ephesus grew so rapidly that the idol-makers feared a substantial loss of income. Obviously there was no more demand for their silver Artemis figures. In their rage, they stirred up a riot, and the city was plunged into turmoil. Apparently it is God's standard for His church to change its surroundings so dramatically that places of darkness stand no more chance and have to go. What would happen if the churches of the Western world had such authority and power? When Paul wrote his first letter to Timothy, the church in Ephesus had probably grown to 60,000. It is hardly surprising that Timothy was shocked when Paul asked him to lead the congregation.[33] In 112 AD, i.e. 80 years after Pentecost, Pliny complains in a letter to the Roman emperor Trajan that in the province of Asia Minor, where Ephesus was located, that most "temples [for idol worship] lie deserted and Christians in vast numbers are found everywhere".[34] We find the same kind of growth all over the Roman Empire. According to the report of the church teacher Crysostom (344–407) there were more than 100,000 believers in Antioch during his day; this was half the city's population.[35] By the end of the first century, the church had spread over the entire Mediterranean and had reached as far as England, India, Ethiopia, just to name a few. What was it that provided the early church with the anointing to change almost the entire known world within 70 years, despite all resistance and outward persecution? I have already given you the answer. It was equipped with the power of the Holy Spirit, and very conscious of its Jewish heritage. It was a church in the "spirit of the sons of Zion".

A House Church Service in the Early Church

Let us visit one of the services of the early church together. Many years ago, I had the opportunity to study this topic for my MA thesis in theology.[36] I was able to expand on much of what I compiled, then and put it into a broader context. When I got saved and became a believer, visiting a lively, spirit-filled service was some-thing extremely fascinating. I was simply thirsty for more of God. Somehow I felt drawn to these special services again and again. The presence of the Holy Spirit was so strong that you could be sure to have an encounter with God there. So if we are to visit a church service in the early church together, we have to be aware that much will be new and surprising for us. Our perception of church or a service is usually formed by our experience. But nobody in the first century had ever seen a belfry, a stained glass window, or a pulpit to preach from. They neither had nor needed a sound system or video projector. I am not saying that these things are necessarily wrong. But on our visit to a service of the early church, we should actually leave behind our old ideas and experiences. So it is Saturday evening, and we come to one of their characteristic services. The church meets in the evenings, as the people have to work during the day. They meet regularly in the various homes of the church members; this is what we find in Acts.[37] So the service takes place in one of the house churches that were scattered all over Jerusalem, Corinth, or Rome. The individual house churches would come together in a rented location for joint meetings every now and then, for instance in a theater. Our service, however, takes place in one of the many homes that are made available by kind hosts. You receive a warm welcome, and are led to the inner courtyard of the house. At first glance it looks like people are having a party. Some people play instruments, others are singing or clapping to the rhythm of the music, others are dancing. It is a family atmosphere, marked by contagious and intoxicating joy. In this house church, they truly "celebrate" the service. We can actually find a quite similar, detailed description of the services in the early church in Acts. Let's take a closer look at these verses.

They devoted themselves to the apostles' teaching and to fellowship, to the breaking of bread and to prayer. Everyone was filled with awe at the many wonders and signs performed by the apostles. All the believers were together and had everything in common. They sold property and possessions to give to anyone who had need. Every day they continued to meet together in the temple courts. They broke bread in their homes and ate together with glad and sincere hearts, praising God and enjoying the favor of all the people. And the Lord added to their number daily those who were being saved. (Acts 2:42-47)

Just how closely connected the early church was with its Jewish roots can be seen from the wording in these verses. The original meaning of the expression "they continued to meet" actually denoted the regular attendance of a synagogue.[38] So this is the indication that the service as described was not a one-time experience or anything exotic, but rather it was part of regular daily church life for the early believers. "Glad and sincere hearts", as the TNIV puts it, in its Greek original meaning signifies "boisterous and exuberant joy", rejoicing and cheering about the fact they had had an encounter with the living God, and were able to worship Him.[39] In the first account of the house church services in Acts, we find the further elements that constituted an integral part of the services besides their times of fellowship: The reading of the Word along with a message and teaching, a meal together ending in communion, as well as times of prayer, worship, and praise. So these are the Biblical findings. I would suggest returning to our New Testament house gathering.

The guests and attendants of the house church sit together at the beginning of the service. They are happy to see each other again and to spend time together. There is a lot to share, and there is much laughter. Then the Jewish dances begin, and everybody is invited to join in. They are Jewish circle dances, similar to the famous Jewish folk dance, the Horah, which is danced in one or several concentric circles.

Many theologians thought that the early church had celebrated quiet, solemn services, mainly consisting of liturgical formulas and beautifully crafted prayers. But their main services were completely different. After the singing and dancing, food is served. Perhaps this amazes you, that food is served in the middle of a service; but this is what we find in Acts (Acts 2:46) and also in Paul's writings (1Cor. 11:33). This weekly meal together is also called a "love feast".

At the beginning of the meal, the lady of the house lights two candles, and says a special prayer of thanksgiving. Then the leader takes the cup, says a blessing, and passes it on to the others, so they too can drink from it. Then he takes a loaf of bread, gives thanks, and then passes it from one person to the next. This reminds us of communion in its original form, with many elements similar to that of the Jewish Passover Seder. At this time, it is all about our love and commitment to Yeshua.

Next comes a time of worship and prayer. You can sense a change in the atmosphere; the presence of God becomes so real that some fall on their knees or lie prostrate on the ground, while others are standing with hands raised in worship. The Holy Spirit rests tangibly on the gathering; every now and then, someone breaks out into a spontaneous song in "new tongues". These "songs of the spirit" are unintelligible at first; but they become clear for everyone when someone interprets them in song.[40] Paul describes the sovereign move of the Holy Spirit during the service in his first letter to the Corinthians in chapters 12-14: Someone gets up to read from the Torah or the writings of the apostles. Sometimes they share memories of the words of Jesus or His miracles. A teacher might get up to explain to the listeners what they heard just now. Prophetic words are shared, a prayer in tongues plus its interpretation. All throughout the service, whenever somebody says something, there is resounding agreement and confirmation. At some point they bring the sick into the midst of the gathering and begin to heal them in the name of Yeshua. First-time guests at such a gathering share how they encountered their redeemer and testify emphatically to wanting to follow Him now!

It has grown late in our service, but still small groups are sitting together to pray. Slowly the first people start leaving the service; they hug each other with a kiss on the cheek. Somehow this service seems to have been like a big family gathering; it is well possible that it has changed their lives profoundly. Would you like to be able to visit such a New Testament gathering once? It is hardly surprising that the house churches had spread rapidly over the entire Mediterranean by the end of the first century. Whether it was in Jerusalem, Corinth, Ephesus, or Rome, their appearance and nature was always similar. For more than three hundred years this kind of service was the way the church gathered. There was no power that could prevent this church from growing.

If we could only take a live look at these services, it probably would not even be the dancing or singing that would surprise us the most. The greatest surprise would surely be the discovery of how Jewish the early church was. They read from a Jewish bible, followed a Jewish Messiah, and accepted the authority of Jewish apostles. Their values, lifestyle, and world view were Jewish. For the first four centuries, they celebrated the Jewish feasts in the church, and kept the Shabbat, i.e. Saturday, as their day of rest. Many members of the church were also involved in the local synagogue, and connected with it.[41] Even though the church in Rome and Corinth, as well as in Jerusalem, was multicultural, mirroring society in the respective cities, it still remained a thoroughly Jewish church. This could not necessarily be taken for granted, as for more than three hundred years both the Jews in the Diaspora, and at home in Palestine, had been subject to the ever-present Hellenistic influence of their surroundings. While Aramaic was the vernacular of the common people, Greek had long since become the official language of the day. By now, due to the rapid growth, the majority of the people in the church were Hellenized gentile believers, compared to the minority of Jewish believers. Despite the strong Greek influence and numerous attacks, the church preserved its Jewish nature until the fourth century AD. Obviously, this provided her with a unique authority. I call this authority the "spirit of the sons of Zion". Their Jewish heritage was obviously the sap of a precious root nourishing the early church that had received its special power by the outpouring of the Holy Spirit in Jerusalem. Even though there had been first warnings all throughout the early church, it was not until the Emperor Constantine (235–337 AD) that the church was finally completely cut off from its Jewish heritage. Constantine accomplished a change of course that was to prove disastrous for the church.[42] At a later point, I will go into more detail. But right now, we should keep in mind something important: If it is true that the early church lost its power and authority because of breaking away from its Jewish heritage, the reverse has to be of vital importance for the church today. I would like to put it as a thesis: 21st-century Christianity will only have authority in its struggle against the spirit of its age if it rediscovers its Jewish heritage again.

To get a clearer estimate of the importance of this issue, we should take a brief look at the Messianic Jewish movement. It is no exaggeration to call this movement unique in church history. The people in this movement are Jews who have found their faith in Jesus of Nazareth – whom they would usually call Yeshua – as the Messiah of Israel, the Son of God and Savior of the world. They are marked by the fact that as Jews they reject conforming to non-Jewish Christianity. Through their faith in Yeshua, these Messianic Jews do not want to diminish their position as part of God's chosen people in any way. So they have found specifically Jewish expressions for their services and faith.[43] The Messianic Awakening in America was birthed from the Jesus People Movement in the 1960s. More than 300 Messianic congregations have been planted all across the United States. At the same time, more than a hundred Messianic congregations have been established in Israel, their number having literally tripled since the beginning of the 1990s.[44] In Germany, the Messianic congregations are among the fastest-growing church growth movements right now. If you add up all these numbers, since 1967-68, more Jews have come to know Jesus as their Messiah than in all other generations since the first century combined! The Messianic movement in itself is a visible miracle in our time. It is the restoration of a heritage that was lost more than 1,600 years ago. At the same time, it is God's call to the "gentile church" in the Western world. Paul writes in Romans[45] about Israel's return to the Messiah, which is not only new life for Israel, but also a sign for the non-Jewish churches to be revived to "life from the dead". If this is true, the authority of the 21st-century church will not necessarily be measured in its size, but according to the restoration of its Jewish roots.

But before we think about how the early church could lose its unique authority and how such a "veil of silence" was able to weigh down on it so heavily, I have to attend to another question that is of vital importance. Why did God choose to raise a priestly nation in Israel, and why did He make our confession of blessing them such a source of our own blessing? Or to put it differently: Why is Israel chosen? And why does the way we treat Israel determine blessing or curse?

Is Israel Chosen?

I can understand that the whole idea of Israel being chosen is very hard to grasp for many Christians. Even though I had started to think about this concept very early on and I had always thought this was not a problem for me, I was so wrong. Whenever I read the Old Testament, it was like a fascinating old story book, but no more than that. My whole image of God was still formed by my Greek humanistic mindset. There was something in me, like an inward filter, that would not allow God's truth to take deep root within me. With respect to Israel's election, it was as if an invisible inner authority was shutting down within me to make me indifferent toward this issue. Many Christians would be shocked to realize how much of their spiritual life is based on the way they have been raised, and not on a revelation of the Word of God. There is no clearer expression of this fact than our understanding of Israel's election.

How was it possible for the world with its "twisted and sinful mind" [46] to get to know God in the first place? God's solution was simple. He chose a priestly nation for Himself that He would raise and form, so they could understand and pass on His Word. They were to learn obedience through difficult ways and special challenges. God promised His people that "nations will come to your light, and kings to the brightness of your dawn".[47] But how would God be able to reveal Himself after the greatest disaster of mankind, after the fall? He called Abraham and gave him the promise of a great people who were to inherit a land. God entered into a covenant with them, clearly predicting the story of this people. He told Abraham that his descendants would not remain in the land, but live as strangers in a foreign land. But because of His covenant with them, He would bring them back to the land of Canaan.[48] It is important for us to know that God has never taken back this covenant, which is valid even to this day. God gave Abraham another promise too, which was that Abraham would be the father of many nations[49]. So here we see a principle that runs through the entire Bible, and we can even find it again with the apostles. God deals with Israel as His chosen people; and He also deals with the nations. Ever since man's expulsion from the Garden of Eden, we can recognize these two recurrent themes that run through the entire Bible like a thread, whether it is in the stories of Cain and Able, Jacob and Esau, or in the account of God's covenant with Abraham. In His election of Israel, God follows a supernatural path. As in the beginning He created the Garden of Eden, throughout Israel's history He prepared a people for Himself, and gave them a new land. In this land, He wanted to reveal Himself through His people, so that Israel would become His model people. God took Abraham's seed,[50] multiplied it, and combined his faith with the revelation of His holy nature. He showed him that He is a holy God, who will never share His honor with any other idol. Through the Torah, He taught His people about a life of righteousness, and gave them principles and direction for all levels of their lives. The reason for God's election is with God Himself. God did not choose Israel because they were a better people than all the rest. God always chooses the weak and lowly, showing His unfathomable love. He chose Israel because He loves them, and because of His covenant with Abraham.

For you are a people holy to the Lord your God.
The Lord your God has chosen you out of all the peoples
on the face of the earth to be his people, his treasured possession.

The Lord did not set his affection on you and choose you because
you were more numerous than other peoples, for you were
the fewest of all peoples. But it was because the Lord loved you
and kept the oath he swore to your ancestors. (Deut. 7:6-8a)

Even though Israel kept turning away from God over and over again, grumbled against Him, and was disobedient, He never stopped loving them and continued His story with them. Because of Israel's disobedience, just as it was with the first man and woman in the Garden of Eden, they were driven from their land time and time again, and had to go into exile. But still God kept His plan that Israel's election was to create a sign and a model for all other nations to never give up. The apostles had understood that God separated mankind into two groups, "Israel and the nations", making a distinction between the one people, Israel, and all other peoples. On all his travels, Paul always went to the Jews first, and then to the Greeks, which included all of the gentiles. He recognized Israel's election, and knew that in Jesus, both parts of mankind were reconciled and formed into a new entity.[51] God wanted to use this small people to be a blessing for all of mankind. With Jesus, God sets out on a new path with Israel; He comes as man and as God, proclaiming the message of the coming Kingdom of God. At the same time, His life is marked by a taunting of His kingship, culminating in the inscription above the cross, "INRI – the King of the Jews"! History has not changed. To this day, God has extended His arm toward His people, Israel and the nations.[52] The return of the Jews after the Holocaust and the birth of Israel as a nation in 1948 emphasize Israel's being chosen and called. He wants to use this people to prepare His way for the coming Kingdom, together with the churches from the nations. His truth will be made manifest in the election of the people of Israel, making it a blessing for the nations. For this reason He decreed right from the start that our attitude toward Israel would determine curse or blessing. To this day, God has never taken back His word or changed it.

I will bless those who bless you,
and whoever curses you I will curse;
and all peoples on earth will be blessed through you.
(Gen. 12:3)

I am convinced that by positioning ourselves appropriately toward Israel, we determine blessing or curse in our lives. I will tell you about the ramifications in our city later in this book. There is just one key experience that I would like to share at this point. After we had come to understand that we are blessed most by joyfully accepting Israel's election, I was to learn an important lesson through an apparently small incident.

For one of our conferences, we had invited a man from Israel as one of our speakers. He is a New York Jew who was saved through a dramatic encounter with Yeshua in the Hippie movement. I met him in Israel, where he introduced us to his ministry then, and we spent a lot of time together. I really have to admit that his way of ministering made me nervous somehow. Sometimes, when I thought he was supposed to preach, he just sat there in silence. At other times – very inconvenient to me – he would ask for the microphone to expand on what I had said. By and by, my inner tension evolved into solid annoyance, which I intended to voice at some appropriate point. But then God said something to me that radically changed my view of Israel. "Jobst, the way you treat your friend is the way you treat Israel!" I knew immediately what He meant. I had wanted to squeeze my friend into my own concept, to make him acceptable for me – and I was trying the same with Israel. To put it differently, it is easy to stand with Israel as long as it fits my religious or even political concept. But what if it does not? I am convinced that most Christians want to bless and love Israel in one way or another. But we need to know that this love only carries weight before God once it is willing to grant His chosen people the first place, regardless of our own opinion and assessment of the situation. Paul warns us as Christians explicitly not to distance ourselves from the Jewish people in any way, or to consider ourselves superior to them.

(...) do not consider yourself to be superior to those other branches. If you do, consider this: you do not support the root, but the root supports you. (Rom. 11:18)

Understanding God's election of Israel means accepting the fact that the church draws its spiritual substance from this root. God has united us with the Jewish people in a unique way. From this root we have received the Bible, the covenant, the promises, and even the Messiah Jesus! The "Church of the Sons of Zion" is nourished by this root. This is the true source of its authority and power. We have seen cities and nations transformed by the power of this root. But the nourishing sap of this root is not limited to spiritual blessing only! It contains God's recipe for success in all areas of our lives. I am convinced that this blessing is made manifest right down to our finances.[53]

Why Did the Early Church Lose Its Authority?

Having realized that our attitude toward Israel's election is crucial to the power and authority of the church, we can return to our initial question. How was it possible for the early church to lose its unique authority? Why did the veil of silence start to cover their colorful and joyful testimony?

There were two reasons that we need to take a closer look at. Despite crises and persecution, the early church throughout the first three centuries was alive, growing, and Jewish. One hundred years later, life in the church was almost completely destroyed. Its gravedigger was the Roman Emperor Constantine (270–337 AD)

59

who officially recognized Christianity, making it the state religion. Because this may seem like a contradiction, we will examine the background more carefully. In 312 AD, Constantine fought the Battle at the Milvian Bridge, where he conquered his enemies. Constantine later reported how he had prayed to the "God Most High" before the battle, which to him was Mithras, the Persian sun god. In answer to his prayer, he was supposed to have seen a vision of a "flaming cross" directly above the sun and to have heard a voice saying, "Under this sign be victorious!" Constantine came to power, and granted the Christians freedom of religion. What a dramatic and apparently lucky turnaround for the early church! Under Emperor Diocletian (236–312 AD), the early church had suffered one of the greatest persecutions to date. Thousands of believers had been tortured and killed. During this time, they had nearly lost their entire spiritual leadership. The Christians had become desperate. Almost every one of them knew someone who had been martyred. But now there was this new emperor, a symbol of hope, displaying strength and charisma. The Christians were overjoyed that he called himself a follower of Christ. Obviously this must have been an act of God! All of a sudden, it was no longer a disadvantage to be a Christian; quite on the contrary, suddenly they were promoted. Constantine made Sunday an official Roman holiday, so the Christians were able to celebrate their services on that day. He closed the pagan temples, and donated vast amounts to build large churches. The church was ecstatic. For them, the new freedom under Constantine was a major paradigm shift. Because of their many new possibilities and privileges, he was their "new apostle". Constantine was to be their first "Pontifex Maximus", i.e. their high priest, who was to lead them from now on. He used his position to control and influence the church, because there was quite a lot he did not like about the new Christian religion. The Christians were too simple and uneducated for him. They were disorderly and in desperate need of the strong hand of a Roman organizational structure. But most disturbing to him was the prominent, powerful Jewish identity of the Christian religion. Like most Romans of his time, he deeply despised and rejected the Jewish people. To him, the Jews were just a "bunch of losers". Especially after the tragedy of two lost Jewish wars, the destruction of Jerusalem and the temple, and the worldwide dispersion of the Jewish people[54], the Romans openly despised the Jews. Constantine began to officially cleanse the church of its Jewish elements. He was the first to introduce a kind of "racial hygiene" system against the Jews. By the time of Constantine, the congregations in Rome and Alexandria were already largely Hellenized. They became the racially pure standard "free of Jews" which was to be imposed on all congregations. All who were unwilling to follow these orders had to expect persecution.

The second reason why the believers in the early church lost their unique authority was the increasing Hellenistic influence on their theology and church life. As I mentioned earlier, after the first century, Greek philosophers and their ideas had begun to play an increasingly important role in the congregations of the great urban centers such as Alexandria and Rome. Rapid church growth increased the ratio of Hellenistic gentile believers to such an extent that the Jewish members of the congregations soon became a minority. Within a short time, Jewish congregational leaders were displaced by Hellenized leaders. The more the congregations turned away from their Hebraic roots, the more the Biblical truth as shared and taught by the apostles was mixed with a pagan world-view and Hellenistic ideas.[55] The destruction of the temple in Jerusalem and the dispersion of the Jews after 70 AD appeared to the church as proof that the Jews had definitely lost their election and spiritual inheritance. Obviously, they concluded, God had removed His hand from the Jews. Their increasing alienation was intellectually reinforced by the writings of the early church fathers, and became their theological foundation. They judged that God had rejected the people of Israel forever as the "Christ killers".

The Christian church was supposed to have taken Israel's place, and was thought to be the only legitimate carrier of all of God's promises and blessings from then on.

This is where we first come across the so-called "replacement theology". It was grounds for one of the most tragic theological misjudgments, and plays a very infamous role in traditional and evangelical churches to this very day. Church fathers of the first to the fourth century, Ignatius of Antioch, Barnabas, Origen of Alexandria, and Chrysostom, just to name some of the most important ones, slowly developed a theology of hatred of the Jews. Anyone who persecuted and killed Jews was made an executor of God's divine wrath. They laid the theological foundation to cut off the church from its Hebraic roots for good. The Jews' increasing deprivation of their rights had begun. Their humiliation and exclusion from public office were only the beginning of a long road of suffering that led to pogroms, inquisition, massacres, and destruction of synagogues in the Middle Ages, and was to culminate in the Holocaust in modern times. I would like to summarize the most important points briefly here. In the fourth century, the church that used to be so full of life and authority became the Roman state church under Constantine. The Jews were subjected to oppressive restrictions and were increasingly deprived of their rights. One hundred years later, the Jewish nature of the early church was almost completely eliminated.

How could that happen? I want to try and explain the Jewish success model of the early church in the form of family-type and spirit-filled gatherings for the services in their house churches. Though there were also larger meetings, there is no doubt that the house services were the backbone of the church. Very soon after Constantine had legalized Christianity, he constructed his first church building in Rome, which needed to be large and impressive. So he had plans designed for a new basilica, as they called it, modeled after the example of a throne room in a Roman palace. In the center of the basilica, there was a throne where the bishop was to sit, who would be a confidant of the emperor, of course. The space right next to the bishop's seat was reserved for the clergy, for the priests and their dependants, while the large area in the front of the basilica was open to the regular church members. They in turn tried to listen to and follow the liturgical services that had become strangely impersonal. The basilica received lavish state funds and quickly spread throughout the entire empire. Constantine subsequently abolished the house services that had been formed and influenced by Jewish believers, and prohibited Christians by law to gather in their homes. The change from a very personal house church to an impersonal basilica also changed the entire concept of the church. Whereas before, the church had been a family of believers, now under Constantine the church became a building where Christians became Christian spectators and only took a minor role.[56]

So Constantine not only separated the early church from its Jewish heritage, he also married it to the pagan mindset of the "Greek spirit". His change of religion to Christianity did not prevent him from continuing to openly worship pagan idols. Constantine's Arch of Triumph that was built after his conversion still contained images of the Persian sun god Mithras, who also continued to appear on Roman coins. In 321 AD, he changed a Roman holiday in honor of Mithras into Sunday. Constantine's change of religion made turning away from other gods unnecessary. The possibility of taking their individual assembly of gods with them into the basilica by simply giving them Christian names made it very easy for many unbelieving pagans to convert to Constantine's church. The church was virtually flooded by converts. Jewish holidays were replaced by pagan holidays that were simply "christened" and turned into Christian holidays. Pagan temples were remodeled and changed into Christian churches. The conversion of gentile believers to Christianity now simply had become a formal step, and no longer had anything to do with the gospel. The life of the Christianized pagans had not changed; they still worshiped the same pagan idols as they had before. Their idols were simply given accepted "Christian names", so it was easy for them to continue their idolatry under a "Christian disguise". All who kept hold of the truth of the gospel and pointed out the fault of the system were slandered and termed "enemies of the gospel". By now, anti-Semitic violence was tolerated on the part of the church. Within 200 years, idolatry and the Greek mindset had completely deceived Christianity. The church increased in power and wealth. The spiritual life in most church leaders had died. It was as if a dark veil had covered the church. The joyful voices of a spirit-filled service and the bold witness of faith had died down. This is what I call the "veil of silence". The heart-to-heart relationship with the living God had given way to the silence of a faith defined by dogmas, completely void of a love relationship with God. The personal times of the family-style, spirit-filled house service had given way to the silence of a formalistic service void of significance. The joy of the Jewish congregation was weighed down by the heavy silence of indifference of a church that had turned anti-Semitic in the meantime.

A Deadly Infection

I keep asking myself where the voices of all those believers went who stood against the anti-Jewish spirit within the young church of the early days. Many of the gentile believers had been friends with Jews; others had learned from their Jewish spiritual fathers and traced their faith back to their ministry and perhaps even to their martyrdom. Did they allow themselves to be deceived by the anti-Jewish attitude of their time? Or were they among the ones who would rather watch in silence how their friends were mistreated, than courageously swim against the current? I come from a nation where a silent majority tolerated the murder of six million Jews. Our silence made us share the guilt. The Holocaust

was the culmination of centuries of anti-Semitism, the beginning of which had been laid right at the beginnings of the church
through the church fathers. Their teachings planted the germ of
replacement theology that can work unnoticed like a destructive
seed until today. This replacement theology is the matrix for a
Christian anti-Semitism whose disastrous harvest became visible
in Germany's Holocaust. The Christians bear the main responsibility because they allowed this evil spirit in, and never cleared
out this negative heritage. Anti-Semitism is not only expressed in
aggressive hatred, but it is much deeper, more hidden, and you can
find it in almost every Western church and denomination. Today,
it puts on a more modern face. It manifests in hidden prejudices
which can then, clad in a political disguise, lead to negative attitudes toward Israel. Anti-Semitism also hides behind an inner
indifference that uses the pretext of negative experiences to avoid
further involvement. Unfortunately, I have come across this kind
of indifference in many pastors, also. Their greatest concern is that
their standing with Israel would mark them as "Israel fanatics". So
they reduce their commitment to Israel and the Jewish people to
waving Israeli flags or blowing a shofar. But as far as their true
attitude toward Israel is concerned, their indifference cloaks them
like a veil of silence. To summarize this in a thesis: The DNA of
the church received a false stamp because it was cut off from its
Jewish roots. Even today, it carries a latent and hidden anti-Semitism that can find its expression in indifference, silence toward
Israel, or simply an attitude of superiority toward the Christian-
Jewish community, the Messianic Body. I know that we can be
quick to argue here. Some have told me, "Don't you know that I
love Israel, and how much we as a church do for Israel?" Others
point out that they allow Messianic Jews the use of their building,
and send annual prayer teams to the Holy Land. Irrespective of
which denomination we belong to or what our theological training
was, there is more of the anti-Semitic DNA of the early church in
our veins than we would like to think.

The Holocaust was neither new, nor the crazy individual crime of Adolf Hitler. German bureaucracy was able to revert to century-old experiences and prejudices. Hitler only had to study the old church fathers to find his justification for the greatest genocide of all times. John Chrysostom (354–407), bishop of Antioch, wrote a series of eight homilies against the Jews. Here is just a brief excerpt. "The Jews are the most worthless of all men. They are lecherous, rapacious, and greedy. They are perfidious murderers of Christ... because they murdered Christ, the wrath of God has rejected them forever... It is the duty of Christians to hate the Jews. The more we love Christ, the more we have to fight the Jews..." [57] Did you know, for example, that in the canonical law of the Catholic Church dated Pentecost 1917, all the anti-Semitic measures, like wearing yellow marks on their clothing or burning of synagogues were described, which the Nazis only had to put into practice? The Pentecost Codex was valid without reservation until the Second Vatican Council (1962–1965). It was not until 1983 that all the anti-Semitic statements were eliminated for good. You can easily recognize Martin Luther's anti-Jewish statements in Adolf Hitler's pamphlet Mein Kampf ('My Struggle'). I am grateful for the many councils and declarations in the church during the past 60 years in taking a clear stand with Israel. And yet many of our churches and congregations still carry the burdensome inheritance of replacement theology like a deadly infection within them. I would like to name just a few marks of this infection.

Formalism Instead of Living Faith

Comparing the experiences of the early church with today, it is shocking to realize that while many of the symptoms may be called by different names now, they are still visible in our time. You cannot undo the painful cutting-off of our Hebrew roots by simply not wanting to be "anti-Semitic" any longer. Rather, it is about renewed spiritual life returning to today's church in a completely new way. In the Western world, we have exchanged our living faith for religious formalism over and over again. Anything that is not born from personal faith in Jesus will turn into outward formalism, just like in the time of Constantine. This is a formalism that might agree outwardly with Christian standards, but is unable to change hearts and will leave them empty, putting an end to any spiritual life.

Belittling Israel's Importance

Even though the church today recognizes the promises to Israel and grants them "their place", it still denies the precedence that God has actually destined for the Jewish people. Instead of giving them the "first place", the church is trying to integrate Israel into their programs, goals, and visions. Many times, it claims the promises given to Israel for itself as an "allegoric exegesis" of the Old Testament, completely missing the fact that its relationship to the Messianic Body is the key to its change. Negative attitudes toward Israel under the pretext of political opinion are usually little else but a subtle attempt to separate Israel from the promises to their fathers.

Open Doors for the "Greek Spirit"

The early church was virtually flooded by the Greek mindset of its time. As long as they were firmly connected to their Jewish roots, the pluralistic, man-centered spirit of Hellenism prevalent at that time was not able to do them any harm. But as soon as they were willing to open up to the "spirit of the sons of Greece", they lost their Hebraic heritage and with it, their spiritual power! Once again, the church of Jesus has flung the doors wide open for the secular humanistic spirit. Its greatest tragedy is that their spiritual weapons against the world have become blunt, and it has largely lost its power of discernment.

The Veil of Silence

A church's silence toward Israel and its own Hebraic roots is an obvious sign that it still carries the Greek-Hellenistic DNA of replacement theology. A church might have lively services, but still be indifferent and trapped under the veil of silence. We are currently witnessing a fresh rise of anti-Semitism unlike anything that we have seen before. How will we act in times when the world stands against Israel? Will we remain silent again?

> *For Zion's sake I will not keep silent,*
> *for Jerusalem's sake I will not remain quiet,*
> *till her vindication shines out like the dawn,*
> *her salvation like a blazing torch.* (Isa. 62:1)

CHAPTER 3

THE VEIL OF SILENCE

The man had visited one of our conferences. He approached me after my teaching session and smiled. "Do you realize that you have just turned more than 20 years of my life upside down with what you said just now?" Up to this moment, he had always thought of his silence as something very positive. Now he realized that it had surrounded him like an invisible veil, and had seriously constrained him in many areas of his life.

The Veil of Silence in the Light of the Bible

There is a proverb that says, "Speech is silver, silence is golden." For some people, this is a good reason to limit their speaking to very little. Others think of silence as something very positive. Someone who can keep silent is thought to be highly principled and strong. But if we think about silence in light of the Bible, we quickly realize that it does not take much pleasure in silence. In Ecclesiastes, Solomon gives the advice that there is a time for silence (Eccles. 3:7) but further mentions of silence are hard to find. In some biblical contexts, silence in a conversation is considered a consent (Num. 30:4.7.11.14); in other incidents, people are silent because they are ashamed (Neh. 5:8), because they want to hide injustice (Judg. 18:19; 2Sam. 13:20), or simply listen (Isa. 41:1; Acts 5:12). Some other passages in the Bible point to the fact that some people were silenced to prevent further spreading of sin, as with the grumbling of the children of Israel (Num. 17:5) or the "lying lips" that were to be silenced (Ps. 31:18). A look into the dictionary[58] might help us to better understand the Hebrew meaning of the word "to be silent". It shows us that often it is used figuratively. The root of the word "deaf, dumb" carries the meaning of "unreasonableness" (Isa. 42:18), being "inactive" and "indifferent" (Hab. 1:13). The Psalmist asks God not to remain silent, meaning He should not remain passive, but act (Ps. 28:1; 35:22; 109:1). But God's silence can also mean punishment and judgment (Isa. 64:12) that can only be broken by one's own confession of sins (Ps. 32:3). In the New Testament, we end up with similar findings: often enough, the command to be silent carries a threatening undertone and wants to prohibit the confession of Jesus as the Son of David (Matt. 20:31; Mark 10:48, Luke 18:39). Other references talk about listening (Acts 12:17) or they focus on preventing the confused babble of prophetic women all talking at once during the service in Corinth (1Cor. 14:34).[59] One incident in the Gospel of Luke completes the picture. The disciples come down from the Mount of Olives worshipping loudly, joyfully praising God, when the Pharisees rebuke them, wanting to silence them. Jesus' reply is exceptionally harsh. "I tell you," he replied, "if they keep quiet, the stones will cry out." (Luke 19:40). To Jesus, silence in this context means not recognizing Him, just as Jerusalem did not recognize Him, and being under a veil of judgment.

When he came near the place where the road goes down the Mount of Olives, the whole crowd of disciples began joyfully to praise God in loud voices for all the miracles they had seen: 'Blessed is the king who comes in the name of the Lord!' 'Peace in heaven and glory in the highest!' Some of the Pharisees in the crowd said to Jesus, 'Teacher, rebuke your disciples!' 'I tell you,' he replied, 'if they keep quiet, the stones will cry out.' As he approached Jerusalem and saw the city, he wept over it and said, 'If you, even you, had only known on this day what would bring you peace —but now it is hidden from your eyes.' (Luke 19:37-42)

Before we think about the question why "silence" can make us sick and can even be dangerous, it is important to point to the terms "quiet" or "stillness", which can also be rendered as "silence" at times, but have an entirely different meaning. To be "quiet" before God is an expression of highest reverence and worship. In Revelation, we read about the angels looking expectantly to Jesus, and how there was silence in heaven for about half an hour (Rev. 8:1). Especially at a time of ever-increasing stress and hectic pace that is rushing by faster and faster, stillness is the key to a successful Christian life, and the sign that one has finally arrived and found peace with God. Some confuse this stillness with empty meditation, or think of a place so silent that you could hear a pin drop. But that is not what this is about. The Bible is talking about stillness when every fiber of one's being is focused on God. This is the hallmark of an intimate and deep communion with God, filled with expectation to have an encounter with Him (Ps. 46:10). A life marked by this kind of stillness will always be exceptional. It will not put itself forward intentionally, but it will never be inconspicuous. It will choose its words carefully, but will never be silent. All who live like that will be able to break the veil of silence wherever they are.

While up to now our focus has been on the "silence", we should now find out how often the words "speak", "talk", or "speech/language" are used in the Bible. And indeed, when we look up these words in any reliable Bible dictionary, there are many more entries than for "silence". In the Hebrew language, there is only one word each for the eye or the ear, whereas for the context of mouth and speech there are entire word groups. There is no other human activity related to such a large variety of terms as speech.[60] This is not too surprising, as the Bible views the human capacity to communicate and turn toward one's counterpart as elementary to the nature of man. Hearing God's Word and being able to respond makes man human. It is his ability to build relationships and have fellowship by speaking to his counterpart and putting his thoughts into words that makes man different from all other creatures. In the creation story, we read about God creating the earth by His word. By His word, He called it out of "tohu-vabohu", the state of being empty, formless, and in darkness (Gen. 1:2). In other words, because creation could not happen in silence, God broke through the darkness with His word; He spoke, and it was so. He created man and breathed His own nature into him, giving him the unique ability to turn his ears, eyes, and mouth toward Him; in other words, to turn his face to Him.[61] In the account of Paradise, we actually see God's model for life. This is how He had planned life for His creation. The ability of direct communication is the highest expression of His love to mankind. We read about Adam and Eve in the garden speaking with God and enjoying fellowship with Him. But after the fall, everything changed; a veil of darkness covered the entire fallen creation, and with it came the great silence. Closed ears, disobedience, and man's own ways cut him off from God – man had turned his face away from God. With the expulsion from Paradise and separation from God, not only sin and death came into fallen creation, but also silence. Man, cut off from God in his very nature, became incapable of relationships and tried to make his way without God.

> *Death and life are in the power of the tongue,*
> *and those who love it shall eat the fruit of it. (Prov. 18:21; MKJV)*

When a man no longer responds to God's Word, it means he has become deaf and mute, and has lost one of his elementary human marks. By declaring their willingness to do what God said when God entered into a covenant with them at Mount Sinai, Israel became His people (Exod. 24:3,7). Whenever there is no response when God speaks, it will come under judgment (Isa. 65:12). David describes the man who is successful in what he does as someone who delights in Adonai's Torah, and speaks it to himself in medi-tation (Ps. 1:2). Especially in the Gospel of John, we can see very clearly that the Word is nothing neutral, but rather corresponds to God's very nature. It actually identifies God Himself with the logos word (John 1:1). Jesus Himself is called the Word that has become flesh (John 1:14). All who content themselves with listening and remain inactive, express their indifference (Matt. 7:21). But all who respond to His word with expressed agreement receive deliverance, salvation, healing, and new life (Rom. 10:9).

In the Gospel of Mark, we read how Jesus is dragged before the Sanhedrin and is supposed to defend Himself against the false accusations of the witnesses. The High Priest is waiting for a justification, and expectantly stares at Jesus. Mark reports, "But He was silent and answered nothing." (Mark 14:61a; MKJV) I had always thought Jesus' silence was a sign of His humility, but is that actually true? Why did He not answer the questions of the High Priest and the scribes? Did He take the silence of the fallen creation upon Himself, just as He had to take their sin, sickness, and poverty? Can I actually throw my speechlessness, my inability to speak, or my silence on Jesus, just as I do my sin, in order to receive back my ability to speak? When Jesus had been nailed to the cross, we read in the gospels that darkness covered the land for three hours (Matt. 27:45). Luke, who as a physician was trained to describe phenomena in detail, gives a more comprehensive picture, and mentions the fact that the sun grew dark. Because the Jewish festival of Passover always takes place at full moon, it could not have been a solar eclipse. What happened in those three hours of darkness while Jesus was agonizing on the cross of Calvary? Nobody will ever be able to comprehend His loneliness and abandonment when all creation's mourning, trauma, pain, and suffering came upon Him. The silent screams of the tormented and abused, the fear of death of the lonely and humiliated, the deep pain that people can cause to one another became a torture for Him that was incomparably greater than anything the Roman executioners and torturers could ever do to Him physically. The darkness that surrounded Him was an expression of the greatest rejection and abandonment ever in the entire universe. For one moment, God had turned away from His beloved son. Darkness shrouded the earth like a garment of mourning, covering it in a veil of silence. Darkness and silence always go together. The prophet Isaiah puts it this way,

> *I clothe the heavens with blackness,*
> *and I make sackcloth their covering.* (Isa. 50:3; MKJV)

A few chapters later, he describes Jesus falling silent under the veil of silence.

> *He was oppressed and afflicted, yet he did not open his mouth;*
> *he was led like a lamb to the slaughter, and as a sheep before its*
> *shearers is silent, so he did not open his mouth.* (Isa. 53:7)

Three hours of agonizing silence. Then His cry rings out. It is the scream of millions of voices going up to heaven from the concentration camps, at the mass executions and pogroms. Not finding an answer there, He cries, "My God, my God, why have you forsaken me?" (Mark 15:34). Jesus' scream breaks through every terror in memory that has ingrained itself deeply into our subconscious. It stands for every unspoken trauma, every abuse, and every pain. And to this day, it stands for all the guilt so unfathomable that there are no words for it, and that is simply repressed and pushed aside. On the cross of Calvary, Jesus had to bear our silence, so you and I would be able to break it. I am asking you to grasp this in your heart; Jesus was silent like a sheep before its shearers, so we would be able to break our silence. Our redemption also includes our silence! We may throw our speechlessness on Jesus, just like our sin, sickness, poverty, and distress. By His silence on the cross, He paid a dear price for our words, even though they may only come slowly, as a stammer at first.

I cannot see anything positive in silence. And for this reason, I actually do not want to let the proverb, "Speech is silver, silence is golden" pass unchalleged. A child who does not learn how to express itself and how to communicate with its environment is in serious trouble and needs help urgently. Married couples who no longer communicate have closed their hearts to one another and are in serious danger of jeopardizing their marriage. A church or congregation has lost its life, once silence has fallen. How much pain, trauma, things not dealt with in the past can be hidden behind a person's silence? And how much healing, restoration, and change can happen when somebody manages to break the silence! Before we think about how the veil of silence can affect each one of us personally, let us take a look into the Bible. It warns us; silence is dangerous, and can have dire consequences.

1. If we remain silent, we will miss our salvation and redemption in Jesus Christ!

Even if you were to agree with every evangelist on the face of this earth, but without wanting to confess Jesus as your Lord with your mouth before God and men, your redemption would be in serious jeopardy.

Because if you confess the Lord Jesus, and believe in your heart
that God has raised Him from the dead, you shall be saved.
(Rom. 10:9; MKJV)

2. If we remain silent, we cannot receive forgiveness!

The foundation of forgiveness is the confession of our sins. Hiding sin in silence, not admitting and confessing it, is living in darkness, even if our lifestyle may have a Christian appearance!

If we confess our sins, He is faithful and just to forgive us our
sins, and to cleanse us from all unrighteousness. (1John 1:9; MKJV)

3. If we remain silent, we will not be able to believe!

The substance of our faith comes by hearing and the spoken confession of the Word of God. Therefore Paul writes in his epistle to the Romans,

> *Faith comes from hearing the message, and the message*
> *is heard through the word about Christ. (Rom. 10:17; NIV)*

4. If we remain silent, we will not be able to overcome the attacks of darkness!

We can only overcome darkness through a combination of forgiveness, our testimony, and our willing self-sacrifice. None of these three ingredients may be missing. As long as the word of our testimony is missing, we will never be able to overcome.

> *And they overcame him by the blood of the Lamb,*
> *and by the word of their testimony;*
> *and they loved not their lives unto the death. (Rev. 12:11; KJV)*

5. If we remain silent, we will not bear fruit!

Jesus' Great Commission to His disciples is still valid for every believer today. To remain silent and to keep the Gospel from others is to miss God's call.

> *And He said to them, Go into all the world,*
> *proclaim the gospel to all the creation. (Mark 16:15; MKVJ)*

6. If we remain silent, we will not be able to be part of God's prayer army for the end times!

God is looking for intercessors who are willing to call out to Him day and night, to stand in the gap for Israel and Jerusalem.

> *I have posted watchmen on your walls, Jerusalem;*
> *they will never be silent day or night. (Isa. 62:6a; NIV)*

7. If we remain silent, we keep God from fulfilling His end time plans with Israel!

Our public confession of our Hebraic roots and God's promises to Israel are more than a political statement. They are the unique calling of the end time church making itself available to God, so He can bring to pass His end time purposes for Israel and the nations.

> *For Zion's sake I will not be silent, and for Jerusalem's sake*
> *I will not rest, until its righteousness goes out as brightness,*
> *and her salvation as a burning lamp. And the nations will see*
> *your righteousness, and all kings your glory. (Isa. 62:1-2a; MKJV)*

8. If we remain silent, we will not be able to resist the spirit of this age!

We are living at a time when the church will have to awaken from its spiritual slumber. In the struggle with the spirit of this age, it will only have authority and the power to overcome if it knows how to break the veil of silence.

> *This is why it is said: "Wake up, sleeper, rise from the dead,*
> *and Christ will shine on you." (Eph. 5:14; NIV)*

The Veil of Silence over Cities and Nations

I have tried to show you a few aspects of the veil of silence in light of the Bible. There is no doubt that God has His story not only with individuals, but also with cities and nations. The Bible describes entire cities, nations, and cultures coming to harm through the behavior and misdeeds of people. In Israel's history, we see how their decision for or against God always brought blessing or curse, life or decay. So quite obviously, there is an invisible reality behind the visible, and that is where the struggle between the church or individual believers and the powers of darkness takes place. Peter warns us not to underestimate this battle. "Be alert and of sober mind. Your enemy the devil prowls around like a roaring lion looking for someone to devour." (1Pet. 5:8) God has given us His armor so we would be able to defend ourselves (Eph. 6:11-17). There is also no doubt that a nation's sin puts darkness over the land that can cover the land like a dark cloud (Isa. 60:2). I do not want to go into a discussion here about whether this darkness is the sum of demonic oppression and obstructions,[62] drawing its rights from the moral sin of the people, or whether it is territorial powers that may vary in each individual case.[63] What seems important to me right now is that the sin of a nation will never just be blown over, i.e. it will never fade away or expire by itself. It continues influencing the people and their descendants, preventing healing and restoration. It is like a sinister heritage that the Bible calls spiritual blindness. It prevents revelation, and keeps a people in demonic bondage. Where there is no vision, the people run wild; this is how the German New Luther translation renders the well-known verse from Proverbs 29:18.[64] According to the original meaning of the word,[65] this denotes "being left to one's own devices" or being like an untended garden. The nation has a "veil on their heart" (2Cor. 3:15-16; MKJV). In the parable of the sower, Jesus speaks about the seed of the Word of God that falls to the ground and does not bear fruit because "the devil comes and takes the Word out of their hearts" (Luke 8:12; MKJV). In 2Cor. 4:4 we read of how Satan can successfully blind the minds of people so they cannot grasp the Gospel. God wants "all people to be saved and to come to a knowledge of the truth" (1Tim. 2:4). At the same time we see God's obvious purpose to heal entire cities and nations (2Chr. 7:14) and to give them the same blessings He gave to Israel (Deut. 28; Col. 1:19). But how can this happen? Our experience in Tübingen was that even through years of focused warfare and intercession, we could not break through the darkness. The more we struggled and strove in our prayers, adding to our commitment in prayer, the thicker and more impenetrable the veil seemed to become. We had not learned yet that darkness is always connected to silence, and that healing can only come once we learn to break the silence. For me, the most striking example of this truth was an experience I had in Argentina.

In 2001, I held a prayer conference in a large church in Buenos Aires, when the Holy Spirit spoke to me while I was ministering. He told me to call 50,000 intercessors to intercede for their nation day and night. In the 1990s, Argentina had become known for an impressive revival that birthed some of the world's largest churches. By then, however, revival had given way to political reality, and the country was paralyzed by corruption, crime, inflation, and economic crises. Every day, people died on the streets. The churches had experienced powerful growth, but had no vision for prayer. Six months later, I had traveled with my friend and translator Ruben Gutknecht to all the provinces, and I called the pastors' networks to participate in a continuous day and night prayer chain. After six months, we had a list of 50,000 registered intercessors. This was the beginning of the first national prayer movement in Argentina. The military government of Argentina had committed inhumane atrocities between 1976 and 1982. Human rights were disregarded. Thousands of people simply vanished; nobody knew whether they had been raped, tortured, brutally murdered, or drowned in the Rio Plata. Finally, Argentina's defeat in the Falkland War led to the fall of the military junta. At that time, however, this part of Argentina's history was almost completely ignored. We set up a one-year prayer program modeled after the Lord's Prayer to help them work through their personal history. They also confessed the history of the cities and, most of all, the nation, and repented for it.[66] During that[67] and the two following years, there were significant changes in Argentina's situation. Political stability and economic reliability returned, and even the newspapers reported on how the nation's past was being worked through. Unfortunately, the prayer movement was valued less than individual church interests, and lost its power. Today, Argentina is in a similar political, economic, and social situation as in the years prior to the beginning of the prayer movement. For me, this is still an example of what can happen when a nation starts breaking the veil of silence.

One of the first key messages I ever heard at a counseling seminar was, the devil will always try to hide sin, keeping it in the dark. Light disperses the darkness only when we are willing to name the truth, calling sin, sin. We had taught the Argentinean intercessors to face both their personal and national sin, confessing it as the truth, in order to humble themselves over it and to repent (2Chron. 7:14). The results had been amazing. For the first time, I had seen there how simple it was to break through a veil of darkness. As long as bloodshed and injustice have not been confessed publicly and made right with God, there will always be a cloud of oppression over the land. We have to be willing to look at the hidden truth about the past, and bring it into the light.

I still remember one prophecy by John Mulinde, a pastor from Uganda, which moved me deeply. To this day it has stayed with me in my ministry. In this prophecy, he saw thick, black billows of smoke spreading over the map of Europe. They produced a thin fog that started covering the land. Suddenly, a light broke forth, and rays of light began to go out in all directions to all the nations of the world. They went across South America, North America, Canada, Africa, Russia, Asia, and on to Australia. Then this picture gave way to a Bible passage:[68]

> *Arise, shine, for your light has come,*
> *and the glory of the LORD rises upon you.*
> *See, darkness covers the earth*
> *and thick darkness is over the peoples,*
> *but the LORD rises upon you and his glory appears over you.*
> *Nations will come to your light,*
> *and kings to the brightness of your dawn. (Isa. 60:1-3; NIV)*

This prophetic picture was the main trigger for the start of a powerful prayer movement. People started praying for our nation in continuous 24/7 prayer in more than 200 cities all across Germany. The vision was to break the dark veil over Germany and Europe. I am very grateful for this prayer movement, that is still today one of the key catalysts for blessing in our land. Since that time, the spiritual atmosphere in Germany has clearly changed. And yet, the foundation for this change is something else. I call Germany today the "country of unmerited grace". Much of the blessing we experience today I trace back to the fact that the post-war generation and their children were actually willing to enter a slow but honest process of working through the past. Today there is hardly a day without a documentary or movie on the events of the past, and also in books and magazines there are numerous contributions. Even though such a long time has passed already, the honest and detailed working through of that era in all levels of society is considered the mark of trustworthiness and a new beginning. Just recently, the German Ministry of Foreign Affairs, the police, the medical association, lawyers, and universities have started to unreservedly expose their roles during the Nazi era. All of a sudden it has become "trendy" in Germany to deal with one's roots. For as long as I can remember, large Christian events with repentance for the sins of our forefathers concerning the sins of the German people have always been part of my spiritual reality. There is no doubt that Germany has changed. And yet there still is a hidden anti-Jewish root deeply ingrained in the hearts of so many people. Even though it is usually well-hidden under a veil of silence, it may erupt violently every now and then.

When we came to Tübingen, more than 35 years had passed since the collapse of the Nazi regime. I have told you how the city had a hard time working through its Nazi past. But during the following years, we were able to watch an increasing public awareness and a working through of the city's past, corresponding to our repentance and the prayers of the church. At this point, we should keep one thing in mind: Whenever the veil of silence is broken over a nation, a city or one's personal situation, it is always the beginning of a spiritual transformation. Start by noting whether people speak openly about injustice, bloodshed, racism, anti-Semitism, or other dark spots in your nation's or city's history, or whether these subjects are taboo. Nobody will be able to break the veil of silence unless the church actually rises to the occasion to humble herself personally, and to expose hidden sin so that the light and mercy of Jesus can shine on it. Somebody once said, "The blood can only cover what we uncover!" So if this is true for countries and nations, how much more for our personal lives!

The Veil of Silence over Churches

Sometimes I go to minister in churches that actually make me want to put on my warm ski suit. I call them "freezer churches". Before the service begins, everybody is happy and relaxed, talking to one another. But as soon as the service starts, much of it seems wintery, cheerless, and rigid. When Jesus entered Jerusalem together with His disciples, He reached the slopes of the Mount of Olives. We read in the Gospel of Luke how the disciples' joy and praises were heard everywhere (Luke 19:37-40). I imagine the Pharisees hearing this and covering their ears. This could not go on. They had to curb this enthusiasm. Finally they turned to Jesus directly and told Him, "Master, your disciples are annoying us with their joy and praises. Put an end to this riot! Rebuke your disciples now and make them shut up!" There is a widespread phenomenon which unfortunately is often confused with spiritual life. It is the religious silence. Religious silence has nothing to do with the presence of God or inner meditation. Instead, it is the expression of a religious, legalistic lifestyle that has a hard time tolerating anything else besides itself. Any expression of joy is eyed suspiciously, and usually classified as superficial. The outward appearance is more important than spiritual life; the religious shell more important than the heart. They do not even like to speak about their faith, as this is something very personal that they would rather work out by themselves. Most of the time, religious silence resists the power of God, always wanting to retreat to the "privacy" of one's personal faith. Someone who lives under the veil of religious silence may hear others praising God and testifying to His wonderful deeds, but then will take offense at outward appearances and not be able to enjoy the praises. This was probably the reason for the Pharisees' harsh reaction. Quite obviously, Jesus had a completely different perspective. I just love His answer.

'I tell you,' he replied, 'if they keep quiet,
the stones will cry out.' (Luke 19:40)

Let us leave behind the "religious silence" of the "freezer churches"! But how can that happen? I have actually found that in "freezer churches" there is a veil of silence drawn over grievances or sins of the past. But as long as these grievances have not been worked through and not been brought to the light, the situation

will never change. Here it is important to take a careful look at the
pastors, elders, and leaders of the church. If in the past they lived
in sin in the church or if they tolerated sin in the church, it is only
by identificational repentance that the "veil of silence" and darkness can be broken. Once they start humbling themselves publicly
before their churches and – if necessary – repenting for their sin,
a "freezer church" can be changed into a "fire church" where the
power of the Holy Spirit can move afresh, and every dark veil is
consumed by fire.

We also need to pay special attention to the role of both traditional and evangelical churches during the time of National
Socialism. Of course, in various churches and denominations
there has been a certain amount of officially working through the
past. But still every church and congregation has to face the question individually in what measure it still is under a veil of silence
in this respect. One mark is that the role of families in the church
during that time is hardly ever talked about, and if so, only with
a maximum potential for conflict. I have been able to help a lot of
people in counseling whose greatest conflict was the fact that their
ancestors had been members of an evangelical church and ardent
Nazis at the same time. I am convinced that some churches and
congregations could see a breakthrough if they were only willing
to repent publicly of their own anti-Semitism and their silence in
the face of the persecution of the Jews in the Third Reich.

Unfortunately far too often we in the churches in the Western
world have softened the radical nature of the cross and let it decay
to a form of "cheap grace", allowing Christians to live without the
challenge to commitment and change. We were taught that the
wonderful promises of God's grace and blessings are for us without
having to pay the price for them. People comforted our conscience
and explained that the message of repentance from sin was too
narrow and only limited our individual freedom. They played
sin and injustice down and preached a "wellness gospel" that has
nothing to do with the message of Jesus any more. Many live a

religious Christian lifestyle in their churches without having ever been convicted of their personal sins. They have never realized that it is impossible to follow Jesus without denying the "world". This results in a spiritually sanctioned life that is still "entangled in the filth of the world and overcome by it"![69] Unless we actively take our sins to the cross, they are like garbage in the basement of our subconscious that we try to hide and preserve at all cost. If we remain silent and do not bring our sins to the light, they will shroud the cross and without fail become a veil of darkness. I am convinced we are on the threshold of a completely new dimension of revival in our churches and congregations. Wherever sin is no longer played down and we repent publicly, our churches will become the revival centers of the future.

But everything exposed by the light becomes visible –
and everything that is illuminated becomes a light. (Eph. 5:13)

The Veil of Silence over Marriages and Families

To what extent silence can tangibly affect us in all areas of our lives is first of all visible in the most intimate partnership that God designed for man: in marriage. In a harmonious partnership, there are times when you talk, and when a joint silence is the sign of intimacy and closeness. But much more frequently, it points to an inner estrangement. Each follows their own daily routine, and only at the end of the day do they have the opportunity to share the other's experiences. But instead, speechlessness enters the relationship. There is no way of putting mutual hurts or disappointments into words, and so the spouses withdraw from one another. Some time ago there was a survey why every other marriage fails: Reason number one was the lack of communication between the spouses. This is not the right place to go into more detail, but it is important for me to show how silence can destroy a marriage, and how breaking the silence can be the beginning of healing and restoration for a marriage.

Perhaps you are aware of the fact that sexual abuse can place an almost impenetrable veil of silence over a family. The victims experience abuse where it is least expected, in the closest family or its surroundings. Research has shown that one in five girls, and between five and sixteen percent of boys are sexually abused once, or over an extended period of time, before the age of 18.[70] The scars left behind by the abuse are deep, and sometimes hard to recognize at first sight. Violations such as sexual violence breach physical boundaries to such an extent that they no longer offer protection for inner boundaries. In response to this violation, the abused person starts building a protective layer around themselves, and hardens their heart. This way, they create some space for themselves in order to be less vulnerable. This in turn leads to behavior that may be hard for others to understand, but that is an expression of a survival mechanism for the person in question. Many of these survival mechanisms are connected to inner withdrawal and silence. But however deep our emotional hurts may be, God can heal them, and wants to heal them. He has the ability to help you to speak about your pain and oppression. On the cross, Jesus paid so we would be able to unburden everything that weighs us down onto Him. You no longer have to carry it yourself. I would like to encourage you, if this concerns you, to start putting the unspeakable into words, and drawing the curtain of silence aside.

In many families, there are certain topics that must never be talked about. These taboo issues weigh heavily on the family's memory and perception like a dense fog. The family members no longer see this as a conscious effort of "not wanting to talk about it"; but rather, reality seems to have adapted to a kind of family truth that is hardly ever questioned, and nobody dares to break away from it. Even right up to the 21st century, the families of both the children and grandchildren born after the war are "contaminated" by the events of two world wars. This is especially true for the time of WWII and National Socialism, when all of Germany was deeply embroiled as the main culprit of the war and a generation of perpetrators. Even though the following generations might not be aware of it, they still carry the emotional and mental load of the "veil of silence" inherited from the fathers and grandfathers. But we also find the same phenomenon with the children and grandchildren of the victims. At best, the Holocaust survivors and victims of the Nazi regime were able to repress the memories of the traumatic experiences and the unimaginable suffering, but could never put them into words. The children and grandchildren of the victims were perpetually haunted by the "ghosts from the past", and suffered even more than their fathers and grandfathers as their emotional and mental heirs. It is surprising to find a certain parallelism between the descendants of the perpetrators and the descendants of the victims of National Socialism that seems tragic to me: In both cases, we find people with comparatively great trouble in bonding or forming relationships because of a blocking or repressing of the truth. They only find relief once they manage to address and name the dark shadows of the past. We will return to this question in a separate chapter later on.

In other families, there are topics that can be the cause of repeated conflict and arguments. They are usually connected to unresolved guilt, unforgiveness, and rejection, that can sometimes go back several generations. Probate disputes can divide families and cause feuds that last for several generations and break up entire families. The most tragic consequences, however, can be seen in families that have never renounced their anti-Semitism and negative attitudes toward the Jews. They live as if they are under an invisible, oppressive veil that seems to isolate them and cut them off from God's promises. I have observed something similar in the U.S. when families were involved in racism, injustice toward others, or bloodshed. This veil can only be broken through earnest repentance, and turning away from the sin. It is about time we break free from old family patterns. We no longer have to live with them. It is only when we put our experiences into words as precisely as possible, giving them their proper name, that we will finally be able to break through this veil, and also break it over our families. In the very moment when we face the Spirit of Truth and allow the mercy of Jesus to enter into all areas of our lives, our lives will change, and we will truly be able to enjoy the riches of God's glory.

The Veil of Silence through the Sins of Our Forefathers

Genealogy, the research of family history, has been booming for years. On German TV, you even find celebrities hunting for their "family secrets". This is also the title of a TV series in which they embark on a trip into the Nazi past of their own families, to bring light into the dark. Ancestry research is no longer just a quirky pastime for aristocrats and retirees. Dealing with one's roots has become trendy, and is considered a symbol of an increased need for identity. Even writers of books have discovered this topic. They describe the generation of grandchildren after the war as those who are constantly suffering from repeated blockages, vague fears, a sense of uprooting, and a heavy sense of guilt or depressed moods, without ever being able to explain where their problems come from. They research their own family past to find a starting point that helps them to get a grip on something that has formed them in a very negative way, and made them sick. Because this issue had been placed under a taboo, they were all the more subtly affected by the after-effects of National Socialism during the war. This important development passes unnoticed by most churches, however. When I talk to people, they ask me again and again why we still have to keep working through our past in Germany. After

70 years, the process of coming to terms with our past is supposed to be finally completed, and we should be able to look ahead again. But many do not understand that this is not about a constantly repeated collective form of repentance; but that it is precisely the personal working through of our own family heritage that is such a vital part of the process. In addition to that, the whole issue of the sins of our forefathers is hardly ever mentioned in most churches. Many do not even realize that there is such a problem, let alone having been taught the steps they can take to be set free from this burden. Others reject this issue because of theological qualms. Millions of believers could be set free of the burdens dating from their forefathers that are causing oppressions in their lives today. It is also possible that there are obstacles for our own spiritual life, that of our nation or our cities, our churches or families, because the sin of our forefathers has never been recognized and rendered powerless at the cross. The guilt we inherited from our forefathers can be the root of distress and lack of freedom in our lives. If we remain ignorant in this area, this can be one of the greatest sources of failure, defeat, oppression, and obstacles for us. To better understand the biblical view of the sins of our forefathers, I would like to explain it with a picture. Our body stores genetic information in the chromosomes in our cells. These chromosomes resemble an invisible cord, the so-called DNA that contains the complete genetic information of each person. Just like on a microchip for a computer, all of our software is stored on this cord. It determines the family characteristics we are born with. This genetic information is passed down from generation to generation. You can also apply the same model to our spiritual lives. Our spiritual DNA is like an invisible storage device that contains more and more data with each successive generation. This information is our spiritual heritage and the "storage space" for the data called "sins of the forefathers".

The Lord is slow to anger, abounding in love and forgiving sin and
rebellion. Yet he does not leave the guilty unpunished;
he punishes the children for the sins of the parents
to the third and fourth generation. (Num. 14:18)

At this point, if not earlier, the critics object that the teaching
about the sins of the forefathers and identificational repentance is
not supported by biblical evidence, and is an adulteration of the
heritage of the reformation.[71] Even though the sins of the forefathers must not be confused with the theological term "original
sin", in my understanding, the actual dispute is about the question of how far the destructive power of sin was able to spread
throughout the world. "Original sin" is the sequence of sin inherited since the first sin through the progenitors Adam and Eve
that is passed on from generation to generation when they lost
the friendship with God for themselves and all of their offspring.
According to biblical testimony, there is no doubt that God regards
all men, without exception, as sinners and transgressors.[72] Adam's
"original sin" was pride, arrogance, and mistrust toward God. The
Bible is just as clear about the fact that mankind fell from grace
through their forefather Adam, and is now inescapably caught
in sin and death (Rom. 5:12,18,19; 1Cor. 15:21,22,49). Here God
had obviously designed mankind to consist not only of the sum
of all individuals, but considered it as a whole entity, a family in
which one person's actions influence everybody else as well. This
common bond also allows Jesus' atoning death on the cross for
all of mankind; but it also shows that the individual's sin actually impacts all. That is why Paul emphasizes that through the sin
of Adam all men became sinners, and through the atonement of
Jesus at the cross, the door to redemption was opened for all men.

For just as through the disobedience of the one man
the many were made sinners, so also through the obedience
of the one man the many will be made righteous. (Rom. 5:19)

Obviously there is a hereditary sin that people suffer from, and that they are invariably captive to. The teaching about the original sin is crucial to our understanding of the Gospel. In a theological compendium, I found the following statement: "Unless there is a radical understanding of sin, there is no radical understanding of grace. 'By grace alone' can only be understood on the backdrop of original sin." [73] In the Apologia of the Augsburg Confession, we read, "Unless we recognize our misery, we cannot understand the greatness and grace of Christ." [74]

During the period of Enlightenment, the concept of original sin was countered by the idea that man was good by nature, and only corrupted by his upbringing of society. In a world that constantly produces new wars, violence, and misery even after the distressful experiences of WWII instead of a proclaimed world peace order, we can safely put this notion aside. The weakening of the term "sin" is the elementary error of liberal theology and Western society formed in the spirit of Enlightenment. No man will be able to free himself from the consequences of this inherited sin that has been passed down through the generations. Because Jesus died for the sin of the world and also for each person individually, the Bible shows us that it always considers both strands, both the collective and the individual, the sin of all mankind and the individual guilt of each person. Once you acknowledge this biblical truth, you will think again about the teaching concerning the sin of the forefathers, and recognize it as a way of rediscovering the greatness of the grace and mercy of Jesus. The key question is with which biblical principle we can explain the hereditary transmission of family guilt. On the one hand, the Bible gives plain judgment on every sinner who is indiscriminately caught up in his sinfulness and will receive God's judgment (Rom. 3:23). On the other hand, the Bible also has very clear standards to measure an individual's personal guilt. So God distinguishes between gradual differences in a person's share of sin that He judges and weighs accordingly. Punishment and forgiveness correspond to the type and degree of the sin committed.[75] In other words, the effects of individual sin in a family can differ in their severity and consequences. The Bible says very clearly that no man can save himself from the curse of sin by his own strength (Gal. 3:22; Rom. 8:2; 11:32). At the same time, he is capable of fighting sin within his own limitations, avoiding evil and living according to a high ethical and moral standard. This is proven by numerous testimonies of people whose lives can serve as examples for many believers. God has never given up on man, even after the fall. His "no" to darkness only applies to man where he has identified with sin and is entangled in it (Rom. 1:18). He hates sin, but He loves the sinner. For this reason, these two always go together – the heavenly Father's boundless grace and love who finds "no pleasure in the death of the wicked" (Ezek. 33:11) and His discipline with which He has to punish and judge sin. Grace and consequences are no more mutually exclusive with God than the perfect redemption in Jesus and the possibility of still having to eat the forefathers' bad fruit. But even though we find so many references to the sins of the forefathers in the Bible, and we also find millions of instances in counseling of sin transmitted to the following generations, we still cannot give a definite answer to the question of why born-again believers many times have to eat the fruit of the sins of their forefathers.

Perhaps we can best compare it to a field that we can inherit in a variety of conditions. We are familiar with the image of the field from Jesus' parable, where He compares the image to the state and openness of our hearts toward the Word of God (Matt. 13:19ff). This field seems to have suffered the impact of inherited family sin of varying degrees, which can seriously obstruct further growth. Each impact is like an invisible fault line, or dent, in our spirit that can only be cleansed and deleted through forgiveness by the blood of Jesus and subsequent deliverance from the sins of our forefathers.

Another image is the one of sowing and reaping. The law of sowing and reaping has been given by God to multiply and pass on His blessing in the hearts of Adam and Eve, just as it was in the Garden of Eden. But when sin came into the world, the same "field" of their hearts suddenly produced evil fruit, that was as specific as it was diverse, and was passed on to the following generation as sin of the forefathers. Paul did not abolish this law, but rather applied it very clearly to the believers living in Galatia.

Do not be deceived: God cannot be mocked.
People reap what they sow. (Gal. 6:7)

The impact of the sins of our forefathers can vary greatly. Some may not even be noticed much; others have such drastic effects on the descendants that they feel deformed in their spiritual lives, and in constant restriction. The results, however, are always the same. We can neither shake them off nor repress them. They will remain part of us until we realize that they are there, forgive, and lay them down at the cross. It is not our goal here to expand on the different kinds of sins of the forefathers; others have done that in great detail.[76] Having said that, I still would like to point out two specific impacts of the sin of the forefathers that have caused devastating deformation in the later generations. The one is what the Bible calls "bloodshed", and the other is "silent complicity". Both can become an almost impenetrable veil, especially in regards to the Nazi guilt of the forefathers.

The Hebrew word for "blood" in the Bible keeps referring to guilt someone incurs by shedding innocent blood. The blood is considered the seat of the soul and of life itself, so hands that shed innocent blood are an abomination in God's eyes, and always result in judgment (Prov. 6:16-17; Ps. 5:6). The innocent blood of Abel has such signal power in the heavenly realm that God says it "cries out to me from the ground" (Gen. 4:10). After the flood, Noah and his family were warned not to shed blood (Gen. 9:6). We find a different context with the Prophet Ezekiel, who was warned not to be negligent as a watchman over the house of Israel. His silence would make him complicit, and he would be held accountable for the shed blood (Ezek. 3:18,20; 33:6,8). The fact that silence makes us complicit and we incur guilt in God's eyes is certainly also a thought found in the New Testament and expressed by Paul (Acts 20:25-27). Our failure to share the Gospel with others is part of it (Acts 18:6). Jesus Himself took into account that bloodshed could be transferred from one generation to the next.[77] So bloodshed can actually be several things; shedding blood, murder, including direct or indirect support of a political party or organization steeped in bloodshed, but also silence and indifference toward the Jewish people. We will see the effects of silence on the following generations in the next few chapters. In any case, bloodshed seems to cause severe deformation in the spiritual heritage of the descendants. In counseling, we have seen devastation again and again. Just to give you an impressive testimony, here is the story of the "holy son" of a mass murderer:

Herbert[78] had been an alcoholic for more than 20 years. His family had broken apart, and he did not expect much more from life. In a soup kitchen for homeless people, he heard of the love of Jesus. He got saved and started following Jesus step by step. His life was transformed, and alcohol was no longer a part of it. Slowly but surely, he became capable of doing little chores again. From behind the destroyed façade of his personality emerged a sensitive man who loved to express his gratefulness with wonderful presents. After a while, a question came up in his mind that he simply could not shake off: What had gone so wrong in his life? Was there a deeper answer to this question than merely his personal failures? At that point, he started working through his personal family history. He knew that his father had been a soldier in the Ukraine – but that was all. He asked for research in a public national archive. A few months prior to the "March of Life" in the Ukraine, he received an official notice. It was there in black and white: His father had been stationed in Kiev during the time of the Babi Yar massacre in 1941-42. Within three days, more than 33,000 Jews had been shot there by machine gun fire. He was informed that his father had belonged to a battalion of the Wehrmacht that had murdered thousands of Jews and prisoners of war in different parts of the Ukraine. Up to this point, his father's history had been covered by a dark veil of silence. But now it was broken. Herbert invested all his money in order to go to the Ukraine for the "March of Life". Shortly before the trip, he was diagnosed with impending heart failure; but nothing could keep him from the most important journey of his life. He discharged himself from the hospital at his own risk. So now he stood at the memorial of Babi Yar in Kiev during the "March of Life" memorial service, the site of those atrocities, and there he faced the survivors of the Holocaust[79]. He had come as the son of a mass murderer to ask for forgiveness, because he himself had received grace and forgiveness. I still remember him standing in the heat of the day at Babi Yar. A young woman spoke out for all of the Germans present whose fathers and grandfathers had been actively involved in the atrocities in the Ukraine. When she asked for forgiveness, scores of TV stations broadcast it, and the whole country was deeply moved. Herbert did not stand at the microphone, and maybe many people did not even notice him. To me, however, he is among those whose history changes an entire nation. His life shows that it is possible to completely leave behind the destructive family inheritance of bloodshed, and to bring forth new life by the power of forgiveness. And his weak heart? Maybe it was a sign of what happened in his life through identificational repentance. From the very first day he entered the Ukraine on his "March of Life", his heart was healed. Today, Herbert is serving the Lord and is a precious part of our church.

Though your sins are like scarlet,
they shall be as white as snow... (Isa. 1:18)

It has been our experience that especially in regards to Nazi sins the "veil of silence" can become an almost impregnable obstacle. Many times, we give in too soon and accept the fact that we will never be able to break our parents' or grandparents' speechlessness. But we have seen amazing miracles here. Sometimes it only takes little steps of faith for us to humble ourselves in prayer for bloodshed or silent complicity during the Nazi era, and ask forgiveness for the sins of our fathers. We will not be able to do this without personal grief and shaking. Only once we discovered that the "silence of the fathers and grandfathers" turned us into silent followers also, we were able to repent and wholeheartedly turn away from it. The willingness to face the personal family past afresh quickly leads to the desire to take our forefathers' guilt to the cross, both personally, but also on behalf of the family. All who take the first steps here will discover how quickly this veil starts tearing, and the silence actually starts disintegrating. Suddenly, grandparents start opening up to the grandchildren, and tragic, traumatic, and even murderous family secrets surface to the light. All who earnestly seek to break this veil will experience the greatest change, and see spiritual breakthroughs first personally, but then also in their families.

The foundation for all change is the power of reconciliation. Paul explains in his letter to the Colossians that everything in Heaven and on earth will be reconciled through Jesus "...by making peace through his blood, shed on the cross" (Col. 1:20). How can the power of reconciliation be activated when we do not honestly face the roots of our own past? Reconciliation and truth are interdependent, and inseparably linked in the redemptive work of Jesus.[80] I do not know whether there are still areas in your family that are not reconciled yet, and that lie in the dark. Jesus wants to come with His light and pierce all darkness. He is the truth, the life and the light. When you embark on this journey, you will no longer fear the truth about your family as a threat, but will be able to have a fresh encounter with the grace of Jesus.

The Veil of Silence over Your Personal Life

I would like to encourage you at this point to pause for a moment to reflect about your own life. Take some time in prayer to think about any areas in your life where you still have to break a "veil of silence". The only way you can do this is by going to the cross. This is the place of grace and forgiveness. As long as people have not made their way to the cross, they will always be caught up in bitterness and accusations. At the cross of Calvary, Jesus took our silence upon Himself, so that with His help, we would be able to speak the unspeakable, and find healing and reconciliation through Him. Your life is far too precious to be wasted under a veil of silence. Perhaps silence has robbed you of your relational abilities. Perhaps you find it hard to develop a lasting heart-to-heart relationship with God and others. Whatever the veil of silence in your life may look like, it is worth the trouble of carefully identifying it, and then expressing it in personal prayer. Here is some advice that you may find helpful.

1. Take an extended time for prayer, preferably several hours, when you set yourself apart for God and keep all disruptive influences away from you, such as your phone, pager, or computer.

2. Ask the Holy Spirit to reveal any "veil of silence" in your life. He is the Spirit of Truth (Jn 16:13), and He loves opening our eyes and pulling away every veil over our lives.

3. When you pray, take a careful look at four areas:

   a) your own conscious silence, e.g. concerning shame, guilt, trauma, fearful experiences, or failure;

   b) your own unconscious silence, i.e. areas in your life you cannot "get a grip on" because they are repressed, dissociated because of traumatic experiences, or eclipsed by other experiences;

c) the conscious silence in your family. Ask yourself whether there are any taboo issues that prevent repentance, reconciliation, healing, and restoration, and;

d) the "fog" over your family you have never been able to clearly identify. You suspect that some occurrences in your family history are the reason behind it, but you do not know where it comes from. It is amazing to see how the first steps toward breaking personal silence usually produce a kind of domino effect that will then cause a lifting of the family curtain.

4. Take a notebook with you when you pray to jot down everything that you discover. This is to document your determination to confess the truth before a witness, thus truly wanting to break the veil.

5. Find an experienced counselor, pastor, elder, or a mature believer whom you trust. He or she should understand the biblical importance of confessing one's sins, and be willing to take time for you. If you have to deal with deeper problems, you should enlist the professional help of Christian therapists on your way to healing and restoration.

6. Pray for the right moment to address taboo issues in your family without accusation or bitterness.

7. Allow the Holy Spirit to lift any further veil, and to speak to you through the Word of God, personal revelation, or even this book, as you continue reading.

CHAPTER 4

THE SILENT GENERATIONS – THE VICTIMS

"Come quickly!" one of the staff members in our center called. "Rose Price from the States is on the phone!" We were in the midst of the preparations for the first "March of Life", where we wanted to take 200 Germans and American participants from Messianic congregations all the way from Tübingen to the memorial at Dachau, following the routes of the death marches after the dissolution of the concentration camps at the end of WWII. As a child, Rose Price had survived six different concentration camps, and Dachau had been among them. The telephone conversation with her was my first encounter ever with a survivor. This opened my eyes to an entirely new understanding of the consequences of WWII that can still be felt today for the children and grandchildren of the former perpetrators and victims. Many of them still carry their family history as a heavy burden, and without realizing it, they live under the shadow of the past, even without ever personally having experienced lack, hunger, persecution, or the necessity to flee. So at the other end of the telephone line, I suddenly heard a German, "Gruss Gott!" In her own unique, humorous way, she shared how she had learned to forgive the Germans, and then she said she would be willing to come to Germany together with her husband Jonathan for the March of Life. This was the beginning of a friendship without which this book surely would never have been written. So first of all, I would like to share her story with you.

The Survivors of the Holocaust

Rose Price was born to a Jewish Orthodox family in Poland. At first, when the Germans occupied her home town in 1939, 11-year-old Rose was put in a labor camp. During WWII, Rose spent five years in different concentration camps. Her entire family, with the exception of her aunt and sister, perished in the death camps. When she was finally liberated in Dachau by Allied forces, she was 16 years old. Through a miracle, she had survived the camps of Bergen-Belsen and Dachau, where she had turned away from God in bitterness. After the war, she emigrated to the United States, built a new life, and started a family. Through her daughter and husband, she met Yeshua as her Messiah, and entrusted her life to Him. But Rose's suffering did not end with her liberation in Dachau. The terrible experiences in the concentration camps had left her deeply traumatized, which caused such bitterness and hate that she had to have 27 operations.

Like most Holocaust survivors, Rose was plagued by nightmares. She shares this in the prelude of her book, A Rose from the Ashes.[81] "I was freezing. The wind howled outside the barracks as my sister Sarah and I huddled together, trying to stay warm and fall asleep at the same time. The barracks teemed with the sounds of other women snoring, crying, in some cases arguing. I was just finally feeling sleep wash over me, when suddenly the barrack door swung open and four Nazi guards marched in. 'Rose! Rose Lubah!' they shouted. My body stiffened with fear. 'Why are they looking for me?' I whispered to Sarah. She didn't answer. ...I could hear the guards coming closer to my bunk, the hollow clomp of the boots on the floor. Then, the footsteps stopped. I lay in the bunk, trying to breathe, hoping they would pass by. 'Rose!' the guard screamed. Startled, I exhaled quickly and loudly. A hand grabbed my arm and pulled me off the bunk to the floor. 'I found her!' the one guard shouted to the others, as he began dragging me from my bunk to the door of the barracks. 'No!' I screamed,

'Please, no! No!' A hand shook me. 'Rose! Rose, wake up!' As the noises of the barracks and the guards faded from my mind, I could hear my husband's voice. 'Rose, shhhhh,' he said gently. 'It was a nightmare. You're safe. Shhhh. You're safe.' I opened my eyes and looked at him, the horror of my dream still clinging to my heart, making it beat fast. 'Hold me,' I told him. 'Please hold me.'"

Almost forty years after her liberation, she received an invitation to come to Germany for a large event at the Olympic Stadium in Berlin. Later, Rose Price wrote about this moment,[82] "Let me give you an idea of what it was like for me. When I was first asked to speak, my reaction was one of horror. For anyone to ask me to set foot on the land where my family was extinguished was more than I could bear. I was torn between obeying the Lord, and holding onto my bitterness and hate; the Lord finally won." In 1981, she returned to Germany for the first time. To quote Rose, "I believe in miracles. I believe the Lord performed one of these miracles when He sent me back to Germany as a speaker for 'Berlin for Jesus '81.' I spoke to over 37,000 German people about forgiveness." Even while addressing the participants at the meeting, she had to fight the hate in her heart. "In Germany, I spoke on a passage in Matthew[83] on forgiveness, and while I was preaching, I felt the hate melting within me. After I spoke, six ex-Nazi soldiers came up to me and asked me to forgive them; one even told me he was a guard in the camp where I was. Everything within me rose against this man. But if God saw fit to forgive them, who was I not to forgive? I shook his hand and forgave. God is, indeed, a miracle working God! To me, this is one of the greatest miracles that could possibly have happened!" Following this reconciliation in Berlin, no further surgery was necessary, and she was completely healed.

A few months after our conversation on the telephone, I met both Rose and her husband Jonathan. They had accepted the invitation to the March of Life, together with numerous other Messianic Jews

101

who ventured on their first trip to Germany, despite their inward concerns and blockages. They were Holocaust survivors of the second and third generation, and were obviously still suffering from the fears and traumas which their parents and grandparents had experienced in Germany during the Nazi era. What was waiting for them in Germany? Had the Germans changed at all after such a long time? The first meeting was a service that many of them will never forget. We wanted to express to our Jewish friends that we, as the descendants of the perpetrators, desired to humble ourselves before them and honor them. In our church, we have some who are grandsons of SS officers who had been actively involved in the Holocaust and the murder of Jews. They knelt before Rose Price and three other descendants of victims of the Holocaust, and asked their permission to wash their feet. They allowed it. And so something happened between the descendants of the victims and the perpetrators that words cannot describe. Hate, rejection, and fears – everything that seemed to have weighed on the children and grandchildren of both the victims and the perpetrators like a leaden cloak, suddenly seemed to melt away in this act of reconciliation. The tent hall was filled with the glory of God, unlike anything I had ever experienced before.

Among those in the first row whose feet were washed by the grandchildren of SS soldiers was the Holocaust survivor Peter Loth. Today, Peter lives in Houston, TX. I had met him a year earlier when we had invited him to be a speaker in our church. I had prepared for our meeting by reading his biography. What I read about him and his story was so gruesome that my spirit could scarcely take it in. We met a few weeks after that, and immediately our relationship was marked by trust. But still there was something within me that refused to believe what I had read about him. So I decided to take the direct approach, and asked him to share his life's story with me.

Peter was born in the concentration camp of Stutthof near Danzig in 1943. When he was supposed to be taken to Auschwitz together with his mother in 1945, partisans attacked the train. His mother did not have the strength to flee together with the baby, and so she entrusted the boy to a Polish lady, who took care of him like her own son. For some time, his Polish foster mother and Peter had to hide in the underground sewer system. "My earliest recollection is that of men who separated me from my 'Matka', my Polish mother. I was taken to an orphanage, where 30 to 40 German children were kept in one room. The Russians and Poles were filled with such hatred toward the Germans that they vented their anger on the little ones. The orphanage lacked everything. The boys were forced to work during the day, and were repeatedly abused at night." [84] Peter himself was raped numerous times, and only escaped death by shooting because his Polish foster mother offered her own body to the Russian soldier in exchange for his life. The girl who was his best friend was shot right next to him. "I saw my little friend with the yellow star. She lay dead on a heap of corpses." When he was six years old, the situation became so unbearable for him that he wanted to kill himself; but then he was allowed to live with his Polish foster mother again. In the meantime, his birth mother had survived the concentration camp and had gotten married to a black American soldier in Western Germany. She lived with him on a U.S. army base, and from there she searched and found Peter's address and wrote him a letter. The American return address aroused the highest suspicion of the Polish authorities, and the 15-year-old was now accused of being a spy. He was put into prison for eight months, where he was physically abused again and again during the course of the many interrogations. Finally he was granted permission to leave Poland, and he was able to cross over to the West through Checkpoint Charlie in Berlin.

When he met his mother for the first time, the only thing he felt for her was hatred. "She spoke German and English, I spoke

Polish and Russian. How could she have abandoned me for the sake of her own freedom? My mother must have noticed my pain and all the questions in my eyes. She unbuttoned her blouse and showed me her back; it was covered with scars. She showed me her breasts; they were mutilated. A number was tattooed on her arm." Suddenly Peter understood that she must have suffered unspeakable things just like he had. "But I didn't know who had done this or why. Weeping I embraced my mama. She asked me, 'Mein lieber Peter, please forgive me.'" At the age of 16, for the first time, Peter had a family. You can imagine how significant this event was for him. And yet, there was another side, a side that most Holocaust survivors have suffered from: Until her death, he and his mother could not find words for the horrors of the Nazi time. But Peter's sufferings were not over yet. In 1959, he emigrated to the United States with his family, followed by years of rejection, contempt, and abuse through the Ku-Klux-Klan, and finally running away from his tyrannical stepfather, who had turned to alcohol. Once again Peter was all alone and without a family. Then a politician found him and took care of him; he even became his mentor. Peter finished his education, completed college, and became an engineer. His first marriage that had produced twins ended in a fiasco. As soon as Peter's wife discovered his black relatives, she filed for divorce. Unanswerable questions tormented his mind. Why had he survived, while "Star", his closest friend, and other children were killed? His own story was buried deep within him. It was hidden under an impregnable veil of silence. "Whenever a memory would flash up – orphanage, abuse, rape, beatings, torture – I experienced a complete blockage and ran away; the pain was simply too great. Often I felt like someone was sticking a burning torch into me." Peter married a second time, and then met Yeshua as his Lord and savior. In 1992, he had a life-changing experience when he received his calling. "God showed me my whole life – going back from the present time right to my mother's womb. He showed me what had happened, and called me to talk about it.

But why should I? I was afraid to expose my inner self. But God promised me that He would always be with me. From the moment I said 'yes', I was able to talk." This was the beginning of a painful journey. After the death of his mother, he met his sister, who told him for the first time that he had been born in a concentration camp. His mother had never told him about this. Peter knew he had to return to Poland. "Without this healing, I would never be able to minister to others." Sometime later, Peter visited Stutthof concentration camp near Danzig. He had been born there, and had been subjected to cruel medical experiments. This was the place where his grandmother had been gassed, and his mother had been brutally tortured. "We went into the office, where we saw our names. It was so painful." At the entrance to the oven where his grandmother had been cremated, he was overwhelmed by anger and mourning. The only thing left in him was hatred. At the entrance to Stutthof concentration camp there was a display of photographs of the guards of the camp, the tormentors of the prisoners. "God appeared to me again, brought me to my knees, and said to me, 'Forgive them!' Peter knelt down in front of those photographs of the camp guards, and found himself in a tremendous inner struggle. "I had to learn that God could only forgive my sin if I forgave those who had sinned against me." So after a long struggle right in front of the photos of the camp guards, he said "yes" to forgiveness, for the first time opening a door for a process of healing in which time and time again he forgave those he had formerly hated. Slowly he regained his inner composure. "I can forgive. Everything was stolen from me; my childhood, youth – everything. But now I am able to forgive. Today I am travelling everywhere to invite people to forgive others, so the Father in Heaven can also forgive their sins."

For if you forgive others when they sin against you,
your heavenly Father will also forgive you.
But if you do not forgive others their sins,
your Father will not forgive your sins. (Matt. 6:14-15)

I have known Peter Loth for many years now, and have heard his story many times. Several times we have ministered together in various places in the U.S. and Eastern Europe. His story is still a living miracle for me today. After having received healing of his emotional hurts and trauma, he is now an ambassador of forgiveness. I will never forget how he ministered in our church for the first time after our initial meeting. After he had told his story and all of us sat in stunned silence, he asked us as Germans for forgiveness. He had hated us, and had realized that this was sin in God's eyes. "Can you forgive me?" I was shocked. For me, it was like the world was turned upside down. How can he ask us, descendants of the perpetrators, for forgiveness? I knew we had to humble ourselves before him and ask his forgiveness. Many of the participants of the service were descendants of SS officers and people actively involved in persecuting Jews, and they carried their ancestors' heritage like an inner burden on their shoulders. I approached and embraced him, proclaiming forgiveness to him representing the Germans. Then the time had come when many of the second and third generation of descendants were able to break their silence and step out of their ancestors' dark shadows. After quickly checking with Peter, I asked all those who wanted to ask his forgiveness for the sins of their ancestors to come forward. Peter wanted to embrace every single one of them and proclaim forgiveness to them. The people came running to the altar, and then they waited patiently in long lines until it was their turn to talk to Peter. Most of them were weeping; others broke down and experienced encouragement and healing. The service went on until 2 a.m. There was an atmosphere of grace and forgiveness, like you usually only read about in books about revival.

There was a spiritual principle behind this: Peter Loth and the descendants of the perpetrators were breaking the veil of silence over their own lives. When victims and perpetrators, as well as their descendants, get to know the power of forgiveness like Peter Loth did, and when they are willing to enter the process of forgiveness and identificational repentance, the shadows of the past lose their power once and for all. The result is a radiant, supernatural presence and glory of God. We have seen this over and over again on the Marches of Life in Europe and America. I wish next time you could be with us. When Peter Loth is speaking, you can feel that he has to deal with the pain all over again. Sometimes he is weeping, and spontaneously he proclaims forgiveness. Often he points out that these presentations help him to receive healing and to work through the past. "Unless we forgive, we will not enter the Kingdom of Heaven. Jesus turns the hypocrites away who know how to talk good, but refuse to forgive." Forgiveness is a matter of the heart, Loth emphasizes. "If you want to do this with your mind, you will fail, because unforgiveness eats away at a man like a cancer." Without forgiveness, we will pass hatred, bitterness or anger on to our children. This is also the reason why he keeps asking, "It is time for forgiveness. Can you accept that?" Every time he shares his story, it cuts me to the heart and causes deep pain. It is the story of a Holocaust survivor whose life stands for millions of others. They have largely passed their suffering and pain to their children. Sometimes they manage to talk about it and to find words for the inexpressible. But most survivors don't. The constant threat of annihilation they have experienced, and the extreme brutality they were exposed to for such an extended period of time, have left them deeply scarred and wounded with an invisible, protective shield and a thick wall of silence around them.

Thirty years after the end of WWII, Israeli and American psychologists first started discussing the effects of the Holocaust on the

children of the victims. They discovered that the long-term consequences of the Holocaust are verifiable to this day, and cannot be
dismissed as a thing of the past. By now, there are numerous scientific papers that document the psychological long-term effects of
the trauma of the Holocaust on the victims and their descendants.
In Israel today there are more than 140,000 Holocaust survivors;
in the U.S. there are 175,000, half of whom live in New York.[85]
Many of them were still children at the end of the war. They
all share the experience of persecution, deportation, selection,
hunger, torture, forced labor, and the murder of their loved ones.
They are generally over 80 years old now. If you take their descendants and close relatives into account, there are several millions
of people today who are still directly or indirectly affected by the
Holocaust. But what does the term 'Holocaust survivor' actually
mean? Dr. Natan Kellermann is a clinical psychologist in Israel
and director of AMCHA[86], the national center for psychosocial
support for Holocaust survivors, plus the second generation. This
is his definition:[87] "A Holocaust survivor is someone who was
persecuted as a Jew under Nazi occupation, whose life was threatened by Hitler's 'final solution', but who somehow managed to
stay alive. Among them are also prisoners in ghettos and forced
laborers deported to labor or concentration camps, or those who
were able to survive in hiding under a false identity. We also
count those refugees among the Holocaust survivors who had to
leave behind their families, fight alongside partisans, or were sent
away by a so-called 'Kindertransport' (Refugee Children Movement)." All of them had to endure a constant state of threat,
humiliation, and degradation, suffering an existential struggle for
survival in the face of death, painful losses, and the annihilation of their families. The years did not lessen the trauma and
intense inner pain, but rather left deep, internal scars in them and
their descendants, until now. Kellermann is currently seeing the
greatest demand for their services by Holocaust survivors seeking
help in the whole of their history.[88] "Especially with increasing

age, the memories come flooding back with full brutal force when a person's career is over and the children are settled and taken care of. Then is the time for the survivors, when they feel the need to address the issue," says Kellermann. After the end of the war, the Holocaust survivors first went looking for their families. Many times there was no one left to find, followed by a deep emotional vacuum that the survivors were unable to face. This went hand in hand with a feeling of guilt, expressed in the question, "Why am I still alive?", that became like a guiding theme in their lives. For many years they hid behind their silence. The Israeli psychologist Dan Bar-On, professor at the Ben Gurion University in Be'er Sheva, describes this condition with the picture of a double wall. "The survivors raise a wall before their memories of the Holocaust; their children sense this wall, and in turn build up their own wall. Now if one side wants to break a window through their wall at some point, they only find a wall on the other side." [89] The parents never spoke about it, and the generation of the children never dared to ask. There was a shadow weighing heavily on the second generation that they could hardly escape. They grew up under an atmosphere of mourning and fear. "The children are the heirs of the pain," says Kellermann.[90] Even though they did not personally suffer the Holocaust, they sometimes sense their parents' repressed pain even more acutely and work it through in their nightmares, as if they had experienced it themselves.

Every Holocaust survivor has their own story. Depending on their character and their experiences during the war, and the time of reintegration after the war, they process the experiences of the Holocaust each in their own way. What they all have in common is that they do not want to be treated as psychiatric patients, and usually have little interest in therapeutic treatment. Many of the survivors showed an "exceptionally high measure" of mental strength.[91] They fought as soldiers in the Israeli wars and helped to the best of their abilities to build the newly-established State of Israel. Somehow they managed to temporarily overcome their traumatic experiences and loss of family members. With their inner protective measures, they did everything to hide the effects they were suffering and to repress the memories. But with increasing age this proved to be more and more difficult. Here is an example taken from AMCHA's psychological counseling: [92] "A survivor came to seek help because of acute sleep disturbance. Every night he woke up drenched in sweat and found it impossible to go to sleep again. Painful memories of the Holocaust came flooding back, along with all of their accessory symptoms. Horror kept overwhelming him every night. He then spoke of recurring nightmares of the Gestapo chasing him on motorbikes. For Jews it had been illegal to be outdoors at night, and in his dreams he was running for his life until he reached the door of his house, but found it locked. While standing before the big door, he called for his father to open the door for him. He shouted, 'Dad, dad!', but no one opened the door. While he was still shouting, he realized that his wife was trying to wake him up, and understood it had all been a dream." But afterwards he was unable to go back to sleep because of the memories of his family who had perished. Over and over again he was crowded by the memory of how he had been forced to do things for which he could never forgive himself. The fact that he was still alive was an absurd accident in his eyes, as his life had actually lost all meaning for him. "It used to be life," he said, "now it is just existing." These are the ten most common effects and symptoms that Holocaust survivors suffer from: [93]

1. A massive repression of their traumatic experiences, even to the loss of memory.
2. Repeated recurring fearful memories and associations.
3. Depression, chronic grief, and idealization of suicide.
4. A feeling of guilt for having survived.
5. Sleep disorders and nightmares.
6. Problems in dealing with interpersonal conflicts.

7. Extreme worries and fears, especially of renewed persecution.

8. Mistrust, isolation, lack of trust, and loneliness.

9. Low tolerance threshold in difficult situations.

10. Panic response at any triggers symbolizing the Holocaust, such as barking dogs, barbed wire, bread that is thrown away, crammed railway stations and trains, but also sudden reactions of grief at happy events, e.g. at Jewish festivals like weddings or family celebrations, stirring memories of people who are no longer alive and have been brutally killed.

Almost all Holocaust survivors had a choice of two basic coping strategies. Either they decided to talk about it, or – as was the case for most of them – they hid behind a thick wall of silence. The children born after the war often became the parents' replacement for what they had lost during the war – their own parents, siblings, or earlier children. The consequences for the children of the "second generation" were immense. Their relationships were marked by an emotional distance, fears, and they lacked the ability to express their emotions. Many of them embarked on a tedious search for their identity.

Holocaust survivors are the most precious people I have met. I love being with them, and I admire how they simply manage to live even despite everything they have been through. And this is what they want: be happy and live! L'Chaim! And dancing is part of it! My wife and I were invited to a banquet with Holocaust survivors in Ashdod by Andre Gasiorowski, director of Helping Hands Coalition, a widely recognized ministry that effectively supports Holocaust survivors. The Israeli Absorption Minister was also present, and I was one of the speakers. We had a team from our bible school with us who were supposed to do a dance there. I had expected an atmosphere of oppression, but far from it! After a festive dinner with lots of laughter, talking, and loud

111

music that rather reminded me of a boisterous family celebration, the Holocaust survivors flooded the dance floor when called by the band. I have seen a fair bit of wild dancing in our church, but the exuberant joy of the 70- to 80-year-olds in their dancing took my breath away. They invited our bible students to join them, and now you could see excited 20-year-olds, who were part of the German generation of grandchildren, whiz across the dance floor together with excited Holocaust survivors. What a picture and what symbolism! The generation of the great-grandchildren, sometimes also called the "fourth generation", is used by God to reach hearts that nobody else is able to reach. This is the generation who breaks the silence and who has left behind the desert years of previous generations.

Behold, I will do a new thing; now it shall sprout;
shall you not know it? I will even make a way in the wilderness,
rivers in the desert. (Isa. 43:19; MKJV)

The "Child Survivors"

All who were able to survive the Holocaust as a child had to cope with completely different experiences compared to those of adult survivors. Children are more vulnerable and more easily deformed than adults, and they found different ways to deal with the extreme trauma of the Holocaust. The "Child Survivors" were under 16 years old when the war ended. Today, they are between 65 and 80 years old. Peter Loth, born in Stutthof concentration camp, and Rose Price, who was 16 years old when she was liberated in Dachau, are such "Child Survivors". The early loss of their parents and siblings is something that is haunting "Child Survivors" for the rest of their lives. They were handed over to foster parents or caregivers, thrown out of trains or hidden in attics and basements, left behind or hidden in forests. Often children were brutally separated from their parents in the concentration camps in many different ways. In contrast to adults, children are both more vulnerable and more adaptable at the same time. Whatever their experiences were – they were deprived of a normal childhood. Early on, they had to experience being at the mercy of alien forces, completely out of their control, ruling over their lives. Many of them had to undergo numerous operations that are undoubtedly the result of the Holocaust. The younger a survivor was at the time, the more traumatic their experiences were, leaving all the deeper traces. The most common problems "Child Survivors" have to struggle with are:

1. Helplessness and a strong victim mentality, feeling at the mercy of others.

2. Existential abandonment and isolation.

3. A permanent sense of "unwantedness", often linked to the need to prove one's worth.

4. Grief that often remains unadmitted, emotionally fading out the losses.

5. Identity trouble, especially with children who were forced to grow up under a false name in another family.

6. Lacking capability to remember.

7. A search for traces of their past in which they hope to revive memories of their parents or childhood through associations, such as familiar smells, a noise, or a picture.

8. Dissociation and isolation of emotions as a survival strategy in order to "go unnoticed".[94]

There are in-depth studies on "Child Survivors". In order to understand, however, what they had to go through and how much they still suffer from the effects of the Holocaust, this may suffice.

The Children of Holocaust Survivors

But let us return to the first "March of Life" that we held in 2007. A well-known TV host and journalist from Dallas got in touch with us, who wanted to know more about our city's history and our ministry, and wanted to produce a TV program with several parts. It was Dr. Jeffrey L. Seif, then the successor and main presenter of Zola Levitt Presents, a TV program that reaches millions of people all throughout the United States. This resulted in the eight-part series "Bad Moon Rising" that became a unique testimony in the United States.[95] Jeffrey himself is a Holocaust survivor of the second generation. I still remember how he kept saying, "You could take mom out of Nazi Germany, but you could never take Nazi Germany out of mom." In one of his messages, he shared how every time he used the flap of a mail box, he was reminded by association of the gas ovens in the concentrations camps.

We visited a kind old man who had survived the Holocaust in a camp in the vicinity of Tübingen. We asked him about his memories. After a very warm welcome, he told us about how both he and his wife had struggled to get a foothold in post-war Germany again. His wife was a survivor of the concentration camp at Theresienstadt. Both threw themselves into reestablishing their lives and tried to repress the dreadful memories, somehow pushing them aside. But they were unsuccessful. Every night the horrible events and the pain would return, like constantly reappearing ghosts in the shape of nightmares. Even their children kept waking from their sleep with a start. They wanted to somehow heal their parents' pain, but they did not know how to fill their vacuum. But the children were weighed down so heavily with their parents' burden, that both died of cancer at the age of 42. "Our children died from the effects of the Holocaust," was the remark that burned itself into my memory during our conversation.

Behind these tragic stories are the traumatic long-term effects of the Holocaust that can be found in the children of the Holocaust survivors and even in their grandchildren.

One woman gives a moving description of how she had to relive her mother's trauma of the Holocaust every day. Even though she was born many years after the war, even more than half a century later she is still haunted by her mother's experiences during the Holocaust. "These images... encroach on me, stifling me. For instance, in the mornings, with all the cars and fumes I think, 'Don't breathe', at the same time sure this is how they would gas people today, by diverting the fumes into the trucks stuffed with prisoners. You have to know that my mother was almost gassed. They dragged her to the showers, but then discovered they didn't have enough Zyklon B.... I remember that... I remember it twenty times a day, a hundred times a day." [96] These recurring images, associations of the Holocaust, and panic attacks are common manifestations in Holocaust survivors. The transmission to their entire family, exercising indirect influence on the lives of their children and even grandchildren, is called "trans-generational trauma transfer" [97] in the professional world. How is it possible that traumatic experiences are transferred despite decades of silence in the families? By now there is a large number of publications, lectures, and professional expertise on the issue. In most reports, the children of the Holocaust survivors are called the second generation. They are born between 1945 and 1960, so today they are over 50 years old.

One of them is Rabbi Chaim Urbach, son of Eliezer Urbach, who was among the founding fathers and advisors of the Messianic movement in America. Eliezer was a Holocaust survivor who had to flee from Poland after he lost his entire family. He wrote a book on the circumstances of how he finally reached Palestine after travelling thousands of miles, and how he helped in the birthing of the State of Israel as a soldier. [98] Chaim Urbach was born in

Israel, where he spent his childhood. In 1967 he came to the States, together with his parents, where he finished his theological studies. Today he serves as rabbi in the Messianic community Yeshuah Tsion in Denver. I met Chaim in Washington, D.C. We were holding a March of Remembrance event on the lawn in front of the Capitol, and he was invited to speak as the representative of the second generation of Holocaust survivors. In his brief address, he presented some very remarkable thoughts coming from his own experience that I would like to share at this point.[99]

"My father, who passed away a little over a year ago, was caught up in the horrific vortex of the Holocaust. I grew up with the Holocaust deeply embedded in my psyche. Why write a paper on the impact of the Holocaust on the second generation, knowing that it would be gut-wrenching, inducing me to dive deeply into national, family and personal pain? The need is infinitely greater than airing my personal story. There are many Messianic Jews who are children of survivors, living in Israel, the U.S., Canada, and elsewhere. Yet our movement, the Messianic Jewish Movement, has been largely silent on the struggles involved in the lives of the second and third generations of survivors. Perhaps this may sound like a simplistic statement, but there is no need for those wounds to remain unhealed. Redemption is available. Our Messiah is waiting to be granted entrance into those dark and broken places to bring healing and restoration... Images of the Holocaust have been embedded in my psyche from childhood. Our generation that grew up in the 1950s and 1960s in Israel was taught about the Holocaust from every possible medium. We were taught songs about the Holocaust, read stories about the Holocaust, and went to Yad VaShem (the Holocaust museum in Jerusalem) where we were shown bars of soap from human fat and lampshades from human skins. Much more personally was the fact that each of our families mourned the death of family members who perished in the Holocaust. The Holocaust's presence was rarely addressed, but nonetheless it was woven into our consciences."

In his presentation, Chaim Urbach points out two phenomena that I think are remarkable. After the end of the war, the survivors returned to a world that was captive under shock to such an extent that it could hardly cope with the suffering of the survivors of the Holocaust. Urbach reports how even in Israel, the survivors were termed "ghetto Jews" over and over again, which was synonymous for all those who did not have the courage to take a stand against the anti-Semitic gentiles and to defend themselves. Wherever they went, they came across the same invisible walls. Generally they were shunned as if they were alien creatures. Many of the survivors got married quickly, trying to replace their lost families with children of their own. Next to their own inability to put the trauma into words, they were faced with the incapability and lacking willingness of anybody to listen to them. It is amazing to see how this double speechlessness is transferred through the generations. Can this be the reason, remarks Chaim Urbach, why until today, the Messianic movement is still under a veil of silence concerning the inner pain and struggles of the second and third generation of the Holocaust?

As a German, I had the privilege of ministering in many different Messianic congregations in America. In almost every congregation I came across reservations, fears, and defense mechanisms that were rooted in the struggles of the second and third generations. I still remember preaching on the "Veil of Silence" for the first time in a large Messianic congregation in Dallas, TX, and sharing how this veil had been broken over our church. While I was speaking, I sensed a tremendous pain in me. What I was feeling was a little of God's pain over all the silence that had been passed on through the generations from the Holocaust survivors to their descendants because of the unspoken suffering and trauma. I sensed the ghosts of the past rising again in many, caused by my speaking German, stirring up painful memories. In Germany I had heard it said many times that we had to let the Holocaust rest, closing our past as Germans, and finally look ahead. But in this service, the reality was a totally different one. Millions of the second and third generations still suffer from the effects of the Holocaust, and at that very moment, I saw some of them right before me! Strangely enough, both the descendants of the victims and the perpetrators suffer the same fate: both generations were caught under a similar speechlessness, living under the veil of silence.[100] I felt the Holy Spirit lead me to say, "It is terrible to say, but you have the veil of silence here just as much as we have it in Germany! It stands between you, parents and children, between you, married couples, and also in your congregations!" The effects of the Holocaust on the second generation cannot be made up for. How much more painful must it be for them, if the second and third generations of German descendants declare themselves rid of any responsibility. While I was repenting as a representative of Germany and the second generation of the perpetrators at the end of my message on the "Veil of Silence", asking for forgiveness, the Holy Spirit spoke to me, saying, "Jobst, as long as the silent generations are still suffering from the effects of the Holocaust, I want to use you to break this veil over them." A few years have passed since then, and I have had the privilege of ministering in many Messianic congregations since then. In the meantime, we have reached hundreds of thousands within America, Israel, and ten other nations with the March of Life Movement. Radio and TV stations have broadcast the reconciliation between generations of descendants of the victims and the perpetrators. We hear of fears disappearing and of traumas being healed through the message about the forgiving "unmerited grace" and of how the fears and traumas are gone from the lives of those still suffering.

In almost every Messianic congregation, I am able to minister to people as they approach me after the message, saying, "I used to hate the German language, and today was the first time I actually enjoyed hearing it again!" Others want to talk to me to tell me of how their fear of Germany has disappeared. At this point, I would like to have Chaim share his experiences as a representative of the second generation.

"In 1986, my father's story was written by his secretary.[101] Before publication, she gave me the manuscript to preview. I was astounded. The vast majority of the story was totally unknown to me. Later on, I discovered that my experience was not unique. Our parents, the survivors, were often incapable of articulating their experience. Helen Epstein, in her ground-breaking book 32 years ago, *Children of the Holocaust: Conversations with sons and daughters of survivors,*[102] presented this trauma as one of the common symptoms in the experience of the second generation of survivors. Epstein, herself an adult child of survivors, grew up with the memories of the horror of the Holocaust, conveyed in brief sketches by her parents. Her parents' pain pervaded her household, but it was never addressed. Growing up, she pictured the trauma of the Holocaust as an ominous presence that was shut up tight in a dark, iron box."

There are essentially two schools of thought trying to find an answer to the mental effects of the Holocaust on the children of the survivors. One assumes that the children of survivors differ from the regular population because of their psycho-social impairment. Others deny this, claiming children of survivors had the same problems as everybody else. After the publication of more than 500 reports describing the transfer of trauma to the children of the second and third generation[103], the focus no longer seems to be on the question of whether, but rather how the transfer takes place. Kellermann describes four basic models[104] of how trauma can be transferred to children and grandchildren.
Psychoanalysis seems to assume that the unconscious mind itself can be "infectious". Experiences that were never worked through are unconsciously transferred to the child. Without noticing, the child absorbs the repressed experiences in his or her own life.

Family systems theory considers dysfunctional family communication as the main reason for trauma transfer. Here the emphasis is on the role of the family environment, where the children of the second generation are emotionally very close to their parents in the "family system" and are excessively concerned about their parents' welfare, and want to protect them from further harm.

Socialization Theory says the transfer happens through the way the parents raise their children. This assumes the direct influence of the traumatized parents. Here, the parents' inadequate behavior in raising the children can have such an influence on the family atmosphere that it has negative repercussions on the behavior of the children. Abbye Silverstein describes this as follows:[105] "It is the second generation and their children who carry the trauma of the Holocaust, as it was transmitted to them from their survivor parents. These Baby Boomer children of survivors grew up in families suffering from post-traumatic stress disorders. Some of their parents' symptoms were survivor's guilt, hopelessness, chronic depression, repressed anger or uncontrolled anger, distrust of human beings, chronic anxiety with recurring nightmares, obsessive thinking about past traumas, difficulty enjoying life, and the inability to show affection. The children of the survivors were exposed daily to their parents' psychological, emotional, and spiritual behavior. Although not experiencing it firsthand, their childhood was shaped by their parents' diluted trauma. It was like being in a room with a smoker and experiencing second-hand smoke without smoking."

The biological model supposes that trauma is transmitted just like a hereditary disease from one generation to the next. One chief witness can be Florian Holsboer of the Max-Planck-Institute of Psychiatry, who researches the transmission of personality changes caused by trauma to the next generation.[106]

It is striking to see how in the three models mentioned above you can expect an improvement even just through the conscious process of working through and putting into words the traumatic issues alone. How much more could happen if the children of Holocaust survivors were given a perspective of hope and redemption? Psychologists agree that a person's mindset has to be changed along the long journey of facing and dealing with the past up to the point of restoration. If the person succeeds in viewing the past not as a curse, but rather as a powerful inheritance, healing could become possible for the survivors, the following generations, and the entire Jewish community who are still struggling with the effects of the Holocaust.[107] Healing begins with a restored identity. What would happen if the identity broken through trauma were touched with the love and shalom of God? And there is no better way for this to happen than through a grace that is so immeasurable, that it is even able to touch and heal the descendants of the perpetrators.

As a representative of the second generation, Chaim Urbach has experienced this. His testimony is encouraging. He writes, "Whereas we grew up with a broken identity because of the trauma transmitted to us by our wounded parents, we now have the potential to experience God's Shalom, completion/relational wholeness. We have the confidence of a love that transcends the brokenness due to the Holocaust. We can revel in God's divine love for us and experience a 're-parenting' by him." I am convinced that this process of redemption and healing can only be released and facilitated through the reconciliation of the second generation of victims and perpetrators. What would happen if churches and congregations made room for that?

See what great love the Father has lavished on us, that we should be called children of God! And that is what we are! The reason the world does not know us is that it did not know him. (1John 3:1)

The Third Generation

Some time ago, I received an interesting letter from Hawaii, and I would like to share a few excerpts with you. "Dear Jobst, I saw an interview that you did online and I was blown away! You spoke about how God convicted you about the sins of your fathers and the silence that was over Germany about the Holocaust. Jesus showed me this interview at a very interesting time. Earlier that week during a time of prayer for Hawaii (my home), he broke my heart as he showed me the condition of my heart toward Germany. I am Jewish and I lived in Germany for most of my life as my parents worked (there) ... So during this time of prayer, God showed me that I (and I hate to use the word) hated Germans. I had wondered my whole life when I saw someone who was older, just what were they doing in the war? Did they stand by and watch while my relatives were murdered? ... When I left Germany to go back to the U.S. for school I did not want to meet Germans, or speak the language. When people heard I had lived in Germany they would say, Oh come meet so-and-so, they are German, and I would want to do anything but that. But then Jesus gets a hold of my heart and shows me a mirror. And I can't believe how much hatred was in me and unforgiveness, and bitterness ... I am called to hope, to believe, and to love, and here I was just hating, and in unbelief that God could ever change Germany. My heart was broken. And then a few days later I found this video of you speaking about this. I have never heard these words coming out of the mouth of a German. You spoke about how the silence of your fathers is still in you, that if you stay silent, the guilt is on you too. I couldn't believe it. 'Ich komme aus dem Land der unverdienten Gnade [I am from the country of unmerited grace].' God can transform curse into blessing. This came after I told God that I was willing to believe that even Germans could change. So I just wanted to send you this letter to thank you ... Thank you for speaking to other Germans, thank you for asking for forgiveness.

This is a ministry that is so needed. I'm crying even now as I think of what Jesus is doing. He is so merciful, He is so full of grace, He is so full of love. How do any of us deserve this kind of grace? ... I just want to ask your forgiveness too. As your sister, I hated you and I didn't believe that you could change. I'm so sorry. God bless you."

The letter was written by a granddaughter of the Holocaust generation; in professional literature this group is also called "the third generation". Demographically these grandchildren of the Holocaust generation are between 35 and 50 years of age. While the second generation of Holocaust survivors came into view for the general American public in the mid 1970s,[108] there is also a clearly identifiable group of the third generation by now. They wanted to talk to their parents about the Holocaust, but soon found out their fathers or mothers were not able to give them any answers. So without hesitation they went to their grandparents and simply asked them to tell their stories. The grandparents did for their grandchildren what they had not been able to do for their children. They spoke about their painful experiences and broke their silence. This produced a phenomenon that numerous psychologists and scientists have researched. It was much easier for the survivors to communicate with their grandchildren than with their own children. Here it makes no difference whether the families live in Israel or America.[109] Apparently, the grandchildren of the Holocaust generation have a freedom their parents never had. They never saw their parents despised and shunned as victims. The second generation, in contrast, frequently had to experience this. For the generation of grandchildren, fears of anti-Semitism and persecution only played a minor role. The second generation had been faced with a much clearer confrontation. The grandchildren know the Holocaust only from documentaries, stories, and books that somehow tend to crowd their parents' bookshelves. And yet they discover that this also concerns them, and that they are more involved than they would care to think. A lawyer, a German "grandson of the Holocaust", reports how the sentence, "My grandmother survived Auschwitz", formed him unlike anything else. "I was a child of the '90s after all, born in 1978. I saw the fall of the Berlin Wall when I was 11, grew up with techno and hip-hop music, with Helmut Kohl [long-term German chancellor] ... Germany is reunited; the French and Poles are Germany's best friends. Why should my grandmother's fate have made itself felt anywhere else but on my bookshelf and in my parents' stories? The answer is, I grew up with the Holocaust. I didn't have to constantly talk about it with my parents; but that was not necessary. I took note of the fact that our bookshelves were full of books on the Third Reich, the Holocaust, Israel, and Judaism. I accepted the fact and read a lot about it." [110] The effects and trauma the second generation had to struggle with are sometimes experienced even more acutely by the third generation. They have to live through associations of the Holocaust, trauma and fears; but due to the long time that has passed, often they are unable to link them to the Holocaust. C. Zimmermann says, "We were not only the grandchildren (of the Holocaust).[111] In some way we were interwoven with it. Our grandmother's story was our family history; the story of the Holocaust was our own." [112] The generation of the grandchildren was removed far enough from the terror of the Holocaust to ask questions that nobody else in the family had ever dared to ask before. Through their innocent asking, listening and working through, they actually managed to develop something like pride in being descendants of Holocaust survivors. In seminars, workshops and scientific research groups, they embark on the search for their identity. I found the following introduction in a workshop for the third generation, 3GH for short. In my opinion, this describes the attitude to life of this generation very adequately:

"The third generation has received all of the fruits of our grandparents' labor. We have enjoyed opportunities they didn't have - personal, cultural and religious freedom - an affluent way of life, abundance of food, education, travel, so many opportunities. In contrast, our parents and grandparents were refugees, and most were denied freedom on all levels. A second level of tension exists because although we have amazing opportunities to flourish and be free compared to our grandparents, we struggle with an 'internal' war – we seek happiness, a sense of purpose, belonging and meaning." [113]

A paradigm shift has taken place between the second and third generation. While the focus of the second generation was still on the suffering and the emotional effects, for the third generation, shame has been changed into self-confidence.[114] The Holocaust is no longer denied or repressed; but rather it has become part of their Jewish identity through the open communication and special relationship with their grandparents. Even though there are studies that show that the awareness of their grandparents' suffering can have positive effects on their social, societal and political actions,[115] the questions still remain as to how they can make the final transition from their inner struggles into God's peace, into His "shalom".

The scientist Mark Yoslow answers this question in his dissertation. According to his findings, all those who have the opportunity to find release from the effects of their Holocaust trauma are those who manage to forgive the Germans and the ones who caused their trauma. By letting go, Yoslow writes, the negative emotional effects of the Holocaust can be changed and transformed into a quest for the meaning of life.[116] God's answer for unhealed wounds is the power of forgiveness. This power, however, must not be confused with "forgetting" or "wanting to cover up". The wounds of the Holocaust are still present in the third generation of survivors. They are the generation who are facing the truth and breaking their silence. All those who discover the power of forgiveness will be able to find peace and healing beyond words.

I was deeply moved by the following report by a young woman in our church: "When I went on the march in 2007, my life was an absolute disaster. Not my outer circumstances, but my inside was a shambles. Since I can remember, I had always been fighting a shadow of fear over me. Outwardly I appeared strong and aloof; but inside I was tormented by the fear that eventually I would be caught and tortured by somebody. Even as a child I suffered from nightmares. When I took my dog for a walk, I would avoid looking into parked cars, for fear of a corpse in there. In fact, I constantly had to look behind me to be sure no one followed me... At some point, I started to cut myself, and tried to commit suicide. The fear increased; I could only sleep with pills, and dying seemed to be a release. At the time of the March of Life 2007 (I had been married by then and had a young son) I was in therapy, and only a few weeks later I was supposed to be admitted to a psychiatric clinic. They told me that I was like someone who had a trauma of war and tried to help me; but I could not understand where it all came from, and cried out to God to get me out of this. On the day we were in Dachau, I walked around the former concentration camp site with a friend. When we were close to the ovens and gas chambers, the ground started shaking under my feet. The atmosphere was charged. The demons were dancing around me; I literally felt them brushing past me, and I collapsed on the spot. As I sat in this place of hell, suddenly everything made sense. My whole life was like a movie in front of me, and I understood what I had always been afraid of. I am Jewish; my grandmother had lived on the Ettersberg in Weimar, where the Buchenwald concentration camp was built in 1937. She was married to a German officer and had concealed her Jewish origins. The truth came to light, and she had to flee. Her husband was killed. In the country, she met a farmer in a small village whom she married, my grandfather. She never spoke about her Jewish heritage or her experiences during the war. Her trauma lived on in me. As I sat there in desperation, I whispered softly, 'Jesus, help me.' All of a sudden, He stood in front of me. I could see Jesus. He smiled at me and held out his hand ... I got up, and His love and peace flowed through me. His presence was so strong that within one moment, all the chains of death and fear that had held me prisoner all my life fell away from me! Since that moment, I am a changed person. Jesus has truly given me new life! No nightmares and insomnia, no more thoughts of suicide or panic attacks, paranoia, or self-destruction! I love living, and every day is a gift, and I am totally in love with Jesus, who gave everything for me to set me free and to break the Veil of Silence. Thank you for letting God use you! It really is a privilege and gift to be in this church. I have experienced so much healing here, and I cannot even put into words what it means to me that you stand by Israel the way you do, and that you love my people and me! Thank you!"

CHAPTER 5

THE SILENT GENERATIONS – THE PERPETRATORS

Even 70 years after the end of WWII, it still affects the life of the German people. Even though the generation born after the war and their children only know about the events from history textbooks, the trauma and fears of the Nazi era still seem to be part of their DNA. A well-known German newspaper wrote about the reasons behind the phenomenon of the "German Angst". The author points to the scientific explanation of the respected molecular biologist and president of the Max-Planck-Society, Prof. Dr. Peter Gruss.[117] According to Gruss, it has been widely accepted for a few years now that stress, nourishment, or trauma can change the chemistry of our DNA. In the same way it is also possible to transmit changes in our psyche caused by psychosomatic factors and nutrition physiology. This is where he starts with his thesis and asks, "Can the reason for the German Angst be found in the trauma that our parents and grandparents suffered more than 60 years ago and were never able to work through? Trauma caused by the suffering they went through, but also by the collective guilt of Nazi Germany?" As with the descendants of the victims, also the descendants of the perpetrators can feel the repercussions that to this day affect them strongly, causing them emotional suffering. It was only in the early '80s that the long-term consequences of the war on the following generations were discovered in Germany.

Most families in Germany today still live under the shadow of the past. Silence seems to be part of their inheritance, just like the "German Angst", and they were never able to shake it off. We will see how the grandchildren of both the victims and of the perpetrators take a healing role, and how their children's generation – the fourth generation – once set free from the inheritance of the past, will have the unique chance to bring forth God's redemptive purposes for their respective nations, working hand in hand.

I realize that presenting the perspective of the perpetrators can cause irritation and pain for many of the victims of the Holocaust and their descendants. In this respect, it can never be about hiding the responsibility of the Germans behind a victim's position. Nor can it be about a moral reckoning or self-justification, even if taking this position was more than justified from the perspective of the Holocaust survivors and their descendants. I want to try and describe a phenomenon that may have different backgrounds and reasons, but that is still true for both the perpetrators as well as the victims. The descendants of both generations only discover slowly how much they have suffered under the burden of their respective family histories. Only step by step do they learn to speak about it, bringing their family story to the light and working it through. As much as many Christians in German churches and congregations would wish to finally close the book on the past of National Socialism, and to avoid it coming back into view over and over again, unfortunately this does not conform to reality. Both the victims and the perpetrators still suffer from their heritage of the past, and they will only be able to experience healing and restoration once they perceive one another, forgive, and come together in reconciliation. This cannot happen unless the veil of silence over them is broken. This is the reason why I am trying to visualize the heritage of the silent generation of perpetrators in this chapter.

Unfortunately, the annihilation of the European Jews never really had a place in German family memory. Their suffering and tragedy are hardly ever mentioned in family stories. In German memory, this produced a stark contrast: People would speak about their nightly fear in the bomb shelters, while they mentioned only in passing their Jewish neighbors who had suddenly disappeared. In their minds, the perspectives of perpetrators and victims were intolerably disconnected. We will see how this perception has changed with the passing generations.

The Generation of Perpetrators

When I first met my wife, it became apparent quite quickly that there was an important aspect where we differed greatly. She was used to communicating openly and freely in her home, while I had great difficulties in that area. Sometimes we would sit together for hours, and I tried my very best to put my thoughts into words. Most of the time, I failed. It was like an inner blockage that would not allow me to simply share with her what was on my heart and what I really thought. Only after a long struggle would I be able to find the right words for my fragmented thoughts. My biography did not provide any satisfactory explanation. Obviously, my communication problem had a deeper cause than I had thought. I am convinced that it had to do with a veil of silence that to this day shrouds entire generations in Germany, keeping them captive. I would like to explain this using the following example. My father returned from American captivity at the age of 28. He had been an officer in the African Corps, where he was seriously wounded as a company commander. Like many others in his generation, he would tell us about his experiences during the war; but deep in his heart, he would clothe himself in silence. Underneath the surface, there were countless untold stories that echoed in the minds in the form of terror or nightmares. His story may serve as an example for the war generation.

131

Most men in this generation, that one I call the generation of perpetrators, had been soldiers in the war, irrespective of whether they were Nazis or not. The mothers in this generation were caught up in the everyday life of the war, and also the post-war era. When the soldiers returned home after the war, many of them remained silent because of shame; others were traumatized and tried to repress their experiences as best as they could. Others, in turn, tried to clear themselves of any personal responsibility, denying their own involvement. After all, they argued, they had only been followers and had to fight for their own survival. Many times their silence was linked to the inner line of argument that they had been forced to go along with what everybody else did and that, even though the "Führer's" speeches might have sent the occasional emotional shiver down their spine, they really had not been interested in politics at all. It was part of this generation's sustained delusion to point to the small group of villains around Hitler in order to explain who had been responsible for all the evil that had happened.[118] The people had actually been powerless against this criminal minority, so they say, and had been helpless before the regime's pressure.

The dimension of their own verve and acceptance that helped to establish, strengthen, and solidify the system, however, was all too often forgotten in the course of family conversation. In the same way, people forgot all too quickly about the suffering of the millions of Jews, and all those who had been persecuted due to racist or ideological reasons and whose enslavement and annihilation had been accepted indifferently. To this day, the vast majority of the war generation uses the apparently exculpatory and yet telltale justification that they never noticed anything. Instead of inwardly working through this time, they pushed aside their memories and dedicated themselves to rebuilding Germany with all their strength.

Then, next to this great majority of the so-called followers, there was the group of perpetrators. They had become guilty of criminal acts during the war, and so there was hardly any reason for them to speak about what they had done. If they were unable to shirk their responsibility by escaping, they made every effort to stay unnoticed. They changed their identity, established inconspicuous, respectable lives, and hoped to remain unchallenged due to the lack of zeal on the part of the German administration of justice in the post-war period, and due to the lack of interest in persecuting Nazi crimes on the part of society as a whole.[119] Those who had actively supported the regime as party members, either out of conviction or opportunism, hid behind a veil of silence after 1945. They managed fairly quickly to retreat into a victim's role, and successfully explained how they had always wanted the best and how in the end Hitler had abused their idealism. They established themselves in a victim mentality that became so dominant that hardly any room remained for regret, let alone remorse, for the suffering of the true victims. "We had to go through so much..." is probably the single most-used phrase for the war generation that felt rather like a generation of victims. In post-war Germany, people were happy to have survived the war. They "rolled up their sleeves" and got to work rebuilding with all their might, which led to the economic miracle in West Germany in the '60s. All who were classified as "followers" by the Allies during the denazification process had made it. Now people wanted to live. Traumas, fears, anxieties, and entanglement in guilt were pushed aside. The responsibility for the victims' suffering was shifted onto others and repressed. Almost every family had untold traumatic stories that vanished behind an almost impenetrable fog. This had incalculable consequences for the following generations. They discovered an unsettled identity, and inexplicable fears in themselves that were not justified by their own biography. Obviously one of the hallmarks that was passed on to the following generation was that they constantly had erupting relational conflicts. To this day, repressed memories are responsible for numerous problems in our families. The ghosts of the past reproduce and affect the generation of children and grandchildren even today.

There was a famous professor of rhetoric of worldwide renown in Tübingen whose lectures I was able to attend as a student many years ago. His phenomenal memory first started failing him in the late fall of 2003. Today, Walter Jens suffers from dementia. The son of this great rhetorician wrote a well-received article titled "Vaters Vergessen" (Father's Forgetting).[120] Tilman Jens sees the reason in the repressing of truth about that "tiny brown spot" in his father's past. Walter Jens had kept quiet about his membership in the NSDAP. "The party member Walter Jens... only slightly retouched the beginning of his biography that later on turned out ever-so upright. Perhaps that was cowardly. He wanted to get ahead. So under the carpet with that stupid Nazi story. He had long since joined the other side anyway. But in the end he was deeply ashamed, and when his little scam was exposed, this shame broke him. He knew that for honesty's sake he should have talked earlier and of his own free will.[121] He suffered from the disease of an entire generation," says Tilman Jens, calling it "the fatal disease of silence." He closes his harrowing article with the following statement, "My father no longer knows who he is." The fact that silence has fateful consequences on body and soul is something that even King David reports in the Psalms.

> *When I kept silent, my bones wasted away*
> *through my groaning all day long. (Ps. 32:3)*

Das Amt und die Vergangenheit (The State Department and the Past) is the title of a book in which the German State Department, for the first time, honestly works through its entanglement in Nazi crimes.[122] It does away with the legend that German diplomats were first and foremost gentlemen, or even involved in the resistance. Instead, many of them had been actively involved in the annihilation of Jews. After the first dust had settled, the diplomats continued their careers after the end of WWII, careful to obtain an honorable discharge at the end of their term of service. No word about their past. Why should German families have been any different?

Children of the War

Almost 70 years after the end of WWII, the traces in Germany still have not faded. Facing National Socialism in political and societal life is part of a vibrant and honest process that continues to this day. It is all the more astonishing that the generation of the children of the war, who are between 60 and 70 today and were born during the war or spent the largest part of their childhood in the war, remained strangely silent about their own biography. A scientific study on the topic of "childhood during the war" shows that the children of the war are still suffering from the effects of their experiences during the war to a much greater extent than previously known. In most cases they have even transmitted the unprocessed trauma to the next generation.[123]

Childhood during the war was experienced in as great a variety of ways as can be. According to a study by the psychotherapist and former director of the Hospital for Psychiatry and Psychotherapy of the University Hospital Munich (KUM), Michael Ermann,[124] children of the war are suffering far more frequently from mental disorders such as fears, anxieties, depression, and psychosomatic trouble than the population average. About a quarter of the respondents stated that their quality of life was seriously impaired; one in ten was traumatized.[125] The children of the war spent their nights in bomb shelters and experienced rape, hunger, and death. They were also deeply affected and marked by their experience of flight and expulsion. The air-raids on refugee treks, cold, hunger, and death all around them went hand in hand with sexual violence. During the winter of 1944-45, millions of women with their children fled westward from the Eastern territories of the former German empire with their children. They were fair game for the soldiers of the advancing Red Army. Hunted, violated, and often raped multiple times; these women were the victims of the Russians, who exercised revenge for the millions of people that had been killed by Hitler's Waffen-SS and the Wehrmacht during the invasion of the Soviet Union. Sources estimate that by the end of WWII, more than two million German women had been raped by members of the Red Army – many times in the presence of their children.

Throughout all of Europe, the war had left behind destroyed families. Men and women were faced with an overwhelming task. The fathers returned from the war inwardly and outwardly broken, the last ones only after ten or twelve years of captivity. They had witnessed incomprehensible things, and many of them had committed terrible atrocities. Most of them never spoke about it and could not find the words for this time. Ermann describes the situation of the children of the war in the post-war era from personal experience. "The main focus was on surviving and rebuilding, clearing away the rubble, creating some kind of shelter. A roof over one's head and food for the children were the bare necessities that counted during those years. But the wounded souls remained undressed – for grandparents, parents, siblings, and the children of the war. What followed immediately after the war experiences were hunger and poverty, being strangers in an unknown surrounding. For refugee children, the new environment constituted a setting in which they were unfamiliar with the people, the language, the customs, and perhaps even the prevalent religious denomination. In any Northern German small town it was considered a stigma to be a refugee child. They had to band together with fellow sufferers in order to be able to bear the teasing. Many became shy and lonely. For many, the post-war era meant being without a father. And when the fathers did return, they were missing a leg or an arm, or had their eye shot through.

They were damaged fathers, broken lives, whose hopes and aspirations for life had vanished. The fathers no longer corresponded to the hopes and ideals that had been expected of them. Many experienced their mother's hidden depression, the mourning that was never shown openly, as they had to be strong and take the father's place for the children. And they did not want the children to know how they were suffering. But the children of the war noticed! These children, who themselves did not dare to weep for an incomprehensible sense of guilt, who roamed the streets and parks alone searching for something they did not know, became the comforters for their mothers, parents, and older brothers and sisters – for hurts and injuries they could only guess." [126]

The economic miracle in Germany helped alleviate the material poverty. At the same time, to a large extent the wounds and traumatic experiences were not even realized, and remained hidden. In most families, people did talk about the war, but only trivialized as adventure stories or funny anecdotes. This deprived the children of the war of the possibility of taking their fate seriously, and if there were any memories left at all, they kept them buried deep within themselves. They tried to comfort themselves with the assurance, "There were others who were far worse off than we." This formed an entire generation. People were functional, busy rebuilding, asked little, never complained, did not want to hear anything about the war – and just could not make themselves throw away bread.[127]

There had never been any generation in Germany before them that were so well off like they were now. They made their careers, had families, and actually there was nothing particular about them. At this point, I would like to quote Ermann once more, who was born in Stettin in 1943 between nights of bombing, and calls himself a typical child of the war.[128] "If there is anything distinctive about us, it is probably the little peculiarities. Hardly any of us is capable of resolutely throwing out clothing or food. With many of us, the way we deal with time shows remarkable relics of flight and air raids: delaying good-byes and decisions, drawing out every moment to the very last second, being completely inde-cisive in travels, chaos just prior to departure. Or there are other strange little phobias that sometimes even go unnoticed, such as going down into a subway station. Or we are sometimes startled by trivial matters: shuddering at the howling of a siren or when the fire-engine rushes by. Or there is this creeping unease when there is a lone airplane cruising the deep blue September sky. Even moods in general; a sudden melancholy that comes with a certain light, an inner stirring when observing an open landscape, the trepidation on some afternoons or quiet evenings, provoked by smells or sounds. But there are also silent symptoms: Many still dream of attacks, falling, violence, battle, flight. Others are startled out of their sleep by a long-forgotten fear summed up in the personal formula, 'The Russians are coming!' Others are marked by depression, low confidence, and anxieties. In part, the symptoms are strange: sensations of cold or recurring high temperature, a sense of tension and restlessness or sudden panic attacks, rigidity, or the feeling of being beside oneself. Today, we recognize such symptoms as the signs of flight or fight responses, recurring memories that try to express themselves in the body, memories of the incomprehensible."

After years of lack of interest and silence, the topic of children of the war now meets a constantly growing awareness in the media, magazines, and books. In her book Die vergessene Generation (The Forgotten Generation), journalist Sabine Bode even calls them the "forgotten generation".[129] The former children of the war, this is her assumption, have been "overlooked in their own country for almost sixty years". Nobody was interested in their story, and so it remained unstudied. Whenever somebody would probe into it and ask questions, the interviewees were unresponsive. This proved to be a difficult subject, as those who had experienced and suffered through the war as children did not want to talk about their experiences, and many of them were actually unable to do so. Many of them did not even realize how deeply they had been formed through their traumatic experiences as children of the war, and how thoroughly they had repressed everything that weighed them down. They did not complain about their fate. It was the time – with trained discipline and the desire to establish a secure existence – to put their own needs on hold. They were grateful for the recently gained freedom, peace, and legal security in the newly-rebuilt Germany. They responded to their unresolved fears with adaptation, sense of duty, and unrelenting rigor toward themselves.[130] "It did not do us any harm!" is one of the statements that showed just to what extent the true sensations of that generation were repressed. "Whatever you do, don't feel anything," one lady said who had grown up during that time. "Whatever you do, don't feel anything," had been the order of the post-war day. For this reason, she flushed the feelings out of her own and her children's lives.[131] The generation of war children was a "quiet generation". They did not complain, weep, or mourn; not for themselves, and certainly not for the victims of National Socialism. It is especially the displaced and refugee children who excel in this respect, as adaptation and achievement was expected from them after they had survived expulsion and flight together with their families. They were to avoid mistakes at all costs, and had to fulfill their families' expectations. The family's honor could not be put at risk for any reason whatsoever, because often it was the only thing that had remained for them. Many times these children turned into "sunshine children", who had no other way of helping their parents but through making their lives easier through their own happy mood. These children in turn were their parents' entire bliss; but deep inside, they too had to come to terms with the terrors of the war. When they started having emotional problems later on in life, they would think of all kinds of reasons – but not their childhood during the war. The generation of the children of the war was doubly silent. They had learned to shut up and fulfill their duties. What they felt inside was not really interesting to anyone – not even to themselves. As they were not able to realize their own hurts and face them, for many of them, empathy and sympathy were like a foreign language that was hard for them to learn. They simply declared the harrowing experiences that had more or less ingrained themselves in their souls as normality. A German boy, so the saying goes, does not cry, and in part he has not learned it to this day. So it comes as no surprise that sometimes for years this generation carried the burden of the terror that they had to live through, until it finally surfaced again, even up to 40 or 50 years later. In the meantime, the children of the war have passed on their unresolved experiences and traumas to their own children. The grandchildren of the war have inherited their parents' fears, and are suffering under their experiences of loss or lack without ever personally having experienced war. After almost 30 years of counseling experience, it strikes me how little awareness there is for this issue in terms of counseling needs within the church. I am convinced that we need to make up for what we missed here, and that there still remains a lot to be spiritually worked through.

Before we start thinking any more about the grandchildren of the war, I would like to add another observation at this point. When I entered the ministry full-time after getting my degree in theology in the early '90s, I repeatedly saw conflicts in so many German pastors and spiritual leaders that I just could not figure out. Even though the issue of "fatherhood" attracted widespread interest, I was amazed to see their obvious emotional barriers and blockages. Many of them had no trouble talking about their spiritual insights and revelations; but when it came to them personally, they seemed aloof and sterile. Apparently it was hardly possible to break through these barriers in counseling. At the same time,

I kept observing relational conflicts toward their "spiritual children", who subsequently turned away from them and had to try and find their own way. They did not feel confident they were taken seriously, or they felt spiritually overwhelmed or emotionally abused. Often they were surprised that their spiritual fathers had never noticed any of these things. In the lives of many of the leaders and pastors formed by this generation of fathers, spiritual breakdowns, burnouts, and family tragedies marked the grim endpoint of their ministries. They were suffering from the fact that they had run dry inside, and found it very hard to establish sustainable relationships. Small wonder; they are part of the "forgotten generation" and had wanted to "function" in their spiritual ministry just as much as all the other children of the war in their generation. They put their own needs on hold, established their respective ministries, and were never able to even see their own limitations and blockages, and so they could never put them into words. It is high time for the veil of silence to break off of them. With their children's help – and I am also talking about spiritual children here – it is possible to break the fathers' silence over them, and to win back their buried emotions.

The Grandchildren of the War

The generation of the grandchildren of the war grew up in an era of prosperity. In fact, they lacked nothing. But behind the façade of economic growth, the generation of the grandchildren of the war was all the more subtly affected by the repercussions of National Socialism. After the war, traumas, fears, and aggressions were lived and passed on in a realm that was closed to the public: in the families. "The generation that was born between 1960 and 1975 has more questions than answers. Why do so many of them feel unsure, that they do not really know who they are and where they want to go? What are the reasons for their vague fear of the future? Why do so many of them remain without children?" These are the questions listed on Simone Bode's book cover on the Grandchildren of the War.[132] For this generation, it is hard to imagine that Germany's disastrous past can affect their lives today, casting its dark shadow over them.

We have seen now how the previous generations put a taboo on family involvement during the Nazi era, and how they remained silent concerning their wartime experiences. Over decades, an entire chapter of war history had been repressed. What followed next in Germany was the "Generation Golf" (contemporaries of the "Generation X" in the United States, named after the favorite car for young people of the time, the VW Golf or Rabbit). They had devoted themselves to consumerism, and expected a golden future. But many of them suffer from recurring blockages, vague anxieties, a sense of rootlessness and leaden guilt, without ever being able to explain what may have caused these problems. It is striking how often they talk about not having solid ground under their feet. For most of them, it is a totally new thought to imagine that their insecure approach to life could originate from their grandparents, who never recovered from their wartime experiences.[133] Perhaps this could also serve to explain yet another phenomenon that can be observed in them. This is the frequent conflicts with their parents that often remain unvoiced, but lead to an ever-increasing alienation. They would all agree in saying that they just feel sure that they are simply unable to reach their parents emotionally, even with their best endeavors.[134] Even though they are aware that something is wrong in their family, they are usually unable to put their finger on it, and do not know what it is. By now we realize the reasons behind this. Many grandparents of the grandchildren of the war had to fight for their survival one way or another. You had to somehow survive, and that was all. They were able to push aside and repress their experiences of guilt, depression, mourning, and

death – but hardly ever could process them. Such was the world
their children were born into. They were given diapers and food,
and that had to suffice. They were alive and had to be grateful
to be better off than their parents. What could they be missing?
Often their pain was not taken seriously because their parents
and grandparents thought, "Your pain can't be anything like we
endured." The grandchildren of the war often report how when
they were not doing well, their parents would not even listen;
or even worse, the parents would not even notice that they were
not happy. Their grandparents were likewise locked in their own
emotional distress, and even if they had loved to do so, they
would have had little to offer emotionally to their children. They
did not necessarily feel something terrible had happened to them
– but still their emotional furnishings were often wanting. To get
a clearer understanding, we will take a closer look at an interesting research paper that the child and youth psychiatrist Karl
Heinz Brisch worked on.[135] Previously, people assumed that small
children are extremely robust and pass even the greatest terrors
without noticing. They were convinced that small children did
not perceive the atmosphere or the emotional state of the adults
around them. But obviously, the exact opposite is true. Children
are extremely sensitive. They sense acceptance or rejection,
openness and love; but also any emotional taciturnity on the
part of their parents, who have not yet recovered from emotional
hurts and traumas in their past. Children are able to sense even
the traumatic experiences their parents have buried deep within
themselves and no longer carry in their consciousness.[136] This
is then reinforced, as the parents' unprocessed experiences can
spring back to life, especially when dealing with the baby.[137] The
traumas that were covered by silence are simply passed on. The
research results leave hardly any doubt that the ghosts of the
past can also be transmitted to the following generations on an
emotional level.

So now the experts no longer deny the possibility that the traumas of both the Holocaust victims and of the perpetrators can be transmitted. The parents' emotional state and attitudes to life can superimpose themselves on the unborn child's spirit even in the mother's womb and unite with it, just as much as with the spirit of an infant or toddler. If father and mother, for understandable reasons, are insecure in their identity and maybe even cold and closed inside, it is no wonder that their children never felt they were taken seriously with their anxieties and inner needs. What is striking in today's 35- to 50-year-olds, according to psychotherapists, is an unclear identity. In other words: they feel uprooted, often incapable of taking life into their own hands, and they are constantly searching for assurance and identity. They sense an emotional vacuum within, and most of them do not know where it comes from or how they can fill it.

The grandchildren of the war have the chance to break the generational silence. Here it is helpful to actively research one's own family history. But often this is opposed by a vague cloud that covers the family past and seems so dense and impenetrable. Usually it is combined with down-playing remarks about the Holocaust and National Socialism. Breaking the veil of silence also means disclosing one's own family history during the Nazi era against all obstacles and resistance. Apparently it is especially easy for grandchildren to talk to their grandparents about this. People who successfully managed to shed some light on their family's Nazi past agree that they are doing much better now, and they were able to shake off a heavy burden. In order to illustrate just how deeply people can be affected, let me give you a few examples.

The mother of a handicapped child kept hearing the word "euthanasia", and had to fight the thought of how much more she would enjoy life if her child were to die. She was hardly able to resist this inner urge. Despite prayer and help in counseling, she did not find any relief. On a sudden impulse she started digging into the veil of silence in her own family. She approached her parents. "Did my grandparents ever have anything to do with handicapped children?" was her question. To her astonishment, the answer was yes. For the first time, she learned that her grandfather, a medical doctor, had been responsible for a children's home that had allowed the murder of hundreds of handicapped children during the Nazi era. No one in her family had ever talked about this. She was horrified. The veil of silence had kept her grandfather's guilt hidden. The light of the truth about her family and her contrite repenting for the sins of her forefathers broke the claims of darkness fostered by generational guilt. The young woman experienced deliverance, and the tormenting thoughts about her child vanished.

In the course of our many years of experience in the field of counseling in our church, we had observed again and again what far-reaching effects the grandparents' Nazi history can have on the grandchildren. The grandchildren of the war have inherited their parents' anxieties, so to speak. They suffer from experiences of loss and lack without ever having experienced war. A good example of this is a young medical doctor. She gave me permission to share her story. "My father had told me about my grandfather being part of the SS, and that he had been on the Russian campaign in WWII. At the end of the war he escaped to Austria, where he lived in hiding for a while, and had his SS tattoos removed. He started a family there and lived unchallenged until the '60s. Then he had a heart attack and died. He had always kept his past secret. During our preparations for the March of Life in the Ukraine,[138] I started delving into my grandfather's past once more, and all of a sudden, I understood my personal connection to my family's history. For years I had suffered from isolation from other people. I carried an inexplicable fear of the truth in me, and always perceived others who were close to me as a threat. It was like I was caught up in myself, and had great trouble sharing my thoughts and emotions. By then I was able to rationally explain many of my problems through my grandfather's history. I had inherited my isolation and fear of being found out from him. Slowly, my emotions and limitations were worked through. The whole process was accompanied and "soaked" in prayer. A few months later, I noticed that my isolation had gone, and the wall between me and others had broken down. But why did I have this sense of carrying a stigma on my life and of not being lovable? I just could not imagine that anyone would ever want to have anything to do with me or enjoy fellowship with me. It was impossible to enjoy fellowship with God, or simply be myself with Him. Obviously there was a connection to my family story. So I started researching again, and received a crucial bit of information from the "Wehrmachtsauskunftsstelle". [139] Even though most of the documents were lost, there was no doubt that my grandfather had been part of the SS tank unit 'Adolf Hitler'. After heavy losses at the beginning of the war, this SS unit was considered one of the best front divisions that would fight 'to the last bullet' for 'every foot of ground'. He remained in this unit until 1942, which means that he was involved in the mass executions and massacres of this unit in the Ukraine and Russia. For the second half of the war, according to the documents found, he was deployed to the training camp Beneschau, about 25 miles Southeast of Prague. More than 30,000 people were expelled from 144 towns and villages and forcefully relocated to make room for the SS training area Bohemia, one of the central training locations for the SS. Right next to it, special detention camps were established that were expanded as sub-camps for Flossenburg concentration camp in 1943. As of August 1943, my grandfather was an instructor on the training ground. It is easy to deduct from his history what kind of atrocities against prisoners he was involved in there. The veil of silence over my family had lifted. Now I was able to repent for my grandfather's guilt with all my heart and ask forgiveness. My grandfather's story had shaken me to my very core. Even though I am still in an inner process here, I suddenly realized I did not have to carry my grandfather's 'stigma' any longer; it was broken by God's love. My attitude toward my profession has changed radically. Whereas I used to reject it as being 'too good for me', I can now accept my qualification as a medical doctor and I am habilitating for a scientific career."

Just how deeply the grandchildren of the war can be affected psychosomatically by their Nazi heritage can be seen in an example mentioned in Simone Bode's book Kriegsenkel (Grand-children of the War).[140] Here a lady reports about her close relationship to her grandfather. While her father was constantly quarreling with the grandfather, whom he would just call the "old Nazi", without realizing it, she was actually formed by her grand-father's Nazi past. With her, he was loving, caring, and patient – toward the rest of the family, he seemed mainly foul-tempered and tyrannical. As she grew up, the young woman slipped into the right-wing extremist camp. While she was able to empa-thize greatly with horses, which were her entire passion, she was completely indifferent to the fate of the six million murdered Jews, and it meant no more to her than a number. Her parents divorced and her grandfather died. After the fall of the Berlin Wall, her father decided to go to Weimar, where he was born. After his return, he looked almost neglected and disheveled. His suit was crushed, his face was swollen, and his hair hung limply about his forehead. He needed two days to recover, and then he wanted to share what had happened. After the first sentences, the young woman just shut off. She did not want to hear about any infamous actions on the part of her grandfather. It was only 15 years later, after a new trust relationship had been established between father and daughter, that he was able to share about his shock in 1990. He had been given an old address, the place where his parents had lived. When he finally found it, he was in a neighborhood on the Ettersberg that had been built for the SS and their families. "It was just a ten-minute walk to the concentration camp of Buchenwald. My grandfather had not only been part of the SS, but also of the 'Totenkopfverbände' (death's-head units). My grandfather had been a concentration camp guard!" [141] When the woman learned about her grandfather's involvement in the concentration camps, she immediately got severe neck-trouble that caused excruciating headaches. "My neck had been my weak spot for years. But this time, no treatment would help. Whether it was massages, injections, conventional painkillers, or homeopathic pills – nothing helped. But still I decided to go to Weimar with my father. ... At the Buchenwald memorial, my father took me to the execution chamber, with the facility for shooting in the back of the neck." Talking to her father, the woman remembered that whenever her grandfather had wanted to end an unpleasant situation, he had always hissed something unintelligible that sounded like "Genickschuss" (a shot in the back of the neck). After this visit, something amazing happened: "The pain never returned. I had no more neck trouble. I am a natural scientist, and usually I stick to clear, hard, verifiable facts. But during the past few years I have heard and read so much about the connection between Nazi crimes and psychosomatic trouble in the following generations, that I am prone to attribute my neck trouble to my grandfather." [142]

When we want to counter the veil of silence over cities and nations, this will only be successful once we start with ourselves. Before we start thinking about the "fourth generation", I would like to summarize my observations at this point: Involvement and guilt, traumatic experiences, as well as flight and expulsion of the war generation, have formed the lives and relationships of the subsequent generations. In many families, they are hidden underneath a veil of silence. Their children and grandchildren still carry the effects of the traumas and inherited identity problems, without ever being able to identify them. Usually, they do not know where they come from, or how they can receive help. About three quarters of German families are more or less affected by them. Their common mark is their silence, the "generational silence". At the same time, the grandchildren of the war have a unique opportunity. Obviously they have the calling to bring forth healing in their families. They are asking questions and suddenly see their grandparents telling them stories they were unable to tell their kids. How many believers are going through seemingly endless deserts without ever seeing real change? They have come to accept the traumas, emotional disorders, anxieties, blockages, sicknesses, relational disorders, work mania, stress, and rigidity that were passed on to them, without ever having found the reasons. Having had an encounter with the liberating power of the cross, all who manage to break the generational silence and who are willing to face the truth will find it easy to experience forgiveness, reconciliation, and restoration.

Today, the generation of the grandchildren of the war has positions of responsibility in public life. They have the great chance to step out of the shadows of the past, and to add the memory of the victims of the Holocaust to their family memory. Ending the family's silence toward the victims of the Holocaust means realizing one's own guilt and involvement in the Holocaust – especially for those who simply looked away. We cannot imagine how deeply the children and grandchildren of Holocaust survivors still suffer from the effects of the Holocaust today. As long as they are still suffering from the consequences, the descendants of the perpetrators can never be released from their responsibility, and can never declare the effects of the Holocaust as over and done with. When the grandchildren of the war ask forgiveness for the guilt of their grandparents, this is no artificial act, and much less a technique. It is birthed from the realization that even against their will, they are still entangled in their fathers' and grandfathers' heritage, and that they are the first ones who are able to break the generational silence. They are the ones who try to find the words their grandfathers never found. The generation of the grandchildren of the war will have to learn to see themselves as important. They have a responsibility that no one else can take. For as long as the victims of the Holocaust and their descendants suffer from the same consequences as they do, they have the mandate to bring forth healing and reconciliation through their humble request for forgiveness for the guilt of their fathers and grandfathers.

While on a trip to Lithuania in preparation for the March of Life there, we had the opportunity to be interviewed by a popular Catholic radio station in Kaunas. One of my friends who was with me had been working through his own family history prior to this visit. He is part of the generation of grandchildren. His grandfather had been a soldier in the Wehrmacht, and had been among the troops that had invaded Lithuania in June 1941. Within six months, almost the entire Jewish population of Lithuania was murdered. Kaunas was one of the key locations for these events. In the radio interview, my friend spoke about his grandfather, and how deeply he was shaken at his involvement. Without playing anything down or glossing over, he confessed his grandfather's guilt with tears, and asked forgiveness. The Catholic priest who interviewed him also wept, and struggled to put his emotions into words. "Thank you for your willingness to share this. Here in Kaunas, we have never heard anything like this before." My friend had started with his own story, and now he has been used by God to break the veil of silence over an entire city. Two weeks later he was able to speak to his parents about their family history for the first time – reconciled and in liberty.

The Fourth Generation – Hand in Hand!

The last witnesses of the Nazi era are dying, and a new generation – the great-grandchildren of the victims, perpetrators, and
followers – is growing up. Does this dark chapter of their history
still concern them at all? A popular German daily newspaper
commissioned a polling institute to carry out a survey among
14- to 19-year-olds that was later published under the title "Was
Great-Granddad a Nazi?" [143] This survey shows that young people
are still moved by the Holocaust and the Nazi era, and yet they
are different from all other generations before them. For them,
National Socialism is simply a part of German history. More than
65 years later, memorial events no longer bring them to tears. At
the same time, an increasing number of them believe that their
own forefathers were involved, and they prove to be much more
willing to correct their traditional family image than their parents.
While seventy-eight percent of the grandchildren of the war aged
45 and older still thought their families did nothing wrong during
the war, only fifty-six percent of the 14- to 19-year-olds still agree
with this statement. Also, the common German exculpatory statement, "It was only a few villains that started the war and killed
the Jews," meets with less and less approval. [144] The more time is
passing, the more the old distorted image of the oppressed German
people is fading in the eyes of young people in the fourth generation. They are able to identify with the victims without feeling
betrayal or rebellion against their own families.

A 17-year-old whose great-grandfather had been an SS Sturmbannführer (assault unit leader), Gestapo Chief of Serbia, and
responsible for the murder of thousands of people, and a 16-year-
old girl whose Jewish grandfather must have been a prisoner
in the concentration camps of Auschwitz, Theresienstadt, and
Dachau meet for the first time to talk. [145] The boy's grandmother
had already started working through her father's Nazi past and

had written a book about it that was used in schools for education. Jon: "I am so proud of my grandma. Everybody needs to know what my great-grandfather did!" Nina's grandfather had also written a book on his time in the concentration camps. But she would rather remember him as a cheerful and good-humored old man, and so she prefers not to read his book while he is still alive. When her grandfather speaks at schools as a survivor witness, he talks about the hunger and pain; but he also speaks about conciliatory thoughts and good experiences. Even though he has been through so much evil, facing his past and passing it on to others seems to have strengthened him, according to Nina. Jon observed the same thing in his grandmother. Facing her father's Nazi past appears to have helped his grandmother. "She says, you don't break when you work through things, but you are strengthened instead." [146] Their actual meeting as great-grandchildren or grandchildren of the victims and perpetrators does not stir much in them. Jon would like to meet Nina's grandfather. He is touched by his story, and, if he were to think further about his own history, he would surely be ashamed of what his great-grandfather did. In Nina's opinion, most people did not do anything during the Nazi era. "Perhaps this is the worst; that doing nothing has such consequences." [147] Nina and Jon are part of the fourth generation. Their conversation is a good example of how their generation is able to turn to one another with sincere interest.

The face of America and the Western world has changed in recent years like never before. According to local observers, Israel is at its lowest in all of modern history. Secular and materialistic thinking, moral scandals in the government, and the years of threats by inner and external enemies have paralyzed the will to fight in most Israelis. In this situation, God is preparing a new generation. The Israeli organization "Yad B'Yad" (Hand in Hand) connects young people from Israel and Germany. One of the highlights for their trips together is a visit to a concentration camp

memorial, where the great-grandchildren of victims and perpetrators literally walk "hand in hand". [148] This is a wonderful picture
for the fourth generation, whether they live in America, Israel, or
Germany. They are the key for God's redemptive plan in these last
days. When the fourth generation stands together in their love and
commitment to Israel, they will have the mandate and spiritual
authority to bring a positive influence and change in America, all
of Europe, and the rest of the world. God will use this generation
to powerfully prepare the way for His return. The German youth
of the fourth generation are able to approach Jews and touch their
hearts like they have never been touched before. Over the past
15 years, we have seen a dramatic increase in spiritual hunger
and openness for Yeshua among young Israelis. [149] Also there is an
unprecedented openness in German hearts for Jews of the fourth
generation, whether they are from America, Israel or any other
nation. As far as we know, today many young people in Germany
are touched by the Holy Spirit and receive a heart for Israel. They
have learned from history – hopefully. By now they are such a
long way off from the Holocaust that it would be easy for them to
push everything aside as irrelevant. That would be a tragedy, as
the way they stand with Israel will determine Germany's future
and destiny for many years. [150]

The fourth generation of German youth honors the Jewish roots of
their faith. They have a new spirit. I call it the "spirit of the sons
of Zion". They know that God has called them out as worshippers
and intercessors, and they stand in the gap on behalf of Israel
in prayer and intercession. They have the authority to break the
veil of darkness over their cities and nations. The fourth generation has a new level of spiritual hunger and authority, irrespective
of where they live. Whether it is in America, Germany, Israel or
any other nation: Jews and Christians, descendants of victims and
perpetrators, are walking "hand in hand". When they do that, they
will produce a movement of revival and evangelism that will light

the fire of God in Israel and the nations like never before. When the fourth generation in Germany turns unconditionally toward Israel and the Jewish people, they may have to go against the flow. But they should always remember: You are the arrows in God's hand, and His answer to the idolatry of secular humanism in this modern age.

I will bend Judah as I bend my bow and fill it with Ephraim.
I will rouse your sons, Zion, against your sons, Greece,
and make you like a warrior's sword. (Zech. 9:13)

Opinion polls show that more than twelve percent of Americans hold anti-Semitic prejudices – that is more than 30 million people. Furthermore, thirty percent of the people questioned believe that American Jews feel greater loyalty toward Israel than toward the U.S. Modern anti-Semitism is hiding behind political attitudes that call for a unilateral recognition of a Palestinian state, and want to push Israel back to the borders of 1967. Israel is a people hated by the world, feared by the enemy, and largely ignored by the church. The right of existence of the Jewish people today is no longer threatened by a Holocaust, but rather by those who deny and fight against it. All who do not want to become followers again at this time, and who do not want to fall under the veil of silence again, will have to take a clear stand with Israel, blessing it. In the next chapter, I will tell you about how the veil of our silence can be broken in our personal lives, and how to go about it practically.

CHAPTER 6

CAN WE (STILL) REPENT FOR THE SINS OF OUR FOREFATHERS?

It was somewhere on the Prayer Expedition from Berlin to Moscow. This reconciliation march was probably one of the most spectacular events we had ever organized. Two hundred participants had joined us to cover 1,300 miles on foot. We wanted to make the most of the period of glasnost and perestroika.[151] The Soviet Union had dissolved into independent states, creating a time-window for the reconciliation march. Numerous participants whose fathers and grandfathers had been involved in the invasion of Russia wanted to ask for forgiveness. At the meetings on the way to Moscow we experienced healing, reconciliation, and an unimagined hunger for the gospel. Several thousand people found faith in Jesus because of this reconciliation march and were saved. The Russian Pentecostal Union we were cooperating with planted many new churches as a follow-up. This was almost 20 years ago now; but next to all the positive memories, I also still remember repeated conflict situations whenever we would touch on the subject of "identificational repentance", repenting for the sins of our forefathers. Back then as now, there is a huge variety of questions on this topic, as well as theological arguments. Does repenting for the sins of our forefathers unnecessarily stir up the past again? Is it possible at all to repent on behalf of previous generations? How much guilt has to be cleared away on behalf of others before a nation can be healed? [152] And is there such a thing as the collective guilt of an entire nation, where the responsibility is not only on an individual perpetrator, but on every member of that particular group? There is a great multi-faceted debate on this subject that is sometimes conducted with great vehemence.[153] Marcel Redling notes in his essay on identificational repentance, "With all due respect for the victims of the Holocaust, we still have to question whether this guilt has not long since been forgiven or whether it is justified to talk about collective guilt in the first place." [154] We will see that in order to deal with the question of identificational repentance, we will have to take a look at the biblical concept of original and hereditary sin. What we will find is that the Bible not only knows collective guilt, but that this concept is actually of crucial importance when considering the sinfulness of man. The more the biblical concept of original sin was watered down by the ideas of enlightenment and the liberal theology nourished by it, the more the radical nature of sin – and with it of grace – was watered down as well. By now, the disintegration of values has progressed significantly and has become the hallmark of a young, enlightened generation. The request for forgiveness seems to be outdated, and self-justification is booming. Modern man decides all by himself what seems attractive and right to him. Anything absolute appears like a monster to him, forcing him to do things and making him captive. But unless he recognizes the monster in himself, he will always be in danger of allowing somebody to abuse him as a hater of Jews, mass murderer, or simply a silent follower, just like our fathers and grandfathers.

A few years ago, the buzzword of a "people of perpetrators" stirred a heated debate in Germany. The term denotes the idea of the Germans' "collective guilt" and says that as a people, they are morally responsible for the crimes committed by their fellow countrymen. After historians started using the term and it became common in political language use, it was voted the "faux-pas word of the year" in 2003.[155] But still the debate about Germany's collective guilt has never subsided.

So what is the question of collective guilt all about? Before challenging you with some theological-dogmatic ideas, I would like to present a more differentiated perspective of the term. We speak about collective accountability or liability as a legal term. This denotes the liability for war damages that are paid by a nation in form of reparations. The Nuremberg Trials for war criminals denied a legal collective accountability in the sense of collective punishment. But there can be no doubt, even for the sheer historic dimension of the Holocaust, about Germany's special collective moral and political responsibility.[156] The famous journalist and Holocaust survivor Ralph Giordano saw the main guilt of the Germans in their silence in the face of the injustice they saw every day, every hour, everywhere.[157] As there had been a minority of Germans who had followed their conscience and not the Führer, it was not permissible to speak about collective guilt. The majority of Germans, however, says Giordano, have no right to feel relieved of their burden because of this, and to benefit from the minority's moral virtue.[158] Likewise, the journalist sees a collective moral responsibility on the part of the Germans that nobody can abscond from. Also when talking about collective guilt, we need to distinguish between the legal terms "collective punishment" and "moral collective responsibility".

To put it into simpler terms: Can we be held accountable for the guilt of our family or even our nation? Is there anything like a hereditary transmission of guilt, i.e. something that Martin Luther described as "locking people into a prison that can only be unlocked from without"?[159] Martin Luther affirms this, referring to the problem of original sin. By their unbelief, every human being is captive to original sin. But this does not relieve them of their own responsibility, as by their daily sinning – according

157

to Luther – they are continuously putting further bricks into the walls of their prison of inherited sin.[160] But how can a person escape this prison and attain freedom? They will never be able to free themselves, so there is only one way. Help has to come from outside! They need a savior, a redeemer! So the only way for them is the call to repentance. The meaning of the Hebrew root of the word "repentance" means "turning around", saying: If you change your mindset and return to God with all of your being, you will be able to find forgiveness, redemption, and freedom in Jesus.[161] It is self-evident that this is something very personal, which nobody can do for another.[162] Next to this individual approach, we find also the collective prophetic call to repentance in the Bible that is addressed not only to individuals, but to an entire nation in keeping with the Old Testament examples. The strongest example of this is surely seen in John the Baptist, who called Pharisees and Sadducees to repentance, challenging them to prove their righteous fruit of repentance by their deeds (Matt. 3:8). Paul later says about John that he had called the entire people of Israel to return to God (Acts 13:24). This is an entire group of people held collectively responsible. Both in the Old and New Testament, we keep finding the principle of collective guilt. But before we study some Bible passages, we first have to take a closer look at original, inherited sin.

The doctrine of original sin is of crucial importance for the entire doctrine of salvation. Without it, we will never be able to understand the radical significance of grace. I would like to mention once again Martin Luther's quote from the apologia in the Augsburg Confession where he stresses, "Unless we have come to realize our misery, we will not be able to comprehend the magnitude of Christ's grace." [163] So again, because it is so important: We will never understand the radicalism of the grace of Jesus, unless we understand the foundational reality of original sin. Let us take a look into the Bible first. Considering the countless passages in both the Old and the New Testament, there is no doubt that all humans, without exception, are considered sinners by God, and He treats them as such.[164] With the same unambiguity, the Bible traces the "original" or inherited sin of man back to Adam and Eve. Since they readily succumbed to the devil's temptation and broke the command not to eat from the "tree of knowledge", they lost their friendship with God due to their pride and mistrust. While before they had been "capable of not sinning", they were now "incapable of not sinning".[165] Adam and Eve had lost everything: their love relationship with God, the assurance of being God's children, and God's pleasure and favor. They were the beginning of the history of mankind that God wanted to make with them. But now they were separated from Him. Since that time, fratricide, selfishness, and hatred have become part of the deadly virus they passed on to all of their descendants. Ever since the first parents' original sin, mankind had to collectively embrace Adam's unfortunate inheritance. Perhaps you are asking yourself what you have to do with Adam's sin. Is not everybody responsible for their own life? But according to the Bible, mankind is much more than a sum of individuals, each separate from the others. It sees mankind as a whole, a unit that belongs together, a family in which the individual's actions carry consequences for the collective entity. The disadvantage here is that an individual's sin also has negative consequences for all. At the same time, this principle opens the only way of salvation: an individual's sacrifice is valid for all. Nobody is excluded! Just as the rotten root of a tree brings forth bad fruit, Adam's original sin is the root sin, and its fruits are the individual sins of each human being.[166] Whatever the sins may be called – there is an innate wickedness and evil in each human being, a disease that nobody can escape. There is only one way out: The prison has to be opened from outside. Jesus died as a sacrifice on the cross in order to counter the inescapable bondage to sin with His radical grace. According to Romans 5:18-19, the sin of the one (Adam) made all men sinners, and by the redemptive sacrifice of Christ (the new Adam) the door of salvation is opened to all. So let us keep in mind: We can only understand the radicalism of the grace of Jesus against the backdrop of original sin. The concept of original sin says that an individual's actions have consequences for all.

Yes, Adam's one sin brings condemnation for everyone, but Christ's one act of righteousness brings a right relationship with God and new life for everyone. Because one person disobeyed God, many became sinners. But because one other person obeyed God, many will be made righteous. (Rom. 5:18-19; NLT)

Many people have problems with the doctrine of original sin, as they have trouble with the historic understanding of the beginnings of this world in the face of scientific findings and theories of natural science on how the world began. You can best counter these problems by first of all taking a closer look at the state of modern man. Obviously, something is wrong with mankind. Despite enlightenment and a humanistic mindset, we are driven by an inner compulsion and are seemingly inseparably bound to evil. Without redemption, man becomes evil. To reach this conviction, you only have to open a newspaper. The consequences of original sin, such as suffering and death, man's desire and his inclination to evil, are still objectively present today, with many very obvious, with others more repressed. Once we realize that on the one hand God is good and consequently has only created good things, and that on the other hand there is nothing good in man, this brings us up against a contradiction that can only be solved through the concept of original sin. If God is good, the evil in man can only come from man himself. Obviously, he abused the freedom God had given him to enable him to turn to Him in love freely and of his own will.[167] If it is true that we have a good God, then the fallen nature of man, with his ability to do evil, can only be deducted from original sin. However, this leads to one important question: Can we not evade responsibility by simply stating that original, hereditary sin is something like fate that we cannot help, a coercive force that we can never change anyway? Paul clearly denies this question: Every human being is responsible for their own actions, not despite, but rather because of hereditary sin, and will be held accountable by God (Rom. 6:12,23). There is only one way to escape this prison. He needs redemption, the unmerited grace he can neither obtain by moral exertion nor by religious achievement, but only through the forgiveness of his sins.

And he is the propitiation for our sins: and not for ours only, but also for the sins of the whole world. (1John 2:2; KJV)

Within the framework of enlightenment developed a counter-concept to the doctrine of original sin. The traditional doctrine of hereditary sin was harshly criticized, because it supposedly overlooked the fact that man can only be held responsible for the deeds committed by him.[168] Man was by nature good, according to the enlightened critics, and it was only bad influences in his upbringing or society that ruined him. The concept of sin became very shallow. Whenever we deny the radicalism of sin, grace becomes irrelevant; if there are no sentenced murderers, there is no need for mercy petitions or an amnesty. The weakening and devaluating of the concept of sin is the foundational error of liberal theology.[169] How can we forget after the Holocaust that sin can turn humans into monsters? From a natural point of view, it is impossible to explain the Holocaust. There was a greater power at work. Those who executed their victims did so with satanic creativity. For their murderous doings they made use of every conceivable technique, anything science could provide. Among them were philosophers, psychologists, lawyers, doctors, artists, and business people. All these people were driven; they indulged in the degradation, humiliation, and extermination of the Jews. The day before, they had been normal people like you and me;

perhaps they were neighbors and loving family fathers. But the following day, they were murderers. It was their own decision. After the experiences of two world wars and the Holocaust, we should be very quick to forget about the secular counter-concept to hereditary sin.

When I was newly saved, I had a conversation with my father that I still remember today. When I said yes to his question of whether I had become a Christian now, he asked me, "So you also believe in evil now?" Being a young teenager, I had not thought about this too much before, so I had no answer, but I promised I would think about it. Who actually defines what is "good" and what is "evil"? How about a definition according to the New Testament? In Greek, there are two different meanings to "evil" that are used both in the gospels and the epistles. In the parable of the royal wedding, the servants went to the highways and byways to invite whoever they could find, both "good" and "bad" (Matt. 22:10). The word for being "bad" or "evil" in an ethical sense, which means being wicked with consequences on the outside, is the Greek word "poneros".[170] In contrast, the word "kakos"[171] describes the evil nature of man. This is someone who is wicked through and through, who carries the festering sores of sin within himself (Rev. 16:2). Therefore, the Bible describes him as "kakos". In the Bible, Satan is personified – he is not an abstract evil, but he is the "evil one", "ho poneros", the initiator of all evil in the world.

Today, the ideas of enlightenment take on a modern disguise. The biblical understanding of sin against God and of man who is in need of grace and redemption has completely changed in today's society. We are currently seeing a complete reinterpretation of values. Modern man defines for himself what is "good" and "evil". "Evil" or "bad" is anything that does not leave him as he is. "Good" is everything he likes, enjoys, and that caters to his desires. In the 21st century, we see man interpreting the terms "good" and "evil" at his whim, giving them a new meaning. Good becomes evil, evil becomes good. What might be evil to one person – for instance, adultery, or cheating on your wife – becomes an act of "self-encounter" to somebody else, and he cannot see anything reproachable in it. We are living in the heyday of justification. A request for forgiveness is hard to find. We should listen very carefully when the same spirits that have robbed our fathers and grandfathers of their consciences reappear in modern guise and try to convince us of who is "good" and who is "bad". We are seeing an unparalleled reinterpretation and erosion of Judeo-Christian values that suspiciously eyes everything opposed to its pantheistic-pluralistic one-world thinking. This mindset will always battle against the God of Israel who says, "I am the Lord, your God; you shall have no other gods beside me." The exclusiveness of Israel as the chosen people will always be anathema to the post-modern spirit. Do we as the church have anything to resist this? What will our answer be? Have we come to terms with the fact that this mindset has wormed its way deep into our churches? I am convinced that we have to discover the key of repentance and the authority of identificational repentance afresh.

At the beginning of this chapter I had promised to take a closer look at some of the foundational Bible passages that speak about trans-generational collective guilt. Surely the explanation to the second commandment is one of the most important passages.

I, the Lord your God, am a jealous God, punishing the children for the sin of the parents to the third and fourth generation of those who hate me, but showing love to a thousand generations of those who love me and keep my commandments. (Exod. 20:5b-6)

There is no doubt that not recognizing God's lordship and majesty, and worshipping other gods in whichever form, will always affect the following generations. The Hebrew term "paqad" is often translated "visit something on someone", but it can also carry a positive or negative meaning in the sense of "look for", "visit", "inquire".[172] This Bible passage actually states very clearly that the Lord will "inquire" of the following generations how it is with the children in the third and fourth generation. Depending on the results of the inquiry, the visitation can well turn into punishment.

Even though Saul had been dead long since, his bloodshed still affected the following generation. The famine, however, did not only affect the "house of Saul", but the entire nation of Israel, until the sin was atoned for by identification: "Afterwards, God had mercy on the land again" (2Sam. 21:14b; translated from German). The following Bible passage and the biblical account that goes with it speaks about a trans-generational collective guilt and the resulting collective punishment:

> *There was a famine during David's reign that lasted for three years, so David asked the Lord about it. And the Lord said, "The famine has come because Saul and his family are guilty of murdering the Gibeonites." (2Sam. 21:1; NLT)*

We can find other examples for identificational repentance in Nehemiah 1:4-7; 9:2; Ezra 9:7 and Daniel 9:8-15. Also in Lamentations, we find trans-generational collective guilt:

> *Our parents sinned and are no more, and we bear their punishment. (Lam. 5:7)*

Here the Bible speaks about the consequences of the parents' sin on the following generations, who in turn obviously tolerated the sins of the fathers and lived with them.

The numerous examples in the New Testament are just as clear. Just as obedience and disobedience determined blessing or curse in a land under the old covenant (Deut. 28), the New Testament shows the law of sowing and reaping. Both in positive and negative respects, at the time determined by God, we reap what we have sown (Gal. 6:7-9). As we are living in a social context, God's laws affect everyone connected to us with blessing or adversity.[173] Probably the most striking example is Jesus' request for forgiveness for those who crucified Him (Luke 23:34). Unforgiveness remains active even after death, and in the following generations. With His identificational priestly prayer, Jesus broke the power of bloodshed over His murderers and their following generations. Thus Jesus cancelled the self-imposed curse over the following generations, "Let his blood be on us and our children!"(Matt. 27:25; NIV).

Jesus said, "Father, forgive them,
for they do not know what they are doing!" (Luke 23:34a)

Critics of "identificational repentance" appeal to Jeremiah 31:29-30 and Ezekiel 18. Both passages seem to speak clearly against collective guilt. It appears as if generational sin had been reckoned up to that time, but now it is abolished. So let us take a closer look at these passages.

In those days people will no longer say, 'The parents have eaten
sour grapes, and the children's teeth are set on edge.' Instead,
everyone will die for their own sin; whoever eats sour grapes –
their own teeth will be set on edge. (Jer. 31:29-30)

The proverb, "The parents have eaten sour grapes, and the children's teeth are set on edge," describes the feeling of life of the generation who had to live in the Babylonian exile and bitterly complained about it. Even though it had been their fathers who had sinned, they had never had to bear the painful consequences. Now they, as the following generation, had to lie in the bed their parents had made. Jeremiah contradicts their accusations and

165

victim mentality, pointing them to their own sin (Jer. 11:10). Collective guilt does not preclude personal responsibility. They had to step out of their fathers' inheritance by active repentance. This is something we can see very well in Ezekiel 18.

In the previous chapters (15-17), Ezekiel had tried to convict the people of their sin with three parables. But chapter 18 is about each individual's personal responsibility before God. Right at the beginning, we come across a saying that Jeremiah had already quoted before then. It was obviously well-known among the people. The people thought their suffering had not come upon them because of their own sins, but because of their parents' sin. So they accused God, thinking He was unjustly punishing them (Ezek. 18:25). But God clearly refutes their accusations. Everybody carries their own responsibility before God, and dies for their own sin (Ezek. 18:20). The fathers' guilt is not an unchangeable fate they have to fatalistically submit to. And it is even less permissible for the descendants to use it as an excuse in order to avoid having to turn from their own sins. But what does this responsibility look like? Are there any prerequisites? Can we deduct a basic rejection of the concept of collective guilt from the principle of individual responsibility which is described very vividly in the example of the three sons in Ezekiel 18? Surely not! So let us take a closer look at the exact wording describing the third son. According to Ezekiel 18:10-13, his father had heaped infinite guilt upon himself. But what about the son?

> But suppose that sinful son, in turn, has a son who sees his
> father's wickedness and decides against that kind of life.
> This son refuses to worship idols on the mountains and does not
> commit adultery. He does not exploit the poor, but instead is fair
> to debtors and does not rob them. He gives food to the hungry and
> provides clothes for the needy. He helps the poor, does not lend
> money at interest, and obeys all my regulations and decrees.

Such a person will not die because of his father's sins; he will
surely live. (Ezek. 18:14-17; NLT)

The third son breaks out of the generational sin through his actions. It is easy to miss this, but just take another look at verse 14. "He sees all the sins his father practiced, but does not follow his example." This speaks about an active repentance of personal responsibility, and about his conscious stepping out of the sins of his fathers.[174] The son had the very real possibility to continue in his father's collective guilt with the same propensity to sin. But the son decided to do otherwise. He looks carefully at his father's sins, which the passage explicitly mentions twice, and then he chooses to act differently. This kind of repentance is the precondition so he will not have to die for the sins of his father.

In this respect, Exodus 20:5b-6 does not contradict Ezekiel 18 in any way. The two passages actually go together very well. According to Exodus 20, the Lord "inquires" (paqad) the fathers' iniquity of the descendants to the third and fourth generation. Depending on the results of the inquiry, the visitation may also bring punishment: If the Lord still finds the fathers' iniquity unbroken and unforgiven in the children and grandchildren, there will be consequences. But on the other hand, there also is the possibility for the Lord to come to a totally different finding. When the children and grandchildren are willing to look at the sins of their fathers, consciously facing them and repenting for them, they break their collective family yoke. They step out of the sins of their fathers and live a different life, by taking responsibility for their own actions, just like the son in Ezekiel 18. Now this does not imply a general rejection of collective guilt, but quite on the contrary; this chapter actually takes it for granted. It describes the way out, how generational guilt no longer has to weigh on a person's life like an inevitable fate, and how by taking responsibility for one's own actions, it can be broken. This makes Ezekiel

18 actually an important advocate for identificational repentance, even though at first it looked like a powerful argument against it – it just takes a bit of a more differentiated approach.

So how can we repent for the sins of our fathers? There are four different levels that we should look at:

The Level of Cities and Nations

The Bible tells us time and time again how the sins and iniquity of individuals can affect entire cities and nations. Progress or decline, rise and success, spiritual disease, or healing of a nation depended on their willingness to humble themselves and repent on behalf of their city or nation (2Chron. 7:14). There is no doubt that behind the visible reality there is an invisible reality where both God and the satanic world are active (Eph. 6:12). People's actions influence the spiritual atmosphere. Their decisions for good or bad, their obedience or rebellion will either give God the legitimate mandate to intervene with blessing, or provide legal grounds for the forces of darkness of the demonic opposition to oppress, debilitate, destroy, and paralyze.[175] Here the matter of bloodshed in a city or nation seems to be of special importance.

*And He said to me, The iniquity of the house of Israel and Judah
is great, and the land is full of blood, and the city is full of
perversity. (Ezek. 9:9a; MKJV)*

We can see in the Word of God how bloodshed can weigh heavily on the land, even long after the perpetrators' death, and how it can lead to collective guilt. The blood of the victims cries out to heaven like the innocent blood of Abel (Gen. 4:10), even if the bloodshed has long since become history.[176] Next to incest (Lev. 20:11), sodomy (Lev. 20:16), and homosexuality (Lev. 20:13), innocent blood shed through human sacrifice, war, and murder defiles the land and has grave consequences. Can we imagine what it means for a family, a city, or a nation if this innocently-shed blood is that of His chosen people? (Gen. 12:3). In the countries where we were invited to do a "March of Life", I have observed the enormous effects of bloodshed there.

Immediately after the German invasion of the Soviet Union in 1941, preparations were made in the Ukraine, Belarus, and the Baltic States to organize the systematic mass murder of civilians, and especially the Jewish population there. Right from the start, the Holocaust followed the victory over the enemy troops, as it was an integral part of the Eastern campaign.[177] In many countries, the German occupying forces found ready helpers who were willing to cooperate with them due to the anti-Semitism that had been festering in their nations for centuries. Following the German invasion, Germans and Lithuanians murdered more than 150,000 Jews within only five months. This number is so enormous that the Germans had to rely on the help of the occupied countries. Even though the invasion first victimized the countries under German occupation, now they had also become perpetrators. This makes a working through of their past so difficult, even to this day. There still is an unbroken anti-Semitism in many of them that is connected to a lacking willingness to face the dark side of their own past.[178] Lithuania is considered one of the countries with the most rampant anti-Semitism. Independent reports trace the higher-than-average rate of suicide, depression, and a largely oppressive atmosphere in these countries back to the unresolved bloodshed. I received similar reports from Riga, where with the help of Latvians 44,000 people were imprisoned in the ghetto of Riga, murdered, or deported to other concentration camps. In one service I had the opportunity to humble myself before them as the descendant of the perpetrators and ask their forgiveness. I am aware that in many places this has happened before. At the same time, I am convinced that Germans can only come to minister to other countries in an attitude of humility and grace to break the veil of silence over them. I have already told you how we as the German nation of perpetrators had received God's "unmerited grace" of healing and restoration for our nation. At an altar call for Latvian families who were still suffering from the bloodshed of their forefathers to repent, many came forward weeping. They were the descendants of Latvian families whose fathers had become mass murderers of the Jews. Their identificational repentance transformed the meeting hall into a place of God's glory. The veil of silence was broken over them. Their repentance caused a release of power and carried tremendous authority. Something had happened in the heavenlies. When I prayed for them, I told the participants of the service that a major shift had occurred in the spiritual atmosphere over their nation because of their identificational repentance that evening. "Do not be surprised if things change in your nation and if you read in the newspapers about a revealing of the works of darkness." Sometimes the Lord gives special prophetic signs to encourage us to continue along the way of working through, repentance, and healing. Soon afterwards, we received an excited report from the Latvian organizer: The day after our meeting, the Latvian president had announced a complete change of the cabinet because of corruption. She wrote, "To my knowledge, no president has ever done this since independence (1990), even though they would have had the right ... Isn't that amazing? I had to think of Pastor Bittner's preaching and prayer, and how he had said, 'Do not be surprised if things change in your nation and work of evil are exposed.'" [179]

Identificational repentance means paying especially close attention to the sins of the forefathers – not to judge it, but in order to break the collective guilt. This is especially necessary if the generation of fathers and grandfathers never managed to admit their own guilt, hiding it under a veil of silence. As long as this guilt still stands unresolved, crying out to God, and as long as nobody has ever asked the victims' forgiveness, a nation or city will suffer under its oppressive effects.

> *For he who avenges blood remembers;*
> *he does not ignore the cries of the afflicted. (Ps. 9:12)*

The Ancestral Level

Just to set this straight: This is not about obtaining God's forgiveness for the dead fathers or grandfathers. The doctrine of identificational repentance would indeed be unbiblical if that were the point. Here it is absolutely true that each one will die for their own sin. Forgiveness can only be brought about by personally confessing and repenting before God. But at the same time, it is important to also break the family's collective guilt. In the previous chapter, I described how much the traumas, but also the guilt incurred in the war generation, can still affect us today. Here identificational repentance becomes something that each one stands before God with, and that concerns us. Many times we see people suddenly learning harrowing details that had previously been unknown to the family. This produces a natural urge to repent before God for the sins of the fathers and to ask His forgiveness. We have experienced that it is only the identificational repentance birthed from a direct, inner shaking and distress which can bring change and healing.

> *But if they will confess their sins*
> *and the sins of their ancestors -*
> *their unfaithfulness and their hostility toward me...*
> *(Lev. 26:40; NIV)*

The Personal Level

"Why should I repent for the sins of my fathers?" is a question that many believers ask themselves, adding, "How many times do I have to repeat that?" But we must not forget one thing: Unless we face the sins of our fathers, we are in serious danger of continuing on the worn and sinful paths of our ancestors. Anyone who just looks away misses the chance of throwing off a dark, inherited family yoke, and of confronting the effects on their own life. So dealing with our fathers' iniquity automatically becomes dealing with our own sin. In the previous chapter, we saw how much each one of us can be affected by this. Even scientists acknowledge that the collective guilt of a nation can be passed on by inheritance.[180] They all agree that the silence of millions of Germans in the face of the injustice they witnessed every day and every hour created a collective moral joint guilt. But is it possible that the silence of the war generation is passed on like an inherited collective Nazi guilt? Apparently that is the case. We had to discover that this silence is widely spread, and has become one of the greatest problems for us Germans – for the war generation, their children, and the descendants, to the fourth generation. Many of us still carry this silence in our DNA. Unless this is broken, we will stand by and watch again while Israel is hated, slandered, and oppressed by enemies. We will be silent again when the world turns right and wrong upside down, when the majority of public and published opinion repeatedly puts the only working democracy in the Middle East on trial with insolent presumptuousness. The silence concerning the Holocaust in the families of the perpetrators continues undiminished in the equanimity and indifference that we still find in many German living rooms today. It is possible to participate in countless reconciliation events and visit numerous Holocaust memorials, and even to completely distance oneself from anti-Semitism – and yet still carry the spirit of one's fathers and the same, unbroken sin in one's life.

But how can we break out of the bondage to the collective guilt of silence concerning the Holocaust? Identificational repentance cannot end with the sins of the fathers. It discovers their thought and deed patterns in one's own life, and leads to a shaking and repentance of one's own sins. This is what breaks the bondage to the collective guilt. Personal repentance for the sins of the fathers becomes an active step of turning away from them. True repentance has taken place once the silence turns into an active and bold confession to stand with the Jewish people and Israel. This is the only way that the Lord will find nothing of the fathers' iniquity anymore when He enquires of the children and grandchildren to the third and fourth generation, according to Exodus 20, because they were careful to face it, deal with it, and personally repented for it with a contrite heart.

Produce fruit in keeping with repentance. (Luke 3:8a)

The Level of the Victims

All who deal with the iniquity of their fathers and the resulting deeper insight into their own sinfulness receive a special mandate for the next step that is vital in the field of collective guilt: the ministry of reconciliation. This ministry is marked by its authenticity. People will realize very quickly how far somebody is truly broken and moved inside. Mere formulas of repentance and words from an unbroken heart are rather empty and repulsive, and cannot bring healing and reconciliation. At the memorial of Babi Yar in Kiev I said that identificational repentance toward the victims of the Holocaust means "finding the words our fathers never found". When the descendants of the perpetrators meet the victims of the Holocaust and their descendants, it is not really a question of personal guilt. But out of their personal brokenness, they can still ask for forgiveness on behalf of their nation and fathers. You may not be able to imagine the intensity with which people are still waiting for words like these today, and how much healing they bring. We had asked 30 members of our church whose fathers or grandfathers had been involved as soldiers in the invasion of the Ukraine to stand in the first row of the memorial event at Babi Yar. Some of them had made horrifying discoveries in the course of their family research, finding that their grandfathers had been involved directly or indirectly in the Holocaust at Babi Yar. Many of them were deeply shaken, and repented wholeheartedly. Others realized why they had kept running into problems and barriers in so many areas of their lives. One young woman, after waiting for a year, had received the official information that her grandfather had been involved in the massacre at Babi Yar only one week prior to the memorial event there. I still remember the roughly one thousand participants from various churches and congregations at the event. The seats of honor were reserved for the survivors of the massacre and the representatives of Jewish organizations, as well as the pastors of many churches. Speakers were official representatives such as the Israeli ambassador; but that was not the main point. I am still moved by this one moment when the young woman whose grandfather had been involved in the massacre stepped up to the microphone. Her simple words changed the entire atmosphere. Everybody could see that her sorrow was real. With tears, she spoke briefly about her grandfather and said, "I am so sorry." Holocaust survivors also wept and embraced her. They received roses, and their painful memories were touched by the love of God through the young woman's repentance. That precious moment brought healing to their pain. The representative of the Jewish association rose to kiss her hand. The request for forgiveness was broadcast by 14 different TV stations and carried as far as the Chinese border by Russian TV. These are the words that are so necessary and that can bring such healing, but were so hard to find for the war generation of our fathers and grandfathers. We are able to speak them and bring healing to wounded and destroyed souls. This is part of the moral responsibility birthed by the guilt of the past that we as Germans carry toward the victims of the Holocaust and their descendants. Irrespective of where they have settled and live now, we cannot be released from it. We do not have very many years left. Most of the survivors are more than 80 years old. Believers of all churches and congregations have the historic responsibility to minister to them in Israel, in the U.S., in Germany, or wherever else they may be living. But we need to act upon our words of reconciliation. It is unbelievable that a large number of the Holocaust survivors in Israel have to live in poverty. It is the churches' responsibility to send helpers and supporters, and to help them to the best of their financial abilities.

If my people, who are called by my name,
will humble themselves and pray and seek my face
and turn from their wicked ways, then I will hear from heaven,
and I will forgive their sin and will heal their land. (2Chron. 7:14)

There is an immovable principle: If we want blessing for our present and future, we must not rest until our past is reconciled on all levels. Perhaps you would argue now that this has already happened a long time ago, and we should learn now to "look ahead". I beg to differ. Wherever I turn, I see a veil of silence: over people still living and suffering under the shadow of their forefathers; over churches and congregations still caught in their indifference toward the Jewish people and often enough in their hidden anti-Jewish attitudes; and last but not least, over cities and nations whose shed blood to this day still cries out to heaven.

We need to be willing to rediscover the secret of identificational repentance. I would like to encourage you to embark on that journey anew.

CHAPTER 7

HOW THE VEIL OF SILENCE CAN BE BROKEN

Our friends in Washington D.C. had worked hard to make the key event of the March of Remembrance happen on the lawn in front of the U.S. Capitol. On Yom HaShoah, the American Holocaust Memorial Day, 40 cities in the U.S. and 10 other countries were going to hold the memorial and reconciliation marches that had been birthed from the German March of Life. Before the March, I visited many Messianic congregations together with my friend Ted Pearce, where I shared the story of our city. Tübingen's testimony served as an encouragement for many and brought healing; but even more so, it became a model of how the veil of silence can be broken.

But before I continue the story at this point, I would like to summarize the thoughts of the previous chapters. I shared how we had to face the veil of silence that weighed upon us like lead in our city. Obviously we did not really have the spiritual authority to be able to break this veil, despite all of our prayer efforts. In the second chapter we explored the unique authority of the early church, and we realized that even despite the resistance in the Hellenistic Mediterranean, it was able to spread rapidly. When it lost its Hebrew roots, it exchanged its spiritual power for secular authority, and became the cause of centuries of suffering for the

Jewish people. To this day, silence and indifference toward injustice against Israel and the Jewish people are the outward signs of a deeply-hidden anti-Semitism that Christianity has carried in its very heart ever since it separated from its Jewish roots. By now, the Hellenistic spirit has penetrated deeply into churches and congregations in the form of postmodern, secular humanism. If they want to regain their original authority, they first have to find the way back to their Hebrew roots. However, and this was the point of the third chapter, we will not be able to break the veil of silence unless we realize its destructive effects within ourselves and learn to call things as they are. In the following chapters we discovered the veil of silence in the families of both the victims and the perpetrators, and were amazed to see that breaking this veil is the prerequisite for a spiritual future and the revival of a new generation. Germany's – and with it, the church's – responsibility toward the victims of the Holocaust is not over for a long time yet. As long as there are still people suffering from the traumatic results of the Holocaust, we are not done with working through the past, even if many Christians in German churches and free churches consider this topic as no longer relevant, and would rather lay it to rest. But how else can the veil of silence be broken, if not through forgiveness? The blood of Jesus can only cover what we uncover. Healing and reconciliation can only happen on the foundation of personal grief, inner brokenness and the resulting repentance. We are not only accountable before God individually, but also collectively. We have to remove all mechanical conceptions from identificational repentance, and need to rediscover it as the powerful, transforming, and healing instrument that it is. This was our topic in the last chapter.

Having reviewed the line of thought in this book once more, we return to Washington D.C. now. There we were sitting on the stage as guest speakers that had been set up in front of the Capitol building. Sitting next to me were my friends, the Holocaust survivors Peter Loth and Paul Argiewicz, as well as Chaim Urbach, a representative of the second generation of Holocaust survivors. It is part of the Holocaust Memorial Day to light six candles in memory of the six million Jews murdered in the Holocaust. I was privileged to do this next to my Jewish friends, which to me was a sign of special honor. Each of us shared over the microphone whom we wanted to remember, and so I commemorated the 600,000 Jews who had been murdered under the direct or indirect influence of Tübingen during the Nazi era. The lighting of the candles carries a specific significance in Jewish symbolism: Light breaks through darkness! Did Jesus not say the same thing about Himself? He is the light, and wherever He is, darkness has to flee! The same thing was true for our city.

All those who do evil hate the light, and will not come into the light for fear that their deeds will be exposed. But those who live by the truth come into the light, so that it may be seen plainly that what they have done has been done in the sight of God.
(John 3:20-21)

I have come into the world as a light, so that no one who believes in me should stay in darkness. (John 12:46)

Visitation

At this point, I would like to take up a thought from Chapter 1 of this book. I shared how our ministry started spreading beyond the borders of Tübingen, but how we did not have a key to break the clouds of darkness over our own city. At one point, we were on a 40-day fast, as we do at the beginning of every year. During one of our corporate times of prayer that we had as a church, the Holy Spirit started speaking prophetically about the sins of our ancestors against the Jewish people. That was nothing new for us, and my response was reluctant. I have to admit that for me at that time, the whole issue of anti-Semitism was over and dealt with. I had to think of the many times in previous years that I had attended meetings and conferences with the main focus on repentance for the sins of our fathers. As most people in my generation, I was ashamed for my country. To me, loving Germany was equal to nationalistic, right-wing extremist attitudes, and so it was out of the question. After so many years of working through the guilt of National Socialism and of repenting, I had just had enough. I loved Israel, this I knew. Just after I got saved, someone gave me a book on the fact that Israel is chosen. From that moment on, I had no doubts about God's covenant with Israel and His calling for the nations. But my love for Israel was not visible on the outside. I did not want to be part of those militant, Israel-flag-waving zealots who in previous years had combined their commitment to Israel with religious oddities and legalism.[181] I did not realize that this was about much more than just a positive attitude toward Israel. During this particular time of prayer, I had to listen more carefully. The Lord reminded us of the silent majority during the Nazi era who had stood by and watched when their Jewish neighbors were deported. The majority of the German population had known about the Holocaust; but afterwards, hardly anybody could remember anything. In almost every German family there are untold stories of guilt and complicity; but the real problems are the indifference and silence. Without this silent majority who simply decided to look the other way, the Shoah[182] in Nazi Germany could never have taken place. When God spoke to us in that precious time of prayer, it hit us like a hammer. He said, "Don't just humble yourselves for the sins of your fathers, like you have done so many times before. Humble yourselves for your own sin – their silence toward my people is in you also!" The Lord pointed at us and said, "You are just as guilty today as your fathers and grandfathers! Your sin is your silence! It is your indifference toward anti-Jewish attitudes and your silence concerning your Hebrew heritage that I have given to you!" You know, there are times of God's visitation that change everything. Because it is hard to put such situations into words, many times you can only recognize them by their effects. Looking back, I realize that God's word to us did not only change me personally, but also completely renewed and changed the ministry in our churches, their authority in prayer and supernatural anointing, as well as their external impact. A spirit of repentance and shaking brooded over us that remained for days and weeks. Just as bigger waves can alternate with smaller ones, our repentance was reinforced by the personal shaking that individuals experienced before diminishing again, only to return all the stronger with the research done for another March of Life. But strange enough, this repentance was nothing oppressive or shattering; but rather, it came with a special sense of the presence of God and a deep, inner joy that could sometimes even turn to boisterous exuberance.

Open Stopped up Wells!

During this fast, we felt we needed to take the entire leadership of TOS Ministries to Israel. Today, I am convinced that this was a time of preparation in which we received a new calling. With our worship band, we wanted to hold a concert for the Lord in the Negev Desert at Abraham's Well near Be'er Sheva – no audience, just for Him. Abraham's Well is situated in a beautiful archeological excavation site called Tel Be'er Sheva. So we set up our speaker system there, powered up the generator, and in the blazing heat we played for hours just for Yeshua, our Lord. At some point during our worship, I felt the urge to take a pick-axe and hack away at the dry desert ground. That was strange, especially seeing as I am not usually keen on weird prophetic acts. After some resisting, I did it; but I still felt very strange. While pursuing my sweaty labor, I was pondering the question, "Lord, why do you want me to do this?" God's reply was like a new calling that He placed upon us as a ministry and church. "I have called you to open stopped up wells and to dig new wells in the desert!" It was at this event that our worship band received a new name. Because of the new calling, we called them BE'ER SHEVA. Since that time, we have travelled to many different countries with the band BE'ER SHEVA, whose members are also our friends and main leaders in TOS, and have witnessed this calling literally come true.

Hanukkah

Right in the center of Tübingen is the Judengasse (Jew Alley) that was first mentioned in official records in 1350 and is still there today. This was the settlement of the first Jews, and it became the heart of the small Jewish quarter with a synagogue. Over and over again, the Jews of Tübingen had to go through persecution, and in 1477, the founder of Tübingen University expelled them from the city altogether. Around the same time, on the broken fragments of Jewish life, the founder of Tübingen University and Count of Württemberg, Eberhard the Bearded (1445–1496), built the venerable city church (Stiftskirche) that still dominates the cityscape today.

Our repentance of the veil of silence had to become very practical now. We wanted to confess the roots of our faith, and as Christians, officially welcome Jewish life in our city. It happened to be the time of the festival of Hanukkah. Hanukkah is also called the "Festival of Lights". In the Jewish calendar, it always starts on the 25th of Kislev, and it lasts for eight days that can be either in November or December.[183] Hanukkah has a very important meaning: The festival commemorates the rededication of the second Jewish temple in Jerusalem in 164 B.C. The Greeks had desecrated the temple and set up an altar to Zeus there. After a successful uprising that became known as the Maccabean Revolt, the altar to Zeus was demolished again. What a tremendous victory! In order to reinstate the temple service, the menorah, the great lamp stand in the temple, was never allowed to go out. For this purpose they needed special, consecrated oil. A search was made, and they found only one jug, which was actually only sufficient for one day. But the preparation of new oil took eight days, which was too long for the menorah not to go out in the meantime. The time could only be bridged through a miracle. And the miracle happened. Once the lamps were lit, the light did not go out for eight days. So the oil kept burning until the new oil had been prepared. This is what the nine arms of the Hanukiah stand for, as the lights may only be lit with the ninth candle, the "shamash" or "servant",[184] after the appropriate blessing. The Hasmonean[185] wars against the Greeks in Jewish history are also considered a spiritual struggle. The Greeks did not intend the physical destruction of the Jews, but rather wanted to Hellenize them and "enlighten" them with Greek culture and philosophy. "Keep your wise books, laws, and customs," they said, "but enrich them with our wisdom and adorn them with our art and way of living. Worship your God in your temple, but also venerate the human body in sports stadiums that we will build for you right next to the temple. Study your Torah, but incorporate it into the principles of our philosophy and into the esthetics of our literature." The Hasmoneans fought for independence from Helle-nistic rule that was prepared to tolerate Jewish life as long as it was willing to be absorbed into the Greek pantheon. In modern terms, the Maccabean Revolt was a rebellion against the Hellenistic plural-istic theological view, and took a stand for the claim to absoluteness of the One God and of His word. As the Jews view the Maccabean Revolt also as a spiritual struggle, the Festival of Hanukkah still is a symbol of their struggle against the Greek spirit.[186] We did not know very much about the background of the festival of Hanukkah. But the first public celebration of Hanukkah in Tübingen was to set a mark in the invisible realm. God's light may never go out. Wherever His light shines, darkness has to flee!

It was freezing cold. A shivering group of about one hundred people had gathered at the "Bended Bridge" (the central place in the former Jewish quarter) and was waiting for a dance performance. We had placed a Hanukiah on a table close by. But the batteries in our boom box had frozen, so a cappella had to do. We started singing quietly, but then clapped more and more enthusiastically to support the dance group's rhythm. The young people were wearing "tallits", the Jewish prayer shawl. You could tell they were freezing, but that did not keep them from passionately dancing to Paul Wilbur's song, "On Your Walls O Jerusalem". This was probably the first time in several hundred years that the Jewish festival of Hanukkah was celebrated at this special place. In the meantime, many curious onlookers had gathered. I stood on a wall and explained what we were doing. To the approving applause of the spectators I called out, "As believers, we welcome Jewish life in our city once again!" I do not remember whether we prayed a lot that day or repented. Our first public Hanukkah was very inconspicuous and sketchy – and yet it produced a crucial opening of the heavens. For the first time, we had broken the silence concerning our Jewish roots. This simple confession was to bring lasting change for ourselves and our life in the city.

The atmosphere in the city changed almost overnight. Looking back, even after many years I can still trace the breakthrough of our ministry back to this date. Unexpectedly, doors that had been closed for years started opening. Years of unsuccessful attempts to even start negotiations with the city authorities concerning a new location for our meetings suddenly came to an end. We needed a new facility urgently! But with all of our efforts, we had only encountered mistrust and kept running up against the wall. But now there was a brilliant solution. We received the permit to set up a large tent hall on a piece of property near the train station as an interim solution. Some said we were crazy and listed the impossibilities: the noise would bother the neighborhood, and both the cold in winter and the heat during the summer months would make services impossible. We prayed and drew up plans for under-floor heating that would be able to warm the tent even with temperatures below freezing, and for air-conditioning that would cool the summer heat in the tent through evaporating water from a sprinkler on the roof. The tent hall was to become a place where we could face the city's past and make the confession of our Jewish roots visible. Everybody who wanted to attend an event in the tent hall had to walk across a little wooden bridge leading across the railroad tracks that had been used to deport Jews to the concentrations camps during the Nazi era. Upon entering the tent hall, the visitor's gaze would first fall on a big Menorah next to the stage. In this tent hall we were able to witness reconciliation, healing, and restoration with Holocaust survivors and their descendants in the many services and conferences up to the dedication of our new Church and Conference Center. Week after week, people would get saved and be filled with the power of the Holy Spirit. Via internet streaming through TOS TV, the services were broadcast around the globe. The March of Life movement started in the tent hall. This place became a testimony of what happens when a church breaks the veil of silence and stands by Israel and its Jewish roots. Ever since that first Hanukkah celebration, we have not stopped the public observance of the festival in our city. In 2006, it was the first time since the destruction of the old Jewish community in 1933 that a Jewish association was founded.

The same year we had the election for a new mayor. A young 34-year-old man was voted into office who had not been given much of a chance at the beginning of the election campaign. His father had still had to fight anti-Semitic animosity in Tübingen, so he was the first-ever mayor of Tübingen with Jewish roots. When we had come to Tübingen in 1982, we had still found many hidden symbols of National Socialism. Streets had been named after Nazi criminals and still had not been renamed. In the first chapter of this book I have written about other examples. It was only approximately 30 years after the end of WWII that the city started facing its past. By now, the past has been thoroughly worked through in essays, books, films, and public lectures, not sparing any details. The new mayor led this process to a peak at a memorial event on the occasion of the 70th anniversary of Kristallnacht, at which almost all churches and a large number of political parties were represented. They organized a whole week of events commemorating the expelled Jews of Tübingen. Six portraits of Jews from Tübingen reminded everybody of the Jewish life that had been systematically destroyed between 1933 and 1945. Their names and pictures were projected on the walls of the same city hall that had played such an infamous part during the Nazi era.

In the old part of Tübingen there is a market square lined with historic, timbered houses. The city hall is one of them, and visitors are invariably drawn to it. In old newspaper photographs you can see Nazi demonstrations and parades in this square. For one of our Hanukkah celebrations, we had planned to form a human Star of David to place it like a fresh seal on our city. Every participant had a light, and joined the shape outlined with string. The Star of David became visible. It was an impressive picture. I am convinced it was a powerful sign for both the visible and the invisible world. At the following procession, we carried a large cross, together with the lit Hanukiah, through the old city, to the place of the former synagogue that had been burned down on Kristallnacht. Finally, after many years of contention, they had set up a worthy memorial "Against Forgetting" there.

Another telltale sign for the changed atmosphere of the city was the fact that all of a sudden, people were able to open up to the gospel. Instead of putting a lot of effort into planning an "Open Air Evangelism" event with a speaker system, we only needed a Bible, our personal testimony, and a stepladder now. We would

set it up in the city center, climb up, read from the Bible, and
share what Jesus had done in our lives. Almost everybody in
our church, housewives, teenagers, retirees, and even kids love
standing on that ladder. The time of defensiveness and rejection is over. People even come to encourage the "ladder team",
asking them to please not stop publicly proclaiming the gospel;
sometimes they even give them some money. People do not want
new religious forms. Their desire to get to know God has not
diminished to this day, and is tremendous. They gather round the
preacher on the ladder, listen carefully, keep asking for prayer
for healing, and they are not ashamed to entrust their lives to
Jesus right there on the street.

Two years after the Hanukkah celebration on the market square,
the doors opened for a construction permit for a Church and
Conference Center that would become a place of encounter for
Jews and Christians. We have taken a piece of the railroad tracks
with us that the people had to cross via the wooden bridge when
entering the Tent Hall. The German railroad company supported
the project. They came with a heavy-duty steel cutter to cut a
piece from the tracks that we mounted under the entrance of the
new center. Everybody attending our events has to walk over
this piece of railroad track that is displayed below walk-on glass.
These were the tracks used to deport Jews to the concentrations
camps. This is to be a visible sign that Christians can never
again be silent concerning anti-Semitism, hatred of Jews and the
restriction of the Israeli right to live.

When we visited Be'er Sheva, I met Arni Klein, who had moved
to Israel with his wife Yonit from New York many years previously. Arni and I became friends. I learned a lot from him. As a
church, we discovered our Hebrew heritage, and found that we had
to make changes in our spiritual lives.

187

The deep repentance we went through as a church sparked an intense three-year process that we could not have foreseen this way. It was as if someone had drawn aside a spiritual curtain. Suddenly our fathers started speaking about their past with weeping, and confessed their guilt to their own children. Hidden sin of the forefathers from the Nazi era surfaced unexpectedly. Every story was a testimony of shaking, conviction, repentance, and deliverance from a prison that had kept the descendants captive up to that time. Almost every week, we would hear reports of how all of a sudden grandparents started sharing their stories, and how guilt that had remained hidden for so long could no longer be covered up. But in none of the reports did I hear of resulting accusations. Quite the contrary, the personal shock led to the desire to repent for the family sin. This repentance was not condemning or oppressive, but rather inseparably linked with a deep touch by the forgiveness of Jesus, which was perceived as unmerited grace.

The pillars of darkness had been shaken through repentance and the simple confession of our Jewish roots. We were finally able to break the veil of silence over our personal lives, and then also over our city. But what had shaken the pillars of darkness? What had happened?

The Veil of Darkness

In order to explain this, I would like to invite you to take a look into the supernatural realm with me. If we want to know what is happening in our city, region, or even nation, we have to understand that we as humans live in two different realms. There is the natural realm that we have to deal with every day, and then there is the supernatural realm, which is the more real one for God. Naturally, we as humans consider reality to be what we can see or touch. And yet the Bible says that everything we can perceive with our natural senses will pass away one day. What will remain is the supernatural and invisible kingdom. Jesus says that heaven and earth will pass away (Luke 21:33). What this boils down to is that for us as believers, the supernatural truth of the Kingdom of God behind the visible reality is absolutely existential.

> *They will perish, but you remain;*
> *they will all wear out like a garment.*
> *You will roll them up like a robe; like a garment*
> *they will be changed. But you remain the same,*
> *and your years will never end. (Heb. 1:11-12)*

So how can we change anything in our visible reality? I am convinced that this will only be successful if we begin with the spiritual realm, the supernatural realm. Cities and nations are not governed by what we perceive as real with our natural senses, but by what rules in the supernatural, spiritual world (Eph. 6:12). When the Bible speaks about darkness that covers the earth (Isa. 60:2), it does not speak about a natural darkness, but the darkness contained in the broad sense translated by the Greek term "skotos". This word denotes spiritual darkness in the sense of a spiritual blindness (Matt. 6:23; Luke 11:35), but also the sphere of Satan, his sinister forces and demons,[187] as well as everybody under his influence (Eph. 4:18; 5:8). At the crucifixion, we see darkness as the extreme form of abandonment by God (Matt. 27:46). The influence of darkness over a city or nation is unmistakable. But vice versa, we also see how human behavior can bring either blessing or harm to a city or nation. The things of the visible realm always influence those in the supernatural world. Their decision to do good or evil, to sin and do wrong, or to obey and lead a godly life will either provide God with the mandate for healing and restoration, or will give the devil a legal right to oppress, destroy, and paralyze.[188]

There is no doubt that God is interested in the well-being of entire cities and nations, wanting to bless, redeem, heal, and draw to Himself in all areas (2Chron. 7:14). No political program, no economic relief, effective as it may be, and no perfectly devised social welfare plan can bring sustainable change to the visible realm of any nation. God created man to entrust him with dominion over the earth (Ps. 115:16). But how should that be possible if not first and foremost in prayer? This calls for active and determined prayer in faith. Christians do not march out to fight in countless battles for what Jesus has already accomplished. They take note of the effects of darkness, and know their authority. Undoubtedly, Jesus has given the authority to tear down walls of darkness to nobody else but the praying church. But how can this happen? Do we need something like a personality profile of darkness? Do we have to call the territorial powers by name before we can command them to be gone? Or is there another, more effective and much simpler way? This is what we will deal with in the next section. But before we do this, let us take note of some important observations.

1. It is God's goal for our cities and nations to visibly change and to become a blessing to his glory.

Behold, I will bring it health and healing, and I will heal them and will show them the riches of peace and truth. (Jer. 33:6; MKJV)

2. The bloodshed in our city was like pillars in the invisible realm that for some reason we were not able to shake. In Habakkuk 2:12, we can read that the people have to bear the consequences if a city was built by blood and injustice in the past.

Woe to him who builds a city with bloodshed and establishes a town by injustice! (Hab. 2:12)

3. Obviously, Tübingen's bloodshed had fostered a resistance that
    we could not overcome through the prayer warfare we knew.
    We simply had not found the right key. We did know all the
    teaching and strategies of spiritual warfare – but to no avail
    in this case. Darkness exercised such control over the minds
    of believers that many times they were discouraged, doubting,
    and robbed of their faith. Another hallmark was silence. In
    Job 37:19, we read how darkness can influence people's minds,
    making them fall silent.

    Teach us what we shall say unto him; for we cannot order our
    speech by reason of darkness. (Job 37:19; KJV)

4. Darkness covers cities and nations like a demonic veil,
    subjecting the inhabitants under its influence. People's decision
    to live in sin and independence from God provides darkness
    with a legal right to exercise its destructive influence.

    See, darkness covers the earth
    and thick darkness is over the peoples. (Isa. 60:2a; NIV)

5. There is a veil covering the nations which can obviously only
    be torn from Mount Zion. In the report of the great feast to
    which all nations are called in Isaiah 25:6-8, Jerusalem is
    the center of the world. The Lord of Hosts has taken up His
    throne there, and reigns from Mount Zion. The nations will
    gather for the "feast of rich food". Then we read something
    unusual: The nations are still covered by a veil. The Lord who
    removes the veil is the God who wages war, YHWH Tzevaot,
    the Lord of Hosts.[189] It seems to be the "power of death" that
    the Lord will overcome in this last, perennial victory celebra-
    tion (Isa. 25:8a). Just as communion is the "pre-celebration" of
    this feast in the coming Kingdom of God, the intercessors who
    have broken the veil of silence over their lives "in the spirit

of the sons of Zion" are the vanguard of the Lord of Hosts through whom the veil of darkness can be removed from cities and nations.

> *On this mountain he will destroy the shroud that enfolds all peoples, the sheet that covers all nations. (Isa. 25:7)*

6. We also find this principle in Isaiah 62:1. This word has become like the theme for the March of Life movement. Breaking the silence for Zion's sake points to the future, but also has a very real rapport with the present.

> *For Zion's sake I will not keep silent,*
> *for Jerusalem's sake I will not remain quiet,*
> *till her vindication shines out like the dawn,*
> *her salvation like a blazing torch. (Isa. 62:1)*

The pillars of the spiritual world are based on solid foundations: It is the silence in our personal lives concerning the Hebrew roots of our faith, and also our silence concerning Israel. Breaking the silence means pulling the ground from underneath those pillars. Wherever this happens, it has incalculable consequences in the invisible world. As soon as God finds someone who breaks their silence, His light will be able to shine in the darkness and completely transform the visible world. A good example can be found in the book of Ester. Haman plotted the first genocide in the history of the Jewish people, bringing the ultimate threat against its very existence. As long as nobody dared to come before the king to tell him about this scheme, the plans were kept secret. But Mordechai knew a way to save the Jewish people. He realized that his plan could have cost Ester her life. For this reason, he gave her a piece of advice that is still valid for us today. The only way was not to remain silent any longer, and to name the truth for what it was.

For if you remain silent at this time, relief and deliverance for
the Jews will arise from another place, but you and your father's
family will perish. And who knows but that you have come to your
royal position for such a time as this? (Est. 4:14; NIV)

In the light of truth, darkness loses its power. Ester decided not
to remain silent, but to boldly come before the king. The hopeless
situation turned around completely. Haman was hanged on the
tree of his own intrigue. We, like Ester, have come to royal position
for such a time as this (1Pet. 2:9). The conditions of our battle are
set: Jesus has conquered Satan and his henchmen once and for all
(Luke 10:18; Eph. 1:20-22; Col. 2:15). His victory over the powers
of darkness is our victory! It is in our hands – or rather, in our
mouths - whether we will have a share in this victory. I wish you
the same courage and determination to speak the truth through
which Queen Ester was able to save her people from Haman's plans
of destruction.

The experiences in our city were like a model for us. We had learned
something about spiritual authority. I call it the authority in the
"spirit of the sons of Zion". We applied our experiences to other
cities and nations and saw amazing results. In order to get to know
the "spirit of the sons of Zion", we will have to go back to the spiritual and cultural roots of the Western world at some point. Why are
we the way we are? What governs our thoughts and minds? Is there
anything like a DNA of the Western world that determines the way
we treat one another and God? In the Western world, we are utterly
Greek-Hellenistic. Usually we do not even realize the influence
on us. The more the Christian world turned away from its Hebrew
heritage in favor of Greek-Hellenistic thinking, the more it became
amputated, and was robbed of its most important inheritance.
Today, liberal, enlightened thinking seems normal in the Western
world, and has almost replaced the ability to believe the word of
God. Mistrust, doubt, and skepticism have become our companions.

193

The spirit of the sons of Greece (Zech. 9:13) wields a much greater influence in our lives than we care to think. I am convinced that we will see a revival in the Western world which will supersede the Azusa Street revival in Los Angeles by far. All signs point to a movement that will be completely different from what we expect. God uses a unique key for this. It is the only means to unlock the gates of the spiritual world. Believers are rediscovering the "key of David". But they will only be able to use it in authority with a renewed spirit, in the "spirit of the sons of Zion".

...These are the words of him who is holy and true,
who holds the key of David. What he opens no one can shut,
and what he shuts no one can open. I know your deeds.
See, I have placed before you an open door that no one can shut...
(Rev. 3:7-8a)

En Route to Greater Authority

There has not been much progress in the discussion of "spiritual warfare" in Germany in recent years. The diverging positions seem locked, and everybody hopes to have finally overcome the constrictions as far as "spiritual warfare" is concerned. Consenting and dissenting opinions have been described in detail many times, so there is no reason for me to repeat them at this point.[190] Spiritual warfare cannot be avoided, as even critics admit, and you cannot make the issue go away by ignoring it. That is why I would like to share some thoughts that can certainly only be fragmentary.

First of all I have to note, as I have mentioned previously, that despite 20 years of spiritual warfare, binding, and loosing of territorial powers, we had not seen any significant results. I believe the Lord respects this kind of prayer if it comes from the heart with commitment, and that He does not reject it due to "theological

194

concerns". The active prayer in faith will win spiritual battles and move mountains (Mark 11:23; James 5:15; 1John 5:4). And yet, I believe that many of the answers to our prayers came "despite", and not "because of", spiritual warfare as we understood it at that time.[191]

At the same time, the symptoms of darkness cannot be overlooked. There is no doubt that believers are caught up in a spiritual battle. This is not directed against humans, but against the enemy in the invisible, spiritual realm. Mankind lives under the dominion of darkness. They are a people dwelling in darkness (Matt. 4:16). Satan is the ruler of this sphere, along with the hierarchy of his demonic host (Eph. 6:12).[192] Darkness in the demonic world operates on two levels:

1. On the human level; next to the physical body it is especially the mind, will, and emotions that can be affected. Their minds are darkened (Eph. 4:18), says Paul, and their deeds are works of darkness (Rom. 3:12).

2. On the global level; here the devil is called the "prince of this world" (John 14:30) and darkness covers the nations (Isa. 60:2).

In proportion to the guilt and crime of a nation and the willingness of the church to humble itself and repent, darkness can seem more or less oppressive, or "broken".[193] The report on the temporal and visible darkness (John 14:30) at the crucifixion (Matt. 26:45-46) can be a good example for this ultimate expression of God-forsakenness.[194]

Oftentimes, critics find it hard to personalize "darkness" or "evil". Joseph Ratzinger, now known as Pope Benedict XVI, has no problem with it. He describes the temptation of Jesus as the first conflict with Satan, as a real spiritual battle that has but one victor.[195] Joseph Ratzinger taught for three years as professor at the Catholic Faculty of Tübingen University. Perhaps this is the reason why I like an image in his book where the devil is depicted as a Bible expert and theologian in the story of the temptation (Luke 4:1-13). In the Brief Tale of the anti-Christ,[196] the anti-Christ receives an honorary doctorate of theology by Tübingen University. According to Ratzinger, this is not a "no" to scientific exegesis as such; but a warning not to subject the Bible to the principles of the so-called modern world view, transferring everything pertaining to God to the realm of the thinkable and subjective.[197] The last request in the Lord's Prayer, "but deliver us from evil" (Matt. 6:13) is the request for the power of darkness to be broken. You cannot separate the two: Satan is "the evil one" and "evil", i.e. the effects of evil on mankind.[198] The Lord's Prayer expected the answer to this prayer here and now (Mark 11:24; Matt. 21:22). We can safely assume that we do not have to put up with an exaggerated "not-yet" mentality. The Lord wants to break the veil of darkness over every individual, every city and every nation, and He will make His victory visible in the "here and now".

Spiritual warfare was often, at least as far as I can tell from my experience, driven by fear. Instead of praying in the assurance that Jesus has overcome Satan and his henchmen once and for all, many times we focused on the "demon behind the next bush". But instead of remaining defensive, we should arise anew and carefully consider the "armor of light" with which we can be on the offensive. We should be the devil's worst nightmare![199] But what is the "armor of light"?

The night is nearly over; the day is almost here. So let us put aside the deeds of darkness and put on the armor of light.

(Rom. 13:12)

196

In Romans 13:12, the night is a symbol of this present age, the sphere of darkness where Satan is at work. But as the day of the return of Jesus has almost come, Paul calls his readers to put on the armor of light. He sees them as soldiers in a battle that requires extreme alertness and readiness to combat (Rom. 13:12). In the following verse, "Let us behave decently, as in the daytime..." (Rom. 13:13), he changes imagery from the battle field to our conduct of life. This is his question: How do you expect to have authority, while you have not done away with the works of darkness and their effects in your lives? The secret of a lifestyle in authority is in clothing yourself with the Lord Jesus (Rom. 13:14). He is the light (John 12:46)! The light that breaks through the darkness does not come by carefully devised strategic prayers, or by authoritarian mannerisms, or a personality profile of darkness. We put on the armor of light by coming into the light ourselves through cleansing, repentance, and our bold confession. But this will only be possible once we get rid of the virus we still carry within us. The veil of silence is not an invention of modern time – it has been the foundation of darkness ever since the fall (Gen. 4:9). That is why the Epistle of John equates confessing of sin with breaking the silence (1John 1:7-9). Once we break the veil of silence over our personal lives, the lives of our families, and over our churches and congregations, and rediscover our Hebrew heritage, making it our confession, the Body of Christ will awaken from its slumber, even when "the night is nearly over" (Rom. 13:12). When the church puts on its "spiritual armor" (Eph. 6:11), it has to know who it is in Jesus. It is the military representative of heaven. It does not fight against men, but for them. Therefore, it attacks.[200] It is the church on the offensive, just as the apostles "turned the world upside down" (Acts 17:6; KJV). When it breaks the veil of silence, it has the real chance to resist the temptations of secular humanism that intend to place man in the center, making him a mind-oriented egotist, and is able to answer with authority.

So what about our prayers? We are called to promote the healing and transforming therapy for our cities and nations with all aspects of spirit-filled prayer – whether that is inspired intercession, prophetic acts, humble identificational repentance, or the loud confession of the Word of God. In prayer we can pull the ground from underneath the pillars of darkness and shake the sinister power structures over cities and nations. In my opinion, it is not important, but secondary what their names and structures are. The main thing is that they have to flee, and that the light of God breaks through the darkness! We need a fresh prayer revival! Perhaps this is surprising to you: We need the same commitment to prayer that we had at the height of "spiritual warfare". In all the criticism I have heard concerning "spiritual warfare", it was very rare for anyone to appreciate the commitment of these intercessors. Their passion for prayer was and is exemplary, and a challenge for any church frozen in its prayerlessness. It is only through a continuous commitment to prayer that we will be able to touch the heart of God, opening the heavens for the presence of God.

The Western world was changed through the prayers of 3,000 monks from Bangor in Ireland, who started with their 24-hour worship and prayer watch in AD 555. Following the pattern of praise, worship, and intercession in the temple in Jerusalem, they came together day and night for more than 300 years. To overcome their tiredness, they would step into the sea at night to bring their songs and prayers to the Lord standing up to their chests in water. Their commitment gave them authority over the hearts of men. Demons were cast out, spells were broken, and healing came.[201] Within three years, they took all of Scotland for Jesus by storm and planted 300 churches! Sources report of a radiant joy on the face of Columba the Younger (543-615), also called Columbanus. When he was 49, he crossed over to the continent with 12 companions, where he found a church devoid of life and power, lacking in repentance, sanctification, and prayer. He was a preacher of repentance with stirring authority, healing the sick, multiplying food or having it appear from out of nowhere, with authority over wild animals, and ministering with powerful prophetic gifts. We know the source of his power and authority. The spiritual power of this revival was so great, that the gospel spread all over Europe from Bangor. It was the commitment of intercessors spending their time before God 24 hours a day, day and night, that opened the heavens over Europe. Are we truly willing to pay the price for revival in America, Germany, and Europe? We should set out for greater authority. It always starts with us – let us start breaking the veil of silence over our own lives.

How to Do It?

Having attempted a glance "behind the scenes" which admittedly can only be fragmentary at best (1Cor. 13:12), I would like to turn to the practical steps now. It is amazing to see what happens when we start breaking the silence.

Situated in the prime location of Tübingen Market Square is our church's Inner City Center. On the first floor, the homeless and drug addicts have been receiving meals for many years; on the ground floor we have a shop where you can browse Israeli products, books, and information on the Jewish festivals over a nice cup of coffee. The building that houses the "Treffpunkt Jesus live" is among the oldest in the city. Some even suspect that the ancient vaulted cellar dated 1475, which can be reached via a narrow staircase from the shop, formerly used to be a Jewish place for prayer. Today there is a little exhibition in the basement, presenting the city's history during the Nazi era on simple panels, as well as the history of the so-called death marches and the working through of the March of Life. At the entrance there are skullcaps ready for visitors from Israel. Since the exhibition was discovered by Israeli tour groups, several hundreds of tourists from Israel have come to visit the vaulted basement. But the real reason for their visit was not the exhibition. Rather, each time they visit us, we share the story of how we personally work through the Nazi guilt in our families, and of our own repentance. Sometimes, Herbert tells his story of how he used to be a homeless alcoholic for twenty years, and then found help in the "Treffpunkt Jesus live". He then asks their forgiveness for what his father did to Jews as part of an execution squad in the Ukraine. After the men put on their kippot, they recite Kaddish. The "Aaronic benediction" played by BE'ER SHEVA on CD usually ends the little ceremony very much like a service. Every time, it produces healing and deep restoration. For the first time, visitors who have lost family members in Auschwitz or other concentration camps hear the request for forgiveness coming from the mouth of a German. Others share how much they or their families were caught under the same veil of silence. During one of the visits, the tour guide gave the following intro- duction, "We used to come to Tübingen because of its historic old city; but now we come because of the exhibition in the 'Treffpunkt Jesus live', and then take a look at the old city afterwards." The letter of another Israeli tour guide to the tourist information in Tübingen may be the best documentation of the changes in the city. Here is a slightly edited and abridged version:

"During my recent trip around Germany, I had the privilege of paying my second visit to your beautiful city. We were welcomed very hospitably by citizens who repeatedly throughout our entire visit kept expressing their love and appreciation both of Israel and its people, history, and heritage. My tour group and I were fasci- nated and overwhelmed by our visit to the exhibition 'March of Life', as well as of the unique shop 'Treffpunkt Jesus live'. Person- ally I can say that this encounter is surely one of my most exciting and memorable experiences ever. Furthermore, this encounter was the most valuable thing that happened to me on all of my trips so far. On a side note – I have been in the business for ten years.

I would like to express my warmest recommendation for a visit to this honorable city and its sacred places, especially the aforementioned shop. The development there is a special recommendation to the people in Israel to develop and strengthen the relationship between Israel and Germany in general and Tübingen especially."

This encouraging testimony shows us that there are several levels of working through the past. We must not confuse them, and have to be very systematic. I would like to encourage you to start with some very practical steps in your own life – this will take endurance, time, and our personal investment. The five levels to work through are:

1. Level: Your personal life
2. Level: Your family
3. Level: Churches and congregations
4. Level: The city
5. Level: The nation

The principles of working through the past are something we can find also in the field of trauma research. I cannot stress enough that there are narrow limits to counseling as far as assisting the process of working through heavy traumatization and its effects on the following generations is concerned. You should absolutely consult a psycho-therapist who works with Christian principles and values. Every process of working through is different. There are some elements, however, that seem to be recurring. AMCHA[202] encourages people to put traumatic experiences into words after a period of building security and trust. Even if there is no general recommendation concerning silence or talking, there is a general consent from a perspective of trauma healing that it is better to let out what has been kept secret for so long than trying to repress and forget painful memories. In other words, "remembering takes precedence over forgetting", and it is amazing to see that even talking alone can bring emotional relief.[203] But of course we must not stop there. If we want to break the veil of silence, we can only do that with a willingness to allow the truth to touch us personally, so personal grief can produce the desire to reach God's throne of grace. Before the throne of grace, the blood of Jesus covers everything we uncover. It is the place where we can repent with all our heart for ourselves or for others. In the New Testament, repentance is "happy business" and has nothing to do with condemnation or religious legalism (Luke 15:10; Rom. 2:4). If it is earnest, it will produce a new lifestyle that can be seen in our confession.

So we can complement each of the five levels with the following four steps:

a) Working through
b) Personal grief
c) Repentance
d) Confession

Now we will take a closer look at each step. You can then transfer them easily to your own situation.

Working Through

I would recommend that you take a quiet moment to note down the things you have realized while reading this book. If you are part of the Holocaust or war generation, or of one of the following generations, it may make sense to read the appropriate literature to find out about the effects of the forefathers' guilt or trauma. Think about instances where you have become a follower and responded with silence. Is there a situation in your life that you have suppressed and pulled a "veil of silence" over it? The Bible reminds us many times to check ourselves, saying, "Examine yourselves... test yourselves" (2Cor. 13:5). Examine yourself to see whether you still have any anti-Jewish attitudes or thoughts. Take time in prayer to personally work through this. In the Holy Spirit you have a precious helper, who loves supporting you in the process. Invite Him, and you will have a wonderful time. He is the Spirit of Truth, who leads into all truth (John 16:13).

> *Search me, O God, and know my heart: try me,*
> *and know my thoughts. (Ps. 139:23; KJV)*

Many people feel that it is helpful here to work through their own family history. This has actually shown tremendous results, and can help to solve many open questions. It takes courage to face the truth about one's own family. This is not about airing dirty laundry. Try to lovingly talk to your family, without accusation, and in the spirit of reconciliation. Often there is still a rich treasure of documents in the family, like photo albums, written documents, or family collections, that are important witnesses of the past. Unfortunately there often is a bitter truth hidden behind the trivializing war-time stories. New scientific findings say that there has been no such thing as a harmless Wehrmacht soldier, not involved in anything.[204] Healing and restoration can only happen once we are willing to face the truth about our families. The resulting blessing is tremendous. The following story is just one precious example of how working through a family's past can happen in a good way. The author is part of our church, runs a senior citizens' home, and has been the chief editor of a Christian radio station for many years.[205] He wanted to find out whether his grandfather had been a war criminal.

"I wanted to know whether my grandfather had been more deeply involved in the crimes of WWII than I had thought up to then. Had he been a victim, a follower or a perpetrator? So together with my parents, I wanted to embark on this research, and I hoped this would provide me with the personal opportunity of facing my family's guilt. Searching the documents we had and other research allowed me to shed some light on the situation.

"My grandfather was killed in the war when my mother was still a baby. We had talked about him in the family every now and then, but my image of him had remained somewhat vague: a 'young doctor' who had had the 'misfortune' of being drawn into the war and who had fallen very soon 'somewhere on the battlefield'. My search began when I first asked my mother where my grandfather had died. It was in Ternopil in the Ukraine. This university city of today was the site of one of the greatest massacres in all of Galicia. In June 1943 alone, approximately 12,000 Jews were shot at the outskirts of the village by German national socialists and their Ukrainian henchmen. Over the entire period of the war, about 200,000 Jews perished in and around Ternopil. Memorial plaques commemorate these pogroms.

"I searched the documents and photos that my mother had only recently discovered in an old box in her attic. All of a sudden, I saw a completely new picture. My granddad was only 25 years old when he was killed in Ternopil in 1944, while taking part in a conference of officers. He was buried with military honors and posthumously promoted to the post of Surgeon Major. The pictures show a self-confident young man who, according to his service record, had been promoted from a simple auxiliary doctor to Surgeon Major. The service record proved to be a detailed documentary of the war events that my grandfather had been involved in. It lists 'breakthrough battles' and 'pursuit fights' right across the modern Ukraine, heading toward Charkov. I was shocked to learn that he had been part of the Army Group South (Heeresgruppe Süd) under the command of Field Marshall Werner von Reichenau, who had issued the so-called 'Reichenau order' in October 1941, calling for the mass murder of 'Jewish subhumans'. Reichenau was the commander in chief of the massacre of Babi Yar, where over 30,000 Jews were shot by the Wehrmacht in Kiev within three days. The

information contained in the service record helped me to recon-
struct my grandfather's path through the Ukraine along places now
infamous for other massacres of Jews. Charkov was another city on
his path – the massacre there cost 20,000 Jewish lives.

"Therefore, it stands to reason that my grandfather was either
directly or indirectly involved in such murderous activities. The
massacres had taken place all over the country, and had been so
violent that I don't believe anyone could have not known. His
successful military career confirms to me that he had not just been
a simple follower or even victim; but very clearly he was a perpetrator, an active partner and operating executor of a murderous
system that destroyed 1.6 million Jews in the Ukraine alone. This
is what I had to face. All of a sudden, I understood where the heavy
burdens had come from that I had noticed in my life time and time
again. I was able to pray in detail and ask forgiveness for my grandfather's bloodshed. I am so grateful to know the living God who
breaks every yoke through the grace of Jesus, and who says, 'I have
swept away your offences [the guilt of your forefathers] like a cloud,
your sins like the morning mist...' (Isa. 44:22)"

The past twenty years have seen a fair bit of progress in Germany
concerning working through city histories. There is a lot of research
being done for scientific reports and presentations, and places of
commemoration are established for the expelled Jews and the Holocaust. But the story that usually remains untold is the story of the
silent majority who watched, and yet was responsible. National
Socialism fell on the fertile ground of anti-Semitic attitudes that
can be traced way back in the city's history. For this reason, every
working through of a city's history should begin with working
through the history of the Jews in that particular city. The following
report by Stefan Haas is an impressive testimony of how a city can
face its history. I think of it as impressive because it shows how the
initial reserve against working through the past changed, first to
personal grief, and then reconciliation:[206]

"Since the 17th century, the little town of Bibra south of Meiningen in Thuringia had seen the peaceful coexistence of a considerable number of Jewish citizens with their Christian fellow citizens. In 1933, about 134 of the roughly 600 inhabitants were Jewish. Only 60 of them survived the Holocaust. 18 houses in the village belonged to Jewish families, and they even had a synagogue. Many of them had to sell their houses under dramatic circumstances, and they tried to flee before the beginning of the Holocaust. On the other hand, young men of the village were drafted into the SS. The functioning village community was torn apart. In 2004, there was a seminar on Israel held in Bibra. Among the participants were Jews from Israel whose ancestors had lived in Bibra until the beginning of National Socialism. It was the beginning of close personal relationships. This encounter gave rise to the idea of putting up a memorial commemorating the Jews of Bibra who had been killed during the Nazi era. The population's first response was reserved. 'Can't we finish with this after 60 years?' But this reserve was actually just a pretext to hide their own insecurities and fears of such an encounter. Before 1933, Bibra had a functioning village community; but then it was polarized and torn apart. What did an encounter mean now, after all the unimaginable suffering that had come over these people? Friends and neighbors had been separated. What would it mean emotionally to meet again now? The fact that the mayor and her deputy took a clear stand for this project was a great help and encouragement. They set a date for the dedication of the memorial, and former Jewish inhabitants from all over the world were invited. Just a few days prior to the set date, you could still sense the tension in the village. But for the celebration itself, many more gathered together than previously anticipated. The inhabitants of the village were given the opportunity to welcome their former Jewish fellow citizens with an abundance of white roses that were provided. With tears in their eyes, warm embraces, great joy, and relief, their hearts opened to one another. Reconciliation happened that nobody could organize, let alone order."

Personal Grief

You cannot produce personal grief. I am touched by the Holy Spirit when I expose myself to Him and honestly face the truth. This is what working through is. Unfortunately, we often try to take a shortcut in order to avoid the part of personal shaking. Sometimes it is easier to say a brief confession of sins than to actually bring our hard hearts before God. Sometimes we lose sight of the fact that we cannot repent from our hearts without this inner shaking, or as Martin Luther put it, having a "frightened conscience". Only a repentance that is birthed from grieving over a matter personally can change our actions. John the Baptist speaks about our repentance bearing fruit (Matt. 3:8). Do not be surprised if there is not much emotion, or even indifference in your heart at first. This is the best sign that you are on the right track. Often the veil of silence is shrouded by a seemingly impenetrable fog. Self-justification, down-playing, and a victim mentality seem to be the invisible fog machines that make it so hard for a deeper shaking to reach our hearts (Luke 18:13). But after personal grief comes honesty, with which we can dare to name the truth unafraid.

I would like to encourage you to start using photo and film material and reports to face these events in history so that they can eventually touch your heart. The most devastating military campaign in history began more than 70 years ago, which cost the lives of 27 million Soviet citizens, mainly civilians. Millions of Jews were shot like cattle and brutally murdered. The slaughter and murder lasted for four years, and had the insane goal to create "Lebensraum" (lit: living space) in the East. This was not a war of conquest, but a racially motivated war of annihilation with the goal of destroying millions of lives. Ordinary men became mass murderers of hundreds of thousands. They were from Germany. But Jews were persecuted, deported, and annihilated on all other fronts also. At that time, there was nobody who was a harmless follower – everybody incurred guilt in one way or another. And we – we could have done the same! Allow personal grief so that you will be able to repent from your heart for yourself and for your ancestors in order to break the yoke on your family.

> *I will give you a new heart and put a new spirit in you;*
> *I will remove from you your heart of stone*
> *and give you a heart of flesh. (Ezek. 36:26)*

Repentance

Many people still have a wrong, I would almost call it "medieval", idea about repentance. They think of God as someone who punishes them and puts a legalistic yoke on their shoulders. When anyone calls them to repentance, they think, "Failed again!" But actually, the gospels see repentance as something completely different. When John the Baptist called, "Repent, for the Kingdom of Heaven is near!" (Matt. 3:2), he said that repentance is the gate to heaven, and the door to return to the father heart of God. Repentance makes the Kingdom of Heaven come near and become visible. As soon as this happens, joy and peace settle in. Mother Basilea Schlink, founder of the Sisterhood of Mary in Darmstadt, says this as follows: Repentance is a gift of the Holy Spirit, who settles on a human heart that has grown hard and secure, breaking it into pieces, only to take it up in His hand again to form a new vessel.[207]

I would recommend you do not stay alone with your repentance. Talk to someone you can trust and who has an understanding of counseling questions. The confession of sins has tremendous power; it "detoxifies" you from silence, and allows you to receive God's promises.

I have summarized a few points here where the Word of God is very clear that silence can become sin. This list is definitely incomplete and can be added to.

Silence can become sin...

1.   ... when I do not confess my sin and take it to the cross.

If we confess our sins, he is faithful and just and will forgive us our sins and purify us from all unrighteousness. (1John 1:9)

2.   ... when I hide my past and keep it in the dark.

But if we walk in the light, as he is in the light, we have fellowship with one another, and the blood of Jesus, his Son, purifies us from all sin. (1John 1:7)

3.   ... when I do not confess my life as a believer and do not stand for the truth of the Word of God.

If any of you are ashamed of me and my words in this adulterous and sinful generation, the Son of Man will be ashamed of you when he comes in his Father's glory with the holy angels.
(Mark 8:38)

4.   ... when I reject the heart of the Father or the Son through my silence.

And he will go on before the Lord, in the spirit and power of Elijah, to turn the hearts of the parents to their children and the disobedient to the wisdom of the righteous - to make ready a people prepared for the Lord. (Luke 1:17; NIV)

5.   ... when I remain silent in the face of injustice, lawlessness, or oppression.

Love does not delight in evil but rejoices with the truth. (1Cor. 13:6)

6. ... when I do not share the precious treasure of the gospel
    without compromising it.

    *He said to them, Go into all the world and preach the gospel
    to all creation. (Mark 16:15)*

7. ... when I do not stand up in the face of anti-Semitism and do
    not confess God's covenant relationship and love to Israel.

    *I will bless those who bless you, and whoever curses you I will
    curse; and all peoples on earth will be blessed through you.*
    (Gen. 12:3)

When Jesus was all alone on the cross of Calvary and heaven was
closed over him, the eclipse placed a dark veil over the land. No
one can even begin to guess His feeling of abandonment. On the
cross of Calvary, Jesus had to bear our silence so you and I would
be able to break it. Our redemption also includes our silence! We
can cast our speechlessness on Jesus, just as much as we do our
sin, sickness, poverty, and need. He has bought our words, even
if they are labored and stammering at first, with the price of His
precious blood.

He was oppressed and afflicted, yet he did not open his mouth;
he was led like a lamb to the slaughter, and as a sheep before its
shearers is silent, so he did not open his mouth. (Isa. 53:7)

Confession

Personal grief and repentance will always change our lifestyle as well. This will inevitably also affect our confession. When we break the veil of silence, it always means rediscovering the Jewish roots of our faith. Jesus will always remain at the center of our worship and adoration, and will remain our Lord. At the same time, our confession of allegiance to Israel and the Jewish people is much more than standing with them and blessing them. It is not about unconditional support for the State of Israel, because just like any other nation, it has its flaws and shortcomings that you can give a name to. And yet there are crucial reasons why Christians today should stand with Israel and publicly confess that.

When the Jewish people returned to the Holy Land and the State of Israel was founded, it was the fulfillment of biblical prophecy. On a merely rational level, this was unprecedented! No other people who had been expelled from their land for centuries and dispersed into all the world had ever kept their national identity to such an extent that it was possible to return to their former country. All of this happened after the annihilation of two thirds of the European Jewry. With the crematoria still smoldering, Israel was born again.[208] Standing with Israel means standing with God's plans and purposes – we should know this! A second reason for standing with Israel is the realization that there is a satanic plan to destroy Israel. We have learned by now that darkness always comes with silence. So we should not repeat the mistakes of the past. We should know that standing with Israel also means coming against its spiritual enemies. Here we are not talking about people, but about spiritual powers that keep trying to rouse destructive, poisonous hatred against the people of Israel.[209] There are enough powers that want to see Jewish blood flow again. Anti-Jewish ideas and conspiracy theories keep surfacing again and again. For this reason, there is a third point why we should break the veil of silence over our families, churches, and cities with our public confession of standing with the Jewish people and Israel: Simply because God has never rejected His chosen people that He loves with all His heart! Every time we take a stand with His Jewish people, when we minister to them, standing with them in unconditional friendship, we touch the heart of God. Blessing or curse, success or failure, depend on how we deal with God's sovereign choice of His people. Our public confession makes the light of God break forth and releases blessing. Our silence, however, will give darkness a mandate and bring on a curse.

I will bless those who bless you,
and whoever curses you I will curse;
and all peoples on earth will be blessed through you.
(Gen. 12:3)

One day, my friend Ted Pearce called me to ask whether I would be willing to write a prayer to be spoken at the end of his song "Forgotten People". It was translated, and found wide circulation in the United States on the CD and later through a music video produced in Nashville. For tens of thousands, this prayer became an unmistakable confession from the city and the country of unmerited grace.

Forgotten People

You shall not bow down to them or worship them; for I, the LORD
your God, am a jealous God, punishing the children for the sin of
the parents to the third and fourth generation of those who hate
me, but showing love to a thousand generations of those who love
me and keep my commandments. (Exod. 20:5-6; NIV)

Lord, I hear the cries of six million of your people. Men, women,
children - murdered, annihilated in the Holocaust, and burnt. We
confess these atrocities as sin and humble ourselves before you in
shame. You have heard our plea, and our repentance has come
before your ears.

Lord, I see black smoke. It rises up and spreads out like a veil of
darkness over our nations again! This dark veil is the sin of our
silence!

Just as we Germans have remained silent, the peoples and nations
are silent once again. Again, your people Israel is hated, despised,
and rejected; and yet we remain silent even in the church. We are
silent concerning the sin of our fathers. We remain silent, and
behold, the black smoke is covering us again.

From the land of unmerited grace we are calling out: Nations arise!
For Zion's sake, open your mouth!

Never again - slander! Never again - hatred! Never again - death!

Israel — we will never forsake you again! You are our inheritance,
our love, the blessing for all nations! Listen! Receive the word! It
will pervade your spirit.

No more silence! Never again! Never again! Never again!

CHAPTER 8

THE MARCH OF LIFE

We had invited Ted Pearce to lead worship in our service. He had come from America especially to visit us in Tübingen. We had discovered his songs about a year prior to this event, so they were well-known in our church. Ted is one of the best Messianic musicians and worship leaders in America, even though he is not Jewish. So we were happily singing along with his songs, and started to dance. Our time of worship turned into a praise festival. That time marked the beginning of a deep friendship with Ted. God used him powerfully to transport the vision of the March of Life beyond the borders of Germany right to America. The way the March of Life began and spread is still a miracle to me. It started in our region and then spread – you could almost say, exploded – to other cities and nations. Within five years, we were able to watch the March multiply, and saw a small prayer assignment turn into a movement that has had tens of thousands involved in at least 80 cities and 12 nations. The March of Life comprises every-thing the Lord has taught us about the veil of silence in previous years. Whether this is the personal working through our family histories, the question concerning the heritage of the generation of perpetrators and victims of the Holocaust, or the joint confession of Jews and gentiles against the modern anti-Semitism of our time and for Israel: The March of Life has become a powerful tool with which we can break the silence and pull the rug out from under-neath darkness.

We currently see a resurgence of a downplaying of the Holocaust and open anti-Semitism in many places. Indifference about the threat toward the Jewish people and silence concerning the injustice done to them can be found again in almost every nation. At the moment, anti-Semitic incidents in Western Europe have reached a new all-time high since the end of WWII. In the United States, the neo-Nazi scene is more radical than ever before. Its goal is a "white America", and it openly propagates an "Aryan race" that is supposed to take over the world one day.[210] The scene makes very clever use of popular communication tools, such as the internet or an increasingly popular music scene, to promote their sinister ideologies. The Turner Diaries, written in the U.S., became a big seller worldwide. The novel divulges racist and anti-Semitic ideas, and is said to be standard literature among the white supremacy movement in America. The well-known American car manufacturer Henry Ford can be called the prophet of this work, and rightly so. His anti-Semitic pamphlets are summed up in the book The International Jew – The World's Problem that had such drastic international influence that even Adolf Hitler adapted parts of it for his book Mein Kampf. Asked by the Detroit News[211] what American industrials meant to him, Hitler answered, "I see Henry Ford as my inspiration." Heinrich Himmler, chief Germanic ideologist and demonic liturgist of the SS Totenkopf divisions, remarked in a letter that for him, Ford was "one of the most valuable, weightiest, and inspired champions".[212] There is a study that says that anti-Semitic statements by American journalists have increased substantially in recent years. But the broad American public has remained largely oblivious to this.[213]

In Latin America, the situation is even more dangerous. Anti-Semitism there is hiding behind a political façade, and hatred toward Israel is disguised as anti-Zionism. A closer look, however, reveals an alarming dimension. Latin America's leading specialist in anti-Semitism, Maria Luiza Tucci Carneiro, presented a 740-page anthology of experts shedding light on the phenomenon of hatred of Jews in North and South America from different points of view.[214] To this day, anti-Semitic views are commonplace in Latin America. When you look up the term "Jew" in some Brazilian dictionaries of foreign words, they seriously give the explanation "bad person". Many men in Latin America have official first names such as Hitler, Himmler, or Eichmann. Again and again synagogues are attacked, the number of anti-Semitic websites and neo-Nazi groups has increased drastically, and Jewish personalities often receive death threats. Even though there are gradual differences between the U.S. and the countries of Latin America, the evangelical and Pentecostal churches usually do not paint a better picture. Of course, there are many among them who recognize that Israel is chosen, and who voice their love for Israel even in public. At the same time, in so many of them you come across indifference in theological disguise that often serves to hide prejudices and anti-Jewish attitudes. So it is hardly surprising that a study discovered anti-Semitic tendencies in evangelical Christian circles, of all places.[215] In Latin America, the situation is similar and even more obvious. When I spoke about the fact that "the Jewish people is chosen" and about the roots of anti-Semitism in Latin America at a conference in Venezuela, the pastors there asked the organizer in all earnestness why he had invited "this old Jew" to speak.

In Eastern Europe, anti-Semitic attitudes are also still rife. It is only very gradually that these governments are starting to face the past. Without wanting to play down the German responsibility for the Holocaust in any way, in recent years there has been an increased focus on the support by local aides and helpers.[216] Hitler's henchmen had willing helpers in the occupied nations, such as the former Ukrainian concentration camp guard John Demjanjuk, who was found guilty of complicity in murder in a thousand cases. The Germans could never have accomplished the millionfold murder of European Jews by themselves. In the huge territories of Eastern Europe, the SS, police, and Wehrmacht had to rely on helpers. Over 200,000 non-Germans were involved in pogroms and mass executions. It is historically undisputed that next to the hundreds of thousands who were abused as helpers and forced into complicity, the Holocaust also had a dimension going beyond Nazi Germany that had its foundation in the anti-Semitic history of the individual European nations that has never been worked through. Only at a very late point in time – most of the perpetrators had died by then – did France and Italy start to thoroughly work through this part of history. Others, such as the Ukraine, Latvia, or Lithuania, still find this very hard, or like Romania and Hungary, they are only at the very beginning of this process. This is hardly surprising, as these countries, attacked by Hitler's Wehrmacht, devastated and covered with millions of dead, became tragic victims themselves. So it was all the more painful to admit that many of their own countrymen were willing aides to the German perpetrators.[217] During the preparations for the March of Life in the Ukraine, pastors and bishops shared about their futile attempts to break the veil of silence concerning their own nation's guilt. But only a few months later, we were going to see this happen in over 17 cities all across the Ukraine in a single day.

Right at the beginning of this book, I shared our city's testimony. We have learned that when we start conscientiously working through our family history on a personal level and take a public stand for the Jewish roots of our Christian faith, it produces an authority that can result in great spiritual breakthroughs. Was the experience of unmerited grace not the key requirement in order to be able to humbly share the message of healing and restoration in other nations? Is it legitimate for descendants of the German perpetrators to help others who had become victims of National Socialism to recognize their own share of anti-Semitic guilt? We have seen this happen through the March of Life in a unique way. Whether it is in America, Germany, or in any other nation – we are experiencing the same thing everywhere. Unfortunately, this process of working through the past is not finished yet. We should make the most of the time we still have left to honor the survivors of the Holocaust. When they and their descendants hear the testimony of facing the past and identificational repentance by descendants of the perpetrators, they experience healing, and many times they open their hearts for the One who alone makes forgiveness possible. In the words of a prayer by the musician and worshipper Paul Wilbur, the March of Life has become an instrument to comfort God's people, setting a mark with its statement of standing with them. I believe there is truth in this.

Comfort, comfort my people, says your God. (Isa. 40:1)

A voice of one calling:
'In the wilderness prepare the way for the Lord;
make straight in the desert a highway for our God.' (Isa. 40:3)

The Death Marches

In order to better understand the complex background to the March of Life, I have to go into some more detail of a phenomenon in the history of Nazi Germany that is rightfully called the final phase of Nazi genocide: the death marches.

Only recently, the Israeli historian Daniel Blatman wrote a long-overdue standard volume on the death marches of 1944-45.[218] He paints a comprehensive and frightening picture of German society at the end of WWII. At that time, the SS evacuated all concentration camps. They wanted to eliminate all traces of the genocide before the concentration camps fell into the hands of allied troops. They left behind weak and sick prisoners or killed them; the rest were marched to other camps or taken there by train. During the harsh winter months of 1944-45, the prisoners were often zigzagged along the highways and byways of a Germany, that was increasingly slipping into chaos, for weeks without appropriate clothes, starving, completely exhausted, and close to collapsing. All who fell by the wayside or attempted escape were killed immediately. The routes of the death marches were drenched in blood and marked by mass murder. Many of the gaunt and worn-out prisoners died of hypothermia or starved to death, and just lay by the roadside. Of the more than 700,000 prisoners who had somehow managed to survive in the concentrations camps until 1945, no less than 250,000 people perished on the death marches at the end of the war. This mass murder was unequalled. More than thirty-five percent of the prisoners in the camps, making it at least a quarter of all victims of the concentration camps, met their death during the last five months of the war on the death marches before the very eyes of the civilian population.[219] They were not only Jews, but also forced laborers, prisoners of war, and political prisoners. Nobody could have missed the endless treks of emaciated and doomed prisoners. The mass murder no longer took place only in faraway Eastern Europe, but on German roads and fields. Now the population was face to face with the genocide that had gone on for years. In his upsetting study, Blatman proves that the murderers did not only come from the ranks of the SS, the police, and the Wehrmacht.[220] The murder took place in plain sight. Nobody could escape. The SS would shoot anyone incapable of walking any further. The Feldpolizei (field police), Hitler youth, and Volkssturm (national militia) saw to it that all who had escaped were caught again and executed. Often it was the civilian population who provided the necessary information. It was the time when even normal people became murderers. Brutalized by Nazi propaganda and the war, even civilians became involved in the massacres and the merciless hunt for "public enemies". As unspeakable as the suffering on the death marches was, they remained covered by silence for a long time, and hardly anybody was held responsible for them. The fate of the hundreds of thousands found hardly any mention. Even in the detailed reports about National Socialism, this chapter remained as good as untouched. The death marches in Germany represent a veil of silence. Tens of thousands were involved in these last massacres, either directly as helpers, or indirectly as onlookers. They took place in full public view, on people's "doorsteps", and they were the final cruel climax of the Holocaust, right under the eyes of the German population.

On the Road to Dachau

About 20 minutes away from Tübingen is the Swabian Alb, a small range of hills with a plateau top that runs through Baden-Württemberg from southwest to northeast. This is also the location of a small church plant of TOS, and this is where the March of Life started. During the Nazi era, dotted across the Swabian Alb were seven extension camps of the Alsatian concentration camp Natzweiler-Struthof, that were all part of the "Operation Desert" which had been established in June 1944. The rock of the Swabian Alb seemed to be suitable for mining oil shale to extract oil. The cruel conditions in the camps were beyond words. Thousands perished just for the sake of a little over 1,200 tons of oil. The project had been doomed to failure right from the start. When the defeat of Germany could no longer be put off in the spring of 1945, the Nazi regime changed its policy of hanging on and issued the so-called "Nero-order". It basically meant the total destruction of Germany. One of the most pressing problems for Hitler was the dissolution of the concentration camps. The prisoners were to be killed off as quickly as possible, so they would not be able to serve as witnesses against the Nazi regime.

One of the hubs for the transfer of the prisoners was Dachau concentration camp just northwest of Munich. The prisoners from the different camps in Germany were supposed to be marched there. By mid-April, Himmler's evacuation order had also reached the Swabian "Desert Camps". Several thousands of prisoners were sent on a death march heading for Bavaria. They had to suffer extreme privation, and hundreds of them were shot or fell by the wayside from sheer exhaustion, where they died.

"The blood spilled on these roads still cries out to Heaven!" or something like this was the prophetic word that first pointed our attention to the death marches. Initially, we had planned on taking a small team to walk along the main route to pray. A short time later, Ted Pearce visited the small church on the Swabian Alb. When he heard about our plan to do this March of Life with only a small team, he was very surprised, to put it mildly. In Ted's eyes, this march was so important that all of his friends in America needed to hear about this. At the time, we thought this was slightly exaggerated; but in the end, this was exactly what happened. So the first March of Life actually took place along the route of the former death marches going toward Dachau. More than 300 people participated, among them the Jewish Holocaust survivors Peter Loth and Rose Price, as well as 20 others from Jewish Messianic congregations in the U.S. In the course of our preparations, again and again we came across indifference and repression, even a flat refusal of support. But during the march, the situation completely turned around. Something had happened. It seemed as if an invisible hand had turned the March of Life into a clarion call against anti-Semitism in our day. Regional, national, and international media reported on it. Numerous personal encounters with eyewitnesses of that time offered a glimpse of their involvement and shame. For many of the Jewish and German participants, these three days became a life-changing experience, transforming anxieties and pain, unadmitted hatred, and hidden bitterness into

friendship. TUBINGEN BEGS FOR FORGIVENESS was the head-
line of a frontline article in the Israeli Jerusalem Post,[221] reporting
on the March of Life. A TV crew led by journalist Jeffrey L. Seif
accompanied the march, and produced an eight-part series titled
Bad Moon Rising. Millions of people all across the U.S. were able
to watch it. People said time and time again, "What you have done
here is one of the strongest statements against re-emerging anti-
Semitism that we have ever seen."

In three days, the 320 participants walked about 220 miles. In
order to make it possible for everybody to join in, each day's route
was split into 30 different sections of varying length. Our route
led us from Tübingen across the Swabian Alb right to Dachau near
Munich. We had planned to have a joint memorial and prayer
march with all the participants in the last few miles leading up to
the Dachau Concentration Camp Memorial, and this was exactly
what we did. This was the same road that tens of thousands of
prisoners had walked to the concentration camp to die there,
among them the 16-year-old Rose Price. Now, more than 60 years
later, we stood at the iron gate of Dachau that still displays the
cynical words "labor makes free". As a teenager, Rose Price had
survived the camp. I shared about her in the earlier chapters. The
final stage of her road of suffering had been Dachau Concentration Camp, where she was liberated by American troops. She had
never been back there since. Together with my wife, we stepped
through the iron gate with her. Later, Rose shared how her legs had
become like lead. Even though she had people at her right and left
who supported her, she did not know how to cope with the overwhelming pain.

At the center of the camp memorial was the roll call yard where
innumerable prisoners had been shot. Our Jewish friends had
showed us pictures of family members who had perished in the
Holocaust, and had asked us to hold them while they recited

Kaddish in the yard in honor of their relatives. Kaddish is one of the most important Jewish prayers and is prayed in memory of the dead. While we were praying, I heard loud wailing. It was Rose. My wife Charlotte put her arm around her and together with some friends tried to comfort her. Obviously Rose had not been able to stand the pain in this place any longer. But when I approached her some time later, the situation was completely turned around. Something peculiar must have happened. Her face was no longer marked by pain and the burden of the past. A radiance had come upon her that I had never seen on her before. Later she shared what had happened.

"Through the experiences in the concentration camps my heart had become so closed and hard that I had never been able to cry ever since I had been in Dachau." I knew that Rose had lost many loved ones throughout her life and that she had had to go through a lot of pain. And yet she continued, "Just now, before my inner eye I saw my heart breaking into six million pieces, and Yeshua lovingly putting it together again and healing it with His touch." At the following meeting, Rose was the main speaker. And there she was, almost cheerful, joking and totally changed. Rose found healing when she faced the truth at the place of her most painful memories.

The Warm Coat of the SS Officer

The former Buchenwald concentration camp is located close to Weimar in Thuringia. The idyllic serenity there belies the horror of this place. Here 56,000 people, among them 11,000 Jews, fell victim to the Nazi terror. The Nazis' answer to the approaching liberators was the death marches. In their attempt to clear out the camp under cover of darkness, the SS sent 28,000 prisoners to their sure death on the roads of Eastern Germany. Hardly noticed by the civilian population, 12,000 to 15,000 people perished – by starvation, exhaustion, or through the guards' bullets. There are a few scattered places where memorials remind us of the fact that German roads are covered with blood. But in all too many places, the former sites of death and torture have been completely forgotten.

Following the liberation of Buchenwald concentration camp, the Soviet military administration took over the camp, and from 1945 until 1950 it was used as a detention camp under the name of "Special Camp 2". During that time, more than 7,000 people died there. Political forgetting was used as a method in the former communist East Germany. During one of her visits to Israel, Chancellor Angela Merkel found some very personal words for this. She said that for the first 35 years of her life she had lived in a country that "considered National Socialism West Germany's problem. It took more than 40 years and was only after the reunification that all of Germany was able both to admit its historical responsibility and to stand by the State of Israel." Just like any other citizen of East Germany, Angela Merkel had lived under a two-fold veil. There was the unprocessed Nazi past, the responsibility for which was shoved onto the class enemy, and on the other hand, there was the ensuing lack of willingness to recognize their own responsibility, which caused the GDR[222] to become a land of silence for 40 years. While the old Federal Republic of Germany had to face the question of guilt despite all of their fathers' repression mechanisms, in the former GDR this issue had been more or less completely denied for 40 years. After the fall of the Berlin Wall and the reunification in 1989, there was an exemplary working through of Nazi history through numerous initiatives in politics and society that seem to even have increased in intensity. At the same time, communist rule had left deep scars in Eastern Germany's spiritual reality. Once again you can find places of Celtic idol worship there, the number of neo-Nazis is increasing dramatically, and people no longer know who Jesus Christ is.

225

It was one year after our first experience with the March of Life. We wanted to also walk in Eastern Germany and follow the routes of the death marches to set a clear mark there. More than 500 people walked a total of about 1,500 miles in four days, symbolically tracing a Star of David over Eastern Germany in 192 stages. Many participants had come from the U.S. especially for this march. Before sharing some of their moving experiences, I would like to give you a brief summary of the vision of the March of Life.

With its message, the March of Life wants to set a mark:

- For a working through of the past and against forgetting
- For reconciliation, healing and restoration between
  the descendants of the victims and the perpetrators
- For Israel and an unmistakable "Never Again!"
  against modern anti-Semitism in our time

In this process, we are depending on God's supernatural intervention. When the veil of silence breaks through identificational repentance and our joint confession, we pull the rug out from underneath darkness, and the March of Life becomes both a forerunner and a powerful tool for a spiritual breakthrough.

The March of Life in Eastern Germany set out from the railroad ramp of the former Buchenwald concentration camp, where the prisoners used to be dragged from the boxcars of the arriving trains. The prisoners had been crammed into the trains like cattle and were completely dehydrated; many of them did not survive this ordeal. The camp guards would then assemble them on the ramp, more dead than alive. From there they were marched into the camp on the so-called "blood road". Among them was 15-year-old Paul Argiewitz. When you visit the camp memorial today, above the entrance you will see a world-famous photograph. It shows the emaciated bodies of survivors who had been photographed lying on their wooden berths just after their liberation. In this picture, you can see both the later Nobel Prize laureate Elie Wiesel and Paul Argiewitz, who I was to meet in Chicago only a few weeks later. Little did I know that this encounter was to produce a deep mutual appreciation and friendship.

The March of Life set out. Five hundred people were marching in silent commemoration from the ramp along the former "blood road" that is part of the memorial site today. The participants were covered by a special presence of God. There were both mourning and tears, repentance, and at the same time, a tangible sense of mercy, a holy earnestness, and deep inner peace that only God Himself could plant in our hearts. We had not informed the press about this kick-off event to the March of Life. But on the same day,[223] there was an exclusive report on the Holocaust survivors of Buchenwald in one of Germany's largest national daily papers, showing this very photograph displayed at the entry of Buchenwald. The headline read, THE SHOCK PICTURE IS ALIVE! Just a few lines into the article, the author wrote, "Now the victims break their silence!" Sometimes we are able to read in the newspapers about the things that happen in the spiritual realm, just like a confirmation from Heaven.

Four days and 1,500 miles later, the final meeting took place on the Teufelsberg (Devil's Mountain) in Berlin. This hill is the highest elevation in the entire city, and is made up of the debris of the former capital of the Reich. There is no other place that could have depicted the unmerited grace shown to Germany more clearly. It does not matter how high our own mountains of debris may be; but God causes new life to come forth! If this promise is true for us as Germans, how much more can any nation, city, or person claim it for themselves!

Yes, you will rebuild the ruined cities that have been in ruins for many generations. (Isa. 61:4; translated from German)

A few months later, I was preaching at a Messianic congregation in Chicago. For someone from Germany, this cannot be taken for granted. Through the American branch of the March of Life, the March of Remembrance, the invitations to speak at Messianic fellowships and congregations had multiplied. Seated in the front row was a special friend of the congregation. It was the Holocaust survivor Paul Argiewitz. I spoke on the "Veil of Silence" and shared about the memorial march along the "blood road" at Buchenwald concentration camp. Afterwards, I led the congregation in an act of reconciliation. When I approached Paul, intending to humble myself and ask his forgiveness for the suffering he endured in Buchenwald, he looked at me with sparkling eyes. Paul spoke German with me, his Bavarian accent was unmistakable. Before I could even ask about his experiences, he said, "I don't have any negative feelings." To my great surprise, he started expressing his appreciation for the Germans. Then he shared a story that continues to move me to this day: Together with many other prisoners, he was forced to leave Buchenwald concentration camp on a death march. There was a lot of snow that winter and it was freezing cold. Paul spoke about the weakened and emaciated prisoners who kept being shot along the road. Then they were supposed to cross a frozen brook. Paul lost his footing and fell into the icy water. He knew this was his sure death sentence. When the SS officer approached him and dragged him into the woods – soaking wet and shivering with cold – he was certain that he was going to be shot. But then something very unexpected happened. The SS officer took off his jumper, and took his leather coat, ripped off the SS insignia and wrapped Paul in his own clothes. Paul could still feel the SS officer's body warmth in the clothes. He stopped shivering. And now I understood the reason behind his appreciation: the warming coat of an SS officer had saved his life on that death march. For me this story is like a modern parable. The mantle of God's love protects, warms, heals, and saves our life. But what if it is given by someone like us Germans, who provoke fears, and whose forefathers were the greatest enemies of the Jews? The mantle of God's love is always a mantle of His mercy and grace. Could it be that this is the reason why He specifically calls the descendants of German perpetrators to place the healing mantle of God's grace and love on the Jewish people? At this point, I would like to share a few moving stories that best describe the experiences of both the descendants of victims and perpetrators whenever such a mantle of God's grace and love is placed around them. A participant from Houston wrote:

"It was because of Hitler, his nation, his perpetrators, and bystanders that my family suffered. Most of my family perished, and my aunt is an Auschwitz survivor in Israel. Some Christians put feet to their faith and hid my parents during Hitler's Hungarian occupation. However, upon our parents' arrival to the USA, due to lack of funds and emotional and mental stress on my mother, my sisters and I were placed in an orphanage and then sent to separate foster homes. I never liked hearing the German language and mistrusted anyone or anything German. Anytime I would meet someone German or with a German name, the first thing that would come to mind was - who were their parents or grandparents and what did they do in the war? Yet, my husband and I produce a TV talk show, "The Crossover", focusing on healing relationships between Jews, Christians and our G-d!!! How could I produce such a program when I myself had such issues that needed healing? G-d gave us the peace and the finances to go to a land that I never would step foot on... Germany's March of Life 2008. Due to the healing testimonies on forgiveness and repentance of the ministers present, especially Peter Loth, the L-rd miraculously revealed hidden things of my childhood the first evening of the march. Throughout the March, G-d kept unveiling hidden moments of my life where I had to forgive and since my return to the United States, G-d hasn't stopped opening up the wellsprings of memories to be pondered, and dealt with His way. Something

else miraculous happened because of the walk ... When I think of
Germany or meeting Germans, my heart is open and the preju-
dice is gone. G-d is faithful and I now have a wonderful German
family in the L-rd to visit and to invite to my home at any time.
Wow! To Pastor Jobst, Charlotte and G-d's amazing German team
– thank you for being so obedient to G-d's call to His people and
His nation Israel. To the one new man in Yeshua ... Ephesians 2:15"

The second story is the story of a Messianic believer in Dallas.
This is a shortened and edited account.

"It all started when I met pastor Jobst at a Shabbat for lunch in
Dallas. He looked me straight in the eye and he asked me if I
would like to come to the March of Life. In that moment I realized that I had to go; however, when I looked at my budget, there
was hardly any money. But the Lord opened the door about a
week and a half before the journey! When I was on the way to
Berlin, a lot of thoughts came into my mind from my last visit in
Germany, about 14 years previously. I was a different man back
then, not a believer. I was just a tourist. Throughout the time that
I visited Germany I travelled with a feeling of great anger toward
the German people, fear, unpleasantness. Every day over there I
just wanted to pack my stuff and leave. Israel is a pretty touristy
place; many times I have met German tourists. But when I visited
in Germany 14 years ago, it was much different; suddenly all this
horrible past bubbled into my soul and I couldn't understand why.
I came to Berlin this time with all that luggage, all that burden,
without being aware of how much I needed to forgive, because
now that I was a believer, I was supposed to forgive everybody.
I didn't know how much I needed to forgive the German people.
Right before I left I decided to take the shofar with me. Blowing the
shofar is a declaration that cannot be put into words. That declaration was "Am Israel Chai", which means "the people of Israel
is alive". When we arrived in Leipzig, I was still tired from the

230

journey, but instantly I felt welcome. I was amazed to see that the church had prepared a Shabbat meal. It was a warm and wonderful feeling. The second day of visit was actually the turning point of my journey to Germany. After I heard Peter Loth's testimony of how he had been able to forgive as a survivor of the Holocaust, I couldn't handle it anymore. Now I hope that you will understand my point. I had always thought that I don't need to forgive the German people because I never was a direct victim of the Nazi regime. For me, forgiveness was only a national issue. So I didn't believe this had anything to do with me personally. When after sharing his testimony Peter Loth asked, "Can you forgive?" and quoted the Scriptures, the Lord spoke directly to my heart. It didn't take long for me to be on my knees. Suddenly, I felt spiritually that a black mush was coming out of my heart. That black mush was my hatred of the German people. That black mush that I had not been aware of bubbled up to the surface. When I saw it, I felt that I had no option but to forgive the Germans personally if I didn't want that mush to remain there. I do not remember how long I was on my knees. I only remember that I cried for quite a while. The Lord did a surgery in my heart during that time. The Lord's presence was obvious, the fear, hatred, and unpleasantness were removed like they had never been there. That was not the end. Peter Loth asked me as a descendant of the victims to stand and to forgive the children and grandchildren of the Nazi perpetrators that stood in line to be forgiven. That was a remarkable moment for me, as in that moment I was able to do it for real for the first time. That event caused me to walk mile after mile in the March like it was just a few yards. The love, the sincerity of remorse that I felt from the people, my German brothers and sisters, caused me to walk and honor the victims that suffered much more than I have. It was very hard for me to say goodbye to my new friends. All I can say is thank you, thank you for standing in the gap. Thank you for your love, thank you for your boldness. May Adonai bless you for everything you do."

The Messianic believer from Dallas met one of the participants in the March of Life over breakfast. She reported their encounter as follows.

"My granddad had been part of the SS and had worked for a publisher in Berlin that printed Hitler's 'Mein Kampf' and anti-Jewish propaganda material. When we arrived in Berlin with the March of Life, I kept waking from my sleep at night because I felt like I was lying in a pool of blood. I didn't really know what to do about this. I kept praying and asking the Lord to somehow intervene in my life. The following morning we had breakfast in the hotel. The American participant from a Messianic congregation in Dallas sat at our table. He only knew my name and had no idea about my background. Suddenly, he looked at me and asked whether he could give me a new name. When I said 'yes', he called me 'Dorit' in Hebrew, and then he added, if I wanted, I could adopt the name. Suddenly, I felt the presence of God so powerfully like I would never have expected. I was completely taken aback. When I asked him what the name meant, he said, 'Dorit means 'Freedom out of this Generation' in Hebrew!' In that moment a burden dropped off my shoulders. I told him about my granddad and how much that prophetic new name meant to me. I also asked his forgiveness for the sin of our family. He declared forgiveness over me and everybody at the breakfast table was in tears, but happy."

A further testimony can give us a brief glimpse of what happened during the regional marches, that is on the shorter sections of the march in Eastern Germany. The groups would stop at significant places to pray. The participants were from different nations:

"We stopped at a memorial for forced laborers, most of them from Eastern Europe. With tears, we asked forgiveness of our brothers and sisters from Belarus, Russia, and the Czech Republic who were in our team on the regional march, for all the oppression and exploitation that we as Germans had subjected them to during the Nazi era. At that moment a participant from Russia broke down screaming and weeping. During the previous night the Lord had given her a dream in which she had seen a black veil break over her own life, and how she was able to see an open Heaven above her."

This story leads us to the Ukraine, where the effects of WWII are still so much alive today that at times I was shocked. In the Ukraine, Germans killed more than 1.5 million Jews bullet by bullet. They call it the hidden Holocaust. More than 100 churches had invited and welcomed the March of Life to the Ukraine. It moved an entire nation.

Mom, Do I Have to Fight against the Germans?

"Mom, do I have to put on my uniform and fight against the Germans?" This was the question of a six-year-old when he heard that German participants of the March of Life were coming to his city. The image was still alive in him that he had inherited from his parents and grandparents. Like all over the Ukraine, the Jewish population in his city had been completely annihilated. If you walk through the Ukrainian woods today, you will find silent witnesses of mass shooting everywhere. They may be mass graves with pretty white fences with a little memorial plaque at the most, mentioning the death of Soviet citizens; but many times it is the cartridges and unburied bones that are reaching out like unbeliev- able memorials of a past never worked through to touch us right now in 2010. On the territory of present-day Ukraine, more than 1.5 million Jews perished between 1941 and 1944.[224] They were murdered by Germans or in the name of Germany, or they died of hunger, exhaustion, and disease.[225] I was standing at the memorial

233

of Babi Yar in Kiev next to the Israeli Ambassador to the Ukraine, Ms. Kalay-Kleitmann. This place represents the largest individual massacre ever committed by Germans. On September 29 and 30, 1941, within 36 hours more than 33,000 Jews were systematically shot by machine gun fire in this former ravine on the outskirts of Kiev. "You know," the Israeli Ambassador remarked, "it comes with the job that I have to attend many such memorial events every year." Then she continued, "But what I have experienced here has touched me so deeply I just couldn't hold back my tears. You can be assured that I will report everything I have seen here to Israel." We had just witnessed a memorial event that truly deserved the name 'historic' in Ukrainian history. More than a thousand participants lined the backdrop to the memorial at Babi Yar where survivors of the massacre, the president of the Jewish Forum of the Ukraine, official representatives of the Baptist and Pentecostal Unions and Messianic congregations, as well as the German Vice-Ambassador to the Ukraine had gathered in unanimity. The press conference in the Independent Press Center prior to the event had been over-crowded. Fourteen TV stations reported for Ukrainian and Russian news networks during prime time, carrying the message of the event as far as the borders of China. European networks like the BBC, Euronews, and Skynews aired reports, as well as the New York Times and Israeli TV. The message of Babi Yar sets a mark of healing and restoration and is directed against anti-Semitism in our modern day. As long as descendants of the victims of WWII still carry their fathers' trauma, fears, and hatred, the descendants of the German generation of perpetrators do not have the option to consider their responsibility and duty fulfilled. "We as Germans have a special responsibility that has not ended to this day. The descendants of the perpetrators are trying to find the words their fathers and grandfathers never found." This was my introduction at the memorial which was later to be broadcast by all the news networks. One participant represented the 40 Germans in the dele-gation whose fathers or grandfathers had been involved in the War of Annihilation or mass executions in the Ukraine, and she shared her personal story. Only a few weeks prior to the March, she had learned through careful research that her grandfather had been an officer in the German army in Kiev at the time of the massacre at Babi Yar. "With all my heart I want to ask you for forgiveness. Something like this must never happen again!" Deeply moved, right there in front of the TV cameras, the Holocaust survivors embraced her.

After the event at Babi Yar, we had lunch together with leading Ukrainian pastors. One of them tried to put the day's experience into words. "You have no idea what this means! This is the first time that different denominations, Jews and Christians, have ever worked together in such unity. Never before have there ever been such positive reports about a Christian event in Ukrainian media across the board. Obviously the Lord has placed His hand on the March of Life in a very special way." But this was only the beginning...

In the Woods of Zhitomir

Two days after our experience at Babi Yar in Kiev, the 200 partici-pants from Germany traveled to 16 different cities all across the Ukraine, where further marches and memorial events had been prepared by the congregations there. In order to understand why the March of Life had to take place not only in Kiev, but also in all the other regions of the Ukraine as well, you should remember that the Jewish population in nearly every Ukrainian city was almost completely annihilated. Countless Ukrainian women and children were forced to help logistically and to watch their neighbors and friends being cruelly shot – bullet by bullet. They tell stories[226] of how the murderers efficiently and systematically planned and dug the mass graves, or they even forced their Jewish victims to dig their own graves. The bodies were piled ten-deep in the trenches.

235

Right before their execution, rigid with panic, they had to lay face-down on the dead bodies beneath them. Witnesses report that the graves "lived" for three more days after the shootings. This means that those who were only severely wounded were buried alive, and slowly and painfully suffocated underground. Still today, people are discovering many yet-unknown mass graves. We were to stand at one of them in Zhitomir. It had only been discovered a few months prior to the March of Life in the Ukraine.

Zhitomir is about two hours away from Kiev, close to the border with Belarus. This city used to be the center of the Hassidic movement, and had an influential Jewish community. About a third of the city's population, more than 24,000 people, was Jewish. On July 9, 1941, Zhitomir was occupied by German troops. Directly behind the tanks, the trucks belonging to the SS special commando 4a advanced into the city. Shortly after that, most Jews in Zhitomir and the surrounding area were killed. Amazingly enough, today Jewish life has returned to Zhitomir once more. The Messianic congregation there cooperated with other churches, and they went to great lengths to prepare the March of Life. In the process they were physically attacked by Ukrainian nationalists, who even knocked down and severely injured one of them. When the pastor of the Charismatic church was riding his mountain bike in the woods a few weeks prior to the March, he discovered several mass graves with white wooden fences. Even though he had grown up in Zhitomir, he had never heard anything about them before. There was no memorial plaque to indicate anything. He decided that the memorial events for the March of Life were going to happen right there. Only a few weeks later, more than 700 participants from a great variety of backgrounds, churches, and denominations were walking on the same paths that the Jews of Zhitomir had walked to their execution. Eyewitnesses told stories of how they were transported on trucks, with one specific truck leading the way that had a music band playing to cover the sound of the shootings. The large group of participants split up into smaller teams that walked to seven different sites of mass graves in and around Zhitomir. Our path led through the Ukrainian woods past other graves until we reached the last one. It was an oppressive situation. One German participant of the March of Life whose grandfather had been a soldier in the Ukraine, and possibly had even been in Zhitomir, finally managed to ask for forgiveness, deeply moved and with tears running down her face. She had brought his diary and read some disturbing lines. Her grandfather had been a Christian and he considered it his duty as an ardent Nazi to help with the final solution of the Jewish question.

An eighty-year-old Ukrainian "babushka" had been an eyewitness to the events at this grave. She said, "This is my grave. I should be lying here. I was 14 years old when we were taken here. But my mother was not with us. So I ran away. They shot after me, and it was like a miracle they only hit my scarf." Ukrainian pastors prayed and humbled their hearts for the guilt of the Ukrainian helpers. In the course of the event, the oppression at this place was transformed into deep, almost inexplicable joy. I believe it was the presence of God. Apparently the Lord had been waiting for this moment for a long time. On the way back, I was talking to the vice governor of the region, who had been the official representative at the event. His words still sound in my ears. "The March of Life brings reconciliation and restoration, just like we need it in the Ukraine, but have never seen until today. Our former president wanted to organize something like this, but it never worked out. Please come back – you will always find open doors here!" The teams in the other cities experienced similar things. In one day, in virtually every region of the Ukraine, it was almost like the word found in Zechariah 3:9 was fulfilled through the identificational repentance of both Germans and Ukrainians and their joint stand with Israel.

See, the stone I have set in front of Joshua!
There are seven eyes on that one stone,
and I will engrave an inscription on it, says the Lord Almighty,
and I will remove the sin of this land in a single day. (Zech. 3:9)

The March of Life united churches and congregations who had never cooperated in this way before. More than one hundred Christian churches and Jewish congregations carried the message of reconciliation, healing, and restoration into the entire nation, as was reported by local TV and radio stations. Their stand against anti-Semitism and for Israel was taken to the remotest corners of the land by almost all news networks and newspapers. At some of the memorial events, they played a particular Jewish song that still resounds in my heart today. It was "Rachim", which in Hebrew means "mercy". Was this not just what we had experienced? Together with our Ukrainian friends we stood before the throne of grace in a priestly ministry, just like Hebrews 4:16 describes it.

Let us then approach God's throne of grace with confidence,
so that we may receive mercy
and find grace to help us in our time of need. (Heb. 4:16)

The March of Life left marks in the Ukraine like an inscription that became visible far beyond the national borders. This was perhaps shown most visibly in one particular memorial march that was designed to place a new seal on the land in a prophetic act. After the memorial event at Babi Yar, the participants split into several teams and walked the outline of a Star of David around Kiev. The descendants of both victims and perpetrators, Ukrainians and Germans, Jews and non-Jews united to walk the 8 to 12 mile sections in joint prayer. Jewish roots are the source of blessing for any nation. When Jews and Christians start reviving them in a spirit of reconciliation and welcoming them anew, the heavens over this nation will open up and release unprecedented blessing.

The March of Remembrance

"Jobst, you have to come to America to tell your story!" Ted was
on the phone, asking me to go with him on some of his concert
tours. "We need a March of Life in every city in America!" he said,
and then he mentioned that the march was supposed to take place
in seven different cities. As the situation in America is different
from the one in Europe, the focus of the March of Remembrance
is on honoring the Holocaust survivors and joining with them in
raising our voices against modern anti-Semitism in our time and
for Israel. At the same time, just like in Europe, it connects the
descendants of German perpetrators with the descendants of the
victims of the Holocaust living in America, and it causes healing
that had not been possible before.

The first year, the main march took place in Dallas, TX. We had
never expected such broad support. On Holocaust Memorial Day,
several hundred participants gathered at the Holocaust Museum for
a memorial march to the city hall, where they voiced their support
for Israel in an open air meeting. Holocaust survivors opened their
hearts for forgiveness and wanted to know more about the secret
behind the grace and mercy of Yeshua. Several trips to the U.S.
later, where I was preaching about the veil of silence, and on Ted's
determined initiative, the following two years we stood on the
stage in front of the Capitol in Washington, D.C. for the main event
of the March of Remembrance. The participants had marched along
the National Mall from close to the Washington Monument right
up to Congress. So I stood at this famous spot outside the Capitol
Building, where most of the American presidents have taken their
oath of office in front of hundreds of thousands. I could hardly
believe it. Initially in 2007, we had only planned on walking along
the Swabian route of the death marches with a few intercessors,
and now here we were, and the March of Remembrance was taking
place in 40 cities all across the U.S. – and also in Paraguay, Peru,

Bolivia, Argentina, in the Philippines, Latvia, and Lithuania as well as many other countries. For all of this there was only one reason: We had broken our silence, personally and then also in our city. I have already told you how we lit six candles in memory of the six million Jews. I reminded the people of the 600,000 Jews that had cruelly perished because of the responsibility of SS executors from Tübingen. As I mentioned at the beginning of this book, they are part of our story. It is the story in which curse was transformed into blessing and darkness into light. Just as our city produced death and destruction in the past, it is destined now to bless the Jewish people and to bring forth healing and new life.

The Pittsburgh Declaration

I cannot finish this book without telling you about the Pittsburgh Declaration. After the March of Remembrance event, I was invited to go to Pittsburgh, PA. This former steel city is still famous for its university and football team, who are contending for their victories on Heinz Field, named after the popular ketchup brand. The city calls itself "City of Champions" – and maybe they are, not only because they have won the Super Bowl so many times. The churches in the city decided to host a March of Remembrance. They drew up a special declaration because they wanted to honor the city's Jewish community on Holocaust Remembrance Day. Following the march, there was a public closing event. A survivor from Auschwitz shared his story. The pastors, ministers, and the Catholic bishop stood up together, and they read the declaration that they had agreed on in the city's pastors' council. I wish such a declaration could be written and read in every city. It stands for a covenant that every Christian, every church and fellowship should have with the Jewish community: [227]

To the Jewish Community of Pittsburgh, Pennsylvania

We know that the Jewish people throughout the centuries have borne the greatest discrimination, the worst persecution, and the most barbaric atrocities of any people group. We are aware that much of this has been done by those who called themselves Christians, sometimes while calling upon the name of Jesus. While those of us standing here with you today deplore and condemn in the strongest terms and way those crimes perpetrated against the Jewish people throughout history, we nonetheless ask for your forgiveness for all of the crimes perpetrated against you which were perpetrated by those calling themselves Christian. These atrocities in no way reflect Jesus, Who Himself a Jew, embraced the Law and the Prophets. As His followers, we too affirm them and embrace them, and in that affirming and embracing we say to you and to the world that we will stand with the Jewish people as long as we have breath.

The concentration camps in Europe stand as silent sentinels to the past barbarity of the human race, not just Christians. Anti-Semitism knows no ethnic, creedal, or political bounds. But we repeat the words engraved and openly displayed at the Dachau Concentration Camp Memorial, "Never Again." By that we mean we are yours. You will never be attacked as a people while we who are Christians stand by and do nothing.

We covenant with you that while others have stood silent during your times of great sufferings, we, the community of those who follow Jesus, will never be silent, never abandon you, and covenant to supply you quarter should any present or future events make that necessary...

Our prayer, as part of the Christian community in Pittsburgh, is that you will always remember this commitment we make to you this First Day of May 2011.

Before I finish this book, there is one important question that remains. Over and over again, I see people – especially in Germany – responding very defensively to the idea of working through the past. Many say, "We as Christians have humbled ourselves for so many years now, repenting for the sins of our fathers! Let's stop that and finally look ahead!" I believe this is not true. As long as there are still people suffering under the consequences of the Holocaust, we can never be acquitted of our responsibility. The foundation for any kind of change is our decision to break the veil of silence. Are you ready? Do you want to do this in your life? I would like to encourage you to do it. On the cross, Jesus made this possible for you and me. He sent the Spirit of Truth so we would not have to remain silent any longer, personally, in our families, churches, or cities. He is the light that pierces any darkness.

With all my heart I believe in a great end-time harvest that the Lord has prepared for the nations of the Western world. Up to now, we have not been able to penetrate the veil over our cities and regions to such an extent as to truly change them. Unless there is a serious working through and setting right of the past, there will be no breakthrough. At a time when the love will grow cold in many (Matt. 24:12), the church with the "spirit of the sons of Zion" will raise its voice in authority and break the veil of silence. We have experienced God's powerful intervention, breakthroughs, and changes. I am convinced it can also happen for you.

The Former Roll Call Yard

The former roll call yard in the former Buchenwald concentration camp is a memorial against forgetting. It is also a witness of what can happen when somebody overcomes their fear and breaks the veil of silence. The Lutheran pastor Paul Schneider is

called the "preacher of Buchenwald". He could be heard loud and
clear all across the yard, where you can still see the prison with
its solitary confinement cells.

Once, he refused the Hitler salute on occasion of a flag salute
on the Führer's birthday and did not take off his cap, stating
his reason, "I will not salute this thug symbol". He was publicly
flogged with a rod and put into solitary confinement. A camp
guard noted, "The prisoner Paul Schneider, currently under
arrest, showed incredible behavior. In the mornings, about
6:30 a.m., when the number of prisoners was reported to me,
Schneider would suddenly open his cell window, climb up the
wall inside the cell until he was able to see the prisoners lined up
for the roll call. With a loud voice, Schneider would then preach
to the waiting prisoners for about two minutes. He completely
disregarded my orders to stop preaching immediately. So I then
ordered the arrest guard to forcefully remove Schneider from
the window." Starting with April 1938, he kept calling out his
passionate sermons from his arrest cell across the roll call yard
of Buchenwald concentration camp, until the beatings forced
him to be quiet. Torture, deprivation of food, solitary confinement – despite all their efforts, the camp guards could not deter
him from his faith in God. The Bible verses he had learnt by
heart gave him strength. From his cell window he spoke encouraging and strengthening words to his fellow prisoners, and he
was not ashamed to shout out the truth even in the presence
of the commanding camp officer: "You are a mass murderer.
I accuse you of murdering these prisoners," and then listing the
individual names of the victims of the previous week. Because of
him, prisoners survived, because his voice reminded them that
God's power reaches further than the power of man. On Easter
Sunday, despite his pain, he pulled himself up at the window of
the arrest cell and called to the thousands of prisoners assembled
on the roll call yard. "Comrades, listen to me. This is Pastor Paul

Schneider. They torture and murder here. But the Lord says, I am the Resurrection and the Life!" On July 18, 1939, Paul Schneider was given an overdose of strophanthin by the camp physician that killed him.

Dietrich Bonhoeffer called him one the first martyrs of the 20th century. Paul Schneider had studied in Tübingen, where he met his future wife in the house of a pastor's family. His fearless confession is a warning for every believer to boldly take a stand and to break any veil of silence with the truth of the Word of God. "Paul's face showed the peace and nobility of the redeemed. At this moment, I was privileged to see Paul with the eyes of faith," his widow later said, who had been permitted to see the body in the concentration camp before the casket was sealed. For a short time, Paul Schneider's widow returned to her mother in Tübingen.

I wish you and all of us will be able to break the "Veil of Silence" in these times of increasing darkness. It is about time that we as the church reclaim God's authority. Let us discover anew what it means to rise together in the "spirit of the sons of Zion" in order to take His light to the nations on our "March of Life".

For I have seen with my own eyes your yeshu'ah,
which you prepared in the presence of all peoples –
a light that will bring revelation to the Goyim
and glory to your people Israel. (Luke 2:30-32; CJB)

APPENDIX

BIBLIOGRAPHY

Berger, Benjamin. *Prophetische Zeichen zur Wende der Zeiten, Heimkehr nach und Aufbruch in Israel*. Zürich: Gemeindehilfe Israel, no year given.

Bittner, Jobst. *Der charismatische Wortgottesdienst in Korinth nach 1. Kor 12-14*. Tübingen: 1991.

Bittner, Jobst, and Ruben Gutknecht. *Guía de Oración para la Argentina*. Buenos Aires: 2001.

Blatman, Daniel. *The Death Marches: The Final Phase of Nazi Genocide*. Belknap Press of Harvard University Press; Tra ed., 2010.

Bode, Sabine. *Die vergessene Generation: Die Kriegskinder brechen ihr Schweigen*. Stuttgart: Klett-Cotta, 2004.

Bode, Sabine. *Kriegsenkel. Die Erben der vergessenen Generation*. Stuttgart: Klett-Cotta, 2010. 7th ed.

Brisch, Karl Heinz and Theodor Hellbrügge, eds. *Bindungen und Trauma*. Stuttgart: Klett-Cotta, 2003.

Brown, Michael L. What Do Jewish People Think About Jesus. Grand Rapids, MI: Chosen Books, 2007

Brunner, Claudia and Uwe Von Seltmann. *Schweigen die Täter, reden die Enkel*. Frankfurt: Fischer, 2006.

Coenen, Lothar, Erich Beyreuther, and Hans Bietenhard, eds. *Theologisches Begriffslexikon zum Neuen Testament* (ThBL), vol. 1. Wuppertal: Neukirchener, 1983.

Conze, Eckart, Norbert Frei, Peter Hayes, and Moshe
Zimmermann. *Das Amt und die Vergangenheit, Deutsche
Diplomaten im Dritten Reich und in der Bundesrepublik.*
München: Karl Blessing Verlag, 2010.

Desbois, Patrick. *Der vergessene Holocaust. Die Ermordung der
ukrainischen Juden.* Berlin: Berlin Verlag, 2009.

Dowgiewicz, Mike and Sue. *Restoring the Early Church. Returning
Intimacy and Power to the Modern Day Church.* Colorado
Springs, CO: Restoration Ministries / Empowerment Press,
1996.

Foerster, Werner. *Das römische Reich zur Zeit des Neuen
Testaments, vol. 2, Neutestamentliche Zeitgeschichte.*
Hamburg: Furche Verlag, 1956.

Gesenius, Wilhelm. *Hebräisches und Aramäisches
Handwörterbuch.* rev. ed. Berlin, Göttingen, Heidelberg:
Springer, 1962.

Häselbarth, Christoph. *Befreiung von Vorfahrensschuld und
Wachstum im Glauben.* Solingen: Verlag Gottfried Bernhard,
2002.

Hauss, Friederich. *Väter der Christenheit, Von den apostolischen
Vätern bis zur Reformation.* vol. 1. Wuppertal: Verlag Sonne
und Schild, 1956.

Hay, Malcolm. *Roots of Christian Anti-Semitism.* New York: Anti
Defamation League of Bnai, 1984.

Heidler, Robert D. *The Messianic Church Arising.* Denton: Glory
of Zion International Ministries, Inc., 2006.

Heschel, Susannah. *The Aryan Jesus: Christian Theologians and
the Bible in Nazi Germany.* Princeton: Princeton University
Press, 2008.

Johnson, Bill. *When Heaven Invades Earth.* Shippensburg, PA:
Destiny Image Publishers, 2005.

Josephus, Flavius. *De bello Judaico, in: Michel, Otto, Otto Bauern-feind*. Darmstadt: Wissenschaftliche Buchgesellschaft, 1959

Junginger, Horst. "Tübinger Exekutoren der Endlösung." In *Tübinger Exekutoren*. http://www.uni-tuebingen.de

Junginger, Horst. "Tübinger Exekutoren der Endlösung. Effiziente Massenmörder an vorderster Front der SS-Einsatzgruppen und des Sicherheitsdienstes", Schwäbisches Tagblatt [Tübingen, Germany], June 18, 2003.

Juster, Daniel, and Peter Hocken. *Der Messianisch-jüdische Aufbruch*. Freilassing, Berlin: Toward Jerusalem Council II, 2005.

Kellermann, Natan P.F. "The Long-term Psychological Effects and Treatment of Holocaust Trauma." *Journal of Loss and Trauma*, 6:197-218.

Kittel, Gerhard. *Die Judenfrage*. rev. ed. Stuttgart: Kohlhammer, 1933.

Lehmann, Ernst. "Die Biologie an der Zeitenwende. " In: *Der Biologe* 4,12. 1935.

Ludwig Uhland Institut für Empirische Kulturwissenschaft, Bechdolf, Ute, Jeggle, Utz . *Nationalsozialismus im Landkreis Tübingen, Eine Heimatkunde*. Tübingen: Tübinger Vereinigung für Volkskunde, 1988.

Luther, Martin. "Concerning the Jews and their Lies (1543)." In *The Jew in the Medieval World: A Source Book 315 – 1791*, edited by Jakob R. Marcus. New York: Atheneum, 1979.

Margies, Wolfhard. *Deutsches Geschichtsbuch für Beter*. Berlin: Aufbruch Verlag, 2000.

Mcdonald, Andrew. *The Turner Diaries*. New York: Barricade Books, 1996.

Melanchthon, Philipp. *Apologia Confessionis Augustanae, AC II: 33*. Translated and edited by Horst Georg Pöhlmann. Gütersloh: Mohn, 1967.

Mulinde, John. *Light or Darkness Over Europe: How Our Prayers Change the Nations*. Seaford, UK: Pillars of Fire Trust, 2000.

Opher-Cohn, Liliane, Johannes Pfäffin, Bernd Sonntag, Bernd Klose, and Peter Pogany-Wnendt, eds. *Das Ende der Sprachlosigkeit? Auswirkungen traumatischer Holocausterfahrungen über mehrere Generationen*. Giessen: Psychosozial-Verlag, 2007.

Pöhlmann, Horst Georg. *Abriss der Dogmatik*. Gütersloh: Gütersloher Verlagshaus, 1985.

Price, Rose. *A Rose from the Ashes: The Rose Price Story*. San Francisco: Purple Pomegranate Productions, 2006.

Ratzinger, Joseph, and Benedict XVI. *Jesus von Nazareth*. Freiburg, Basel, Wien: Verlag Herder, 2006.

Redling, Marcel. *Stellvertretende Buße: Biblisches Konzept oder wiederauflebender Irrtum?* MBS Text 6, Martin-Bucer-Seminar, 1st year 2004.

Richter, Adolf Martin. "Der Briefwechsel zwischen Trajan und Plinius an Trajan." In the *Alte Kirche, Kirchen- und Theologiegeschichte in Quellen,* edited by Heiko Obermann, vol. 1. Neukirchen–Vluyn: Neukirchener Verlag, 1977.

Sandford, John Loren. *Healing for the Nations*. Grand Rapids: Chosen, 2000.

Schlink, M. Basilea. *Buße – glückseliges Leben*. Darmstadt/ Eberstadt: Evang. Marienschwesternschaft, 1965.

Schönhagen, Benigna, and Wilfried Setzler. *Jüdisches Tübingen, Schauplätze und Spuren*. Haigerloch: Klaus Schubert, 1999.

Schönhagen, Benigna. *Tübingen unterm Hakenkreuz. Eine Universitätsstadt in der Zeit des Nationalsozialismus*. Tübingen: Theiss, 1990.

Szymanski, Tekla. Notizen aus den USA, in: *Tribüne – Zeitschrift zum Verständnis des Judentums*. Frankfurt, June 2004.

Tucci, Carneiro, and Maria Luiza. *O Antisemitismo nas Americas*. EDUSP: São Paulo, 2008.

Warner, Timothy M., "Dealing with Territorial Demons," in Wagner, C. Peter, ed. *Territorial Spirits: Insights Into Strategic Level Spiritual Warfare & Intercession*. Chichester, UK: Sovereign World Ltd, 1991.

Weigand, Edith S., and Eliezer Urbach. *Out of the Fury: The Incredible Odyssey of Eliezer Urbach*. Denver: Zhera Publications, 1987.

Wiesing, Urban, Klaus-Rainer Brintzinger, Bernd Grün, Horst Junginger, and Susanne Michl, eds. *Die Universität Tübingen im Nationalsozialismus*. Stuttgart: Franz Steiner Verlag, 2010.

Willi, Hans-Peter. *Bücher sind manchmal so lieb wie Kinder, Johannes Reuchlin (1455-1522) und sein Augenspiegel gedruckt bei Thomas Anshelm in Tübingen 1511*. Tübingen: HP Willi, 2011.

Wolff, Hans Walter. *Anthropologie des Alten Testaments*. Munich: Chr. Kaiser, 1984.

Yoslow, Mark. *The pride and price of remembrance: An empirical view of transgenerational post-Holocaust trauma and associated transpersonal elements in the third generation*. Palo Alto: Institute of Transpersonal Psychology, 2007.

Zimmerling, Peter. *Die Charismatischen Bewegungen*. rev. ed. Göttingen: Vandenhoeck & Ruprecht, 2003.

IMPORTANT FACTS ABOUT THE MARCH OF LIFE

Information

Bringing the March of Life or the March of Remembrance to your city!

The March of Remembrance

Remembering, honoring the Survivors, praying for Israel and standing against Anti-Semitism in the United States, Latin America and worldwide.

Visit the website for coming events and to find out how to organize a March in your own city: www.marchofremembrance.org

The March of Life

Memorial and reconciliation marches at historic locations of the Holocaust in Europe. Descendants of Nazi perpetrators finding words their fathers and grandfathers could not find. A clear symbol for Israel and against modern anti-Semitism.

Visit the website of the March of Life for documentation, reports, background information and dates for coming events:
www.marchoflife.org

Contact

For any further questions or information
please get in touch with us:

USA:
TOS Ministries
P.O. Box No. 20051
New York, NY 10017
USA
Phone: (212) 419-0932
E-Mail: tosamerica@tos.info

Europe and worldwide:
TOS Ministries
Eisenbahnstr. 124
72072 Tübingen
Germany
Phone: +49 7071 35600
E-Mail: mailbox@tos.info

END NOTES

1   *Pogrom is a Russian word meaning "to wreak havoc, to demolish violently." Historically, the term refers to violent attacks by local non-Jewish populations on Jews in the Russian Empire and in other countries."* Source: United States Holocaust Memorial Museum, http://www.ushmm.org/wlc/en/article.php?ModuleId=10005183

2   Hans-Peter Willi, *Reuchlin im Streit um die Bücher der Juden. Zum 500jährigen Jubiläum des Augenspiegel* (Tübingen: HP Willi, 2011), 9 et sqq.

3   Urban Wiesing, et al., eds., *Die Universität Tübingen im Nationalsozialismus* (Stuttgart: Franz Steiner Verlag, 2010), 740.

4   Ibid.

5   *Tübinger Chronik* [Tübingen, Germany], April 3, 1933.

6   Ludwig Uhland Insitut für Empirische Kulturwissenschaft, Ute Bechdolf and Utz Jeggle, eds., *Nationalsozialismus im Landkreis Tübingen, Eine Heimatkunde* (Tübingen: Tübinger Vereinigung für Volkskunde, 1988), 311.

7   Ernst Lehmann, "Die Biologie an der Zeitenwende", *Der Biologe 4,12* (1935), 376.

8   "Die Wissenschaft geht ins Volk. Maßgebende Beteiligung Tübinger Dozenten an der Berliner Vortragsreihe 'Judentum und Judenfrage'," *Tübinger Chronik*, Feb 9, 1939.

9   Benigna Schönhagen, "Zwischen Begeisterung und Opportunismus - Die Universitätsstadt Tübingen in der Zeit des Nationalsozialismus," Psychologie und Geschichte, http://journals.zpid.de/index.php/PuG/article/view/292 (June 2002): 12.

10   See also: Horst Junginger, "Tübinger Exekutoren der Endlösung," in Tübinger Exekutoren. http://www.uni-tuebingen.de

11   Ibid.

12   Gerhard Kittel, *Die Judenfrage*, rev. ed. (Stuttgart: Kohlhammer, 1933), 13.

13   Martin Luther, as quoted in Jakob R. Marcus, "Concerning the Jews and Their Lies," in Jakob R. Marcus, T*he Jew in the Medieval World: A Source Book 315-1791* (New York: Atheneum 1979), 167-169.

14   See also: Susannah Heschel, *The Aryan Jesus: Christian Theologians and the Bible in Nazi Germany* (Princeton: Princeton University Press, 2008).

15   Horst Junginger, "Tübinger Exekutoren der Endlösung. Effiziente Massenmörder an vorderster Front der SS-Einsatzgruppen und des Sicherheitsdienstes", *Schwäbisches Tagblatt* [Tübingen, Germany], June 18, 2003, 29.

16   Ibid.

17   Wiesing, et al., eds., *Die Universität*, 513ff.

18   Junginger, "Tübinger Exekutoren," 4.

19   Walter Mayr, "Halbgott in Feldgrau," Spiegel-Online, April 3, 2010.

20   Wiesing, et al., eds., *Die Universität*, 801.

21   Cf. Nazi Glossary in Wikipedia, http://en.wikipedia.org/wiki/Nazi_Glossary#S

22   Wiesing, et al., eds., *Die Universität*, 527.

23   Benigna Schönhagen and Wilfried Setzler, *Jüdisches Tübingen, Schauplätze und Spuren* (Haigerloch: Klaus Schubert, 1999), 17.

24   Ibid., 5.

25   Ibid., 24-26.

26   Press Service of the City of Tübingen on September 9, 2003: www.tuebingen.de.

27   Wiesing, et al., eds., *Die Universität*.

28   See also: Werner Foerster, "Das römische Reich zur Zeit des Neuen Testaments," vol. 2, *Neutestamentliche Zeitgeschichte* (Hamburg: Furche Verlag, 1956), 108ff.

29   Just a few Bible passages as examples: Col. 2:8; 2Tim. 2:25; 4:3-4.

30   Dr. Robert D. Heidler, *The Messianic Church Arising* (Denton: Glory of Zion International Ministries, Inc., 2006), 15ff.

31   Acts 4:4 speaks about an increase to 5,000 men. As women were customarily not counted at that time, we can safely estimate a church of ten thousand members.

32   Heidler, *Messianic Church*, 18.

33   2Tim. 1:3-7.

34   Adolf Martin Richter, "Der Briefwechsel zwischen Trajan und Plinius an Trajan 10,96 (9)," in Heiko A. Obermann, ed., *Alte Kirche, vol. 1, Kirchen- und Theologiegeschichte in Quellen* (Neukirchen–Vluyn: Neukirchener Verlag, 1977), 14-16.

35   Antioch, at the time, had 100,000 Christians and as many pagans; these he fed with the word of God: Coptic Orthodox Church Network, "Saint John Chrysostom," www.copticchurch.net/topics/synexarion/john.html

36   Jobst Bittner, *Der charismatische Wortgottesdienst in Korinth nach 1.Kor 12-14* (Tübingen, 1991).

37   Acts 2:46 ff.

38   *proskarteréo* (participle with dative): 'to keep hold of something'

39   Bittner, *Der charismatische Wortgottesdienst*, 46.

40   1Cor. 14:15.

41   Acts 15:5; 21:20.

42   Cf. Heidler, *Messianic Church*, 12ff.

43   Daniel Juster and Peter Hocken, *Der Messianisch-jüdische Aufbruch* (Freilassing, Berlin: Toward Jerusalem Council II, 2005), 11.

44   Ibid., 17.

45   "For if their rejection brought reconciliation to the world, what will their acceptance be but life from the dead? If the part of the dough offered as first fruits is holy, then the whole batch is holy; if the root is holy, so are the branches." (Rom. 11:15-16)

46   The original meaning of the word *iniquity* is actually a 'twisted and sinful mind' that is passed on through the generations.

47   Isa. 60:3.

48   Gen. 15:13f and 17:1-8.

49   Gen. 17:4-6.

50   Gen. 12:1-3.

51   Benjamin Berger, *Prophetische Zeichen zur Wende der Zeiten, Heimkehr nach und Aufbruch in Israel* (Zürich: Gemeindehilfe Israel, no year given), 14ff.

52   Ibid., 21.

53   Cf. Heidler, *Messianic Church*, 32ff.

54   In 70 AD Jerusalem was conquered and destroyed by the Roman Emperor Titus. In the battles and subsequent executions, 600,000 Jews (a quarter of the Jews in Palestine)

met their death. In 130 AD Emperor Hadrian planned to erect a temple to Jupiter on the ruins of the temple. This triggered the Second Jewish Revolt (132 - 135 AD) under Simeon Ben Koseba (Bar Kochba). As a consequence, the Romans expelled all Jews from Palestine and sold them as slaves into all parts of their empire. See also Flavius Josephus, "De bello Judaico" in Otto Michel, Otto Bauernfeind, eds. (Darmstadt: Wissenschaftliche Buchgesellschaft, 1959).

55 Mike and Sue Dowgiewicz, *Restoring the Early Church. Returning Intimacy and Power to the Modern Day Church* (Colorado Springs, CO: Restoration Ministries / Empowerment Press, 1996), 146ff.

56 Heidler, *Messianic Church*, 44.

57 Malcolm Hay, *Roots of Christian Anti-Semitism* (New York: Anti Defamation League of Bnai 1984), 27.

58 Ernst Jenni and Claus Westermann, eds., "Schweigen", in *Theologisches Handwörterbuch zum Alten Testament, vol. 1,* (Munich: Gütersloher Verlagshaus, 1984), 639.

59 See also: Bittner, *Der charismatische Wortgottesdienst,* 108ff.

60 Hans Walter Wolff, *Anthropologie des Alten Testaments* (Munich: Chr. Kaiser, 1984), 121.

61 Ibid., 116.

62 This is what Wolfhard Margies says in *Deutsches Geschichtsbuch für Beter* (Berlin: Aufbruch Verlag 2000), 17.

63 Timothy M. Warner, "Dealing with Territorial Demons," in C. Peter Wagner, ed., *Territorial Spirits: Insights Into Strategic Level Spiritual Warfare & Intercession* (Chichester, UK: Sovereign World Ltd, 1991), 51-54.

64 *Neue Luther Bibel,* 2009.

65 Cf. Wilhelm Gesenius, *Hebräisches und Aramäisches Handwörterbuch, rev. ed.* (Berlin, Göttingen, Heidelberg: Springer, 1962), 660.

66 Jobst Bittner and Ruben Gutknecht, *Guía de Oración para la Argentina* (Buenos Aires: 2001).

67 i.e. April 2002 – April 2003.

68 John Mulinde, *Light or Darkness Over Europe: How Our Prayers Change the Nations* (Seaford, UK: Pillars of Fire Trust, 2000), 36.

69 2Pet. 2:20 (translated from German).

70 http://member.preventchildabuse.org/site/DocServer/sexual_abuse.pdf?docID=126.

71 Cf. Marcel Redling, Stellvertretende Buße: *Biblisches Konzept oder wiederauflebender Irrtum?* (MBS Text 6, Martin-Bucer-Seminar, 1st year 2004), 30.

72 Gen. 8:21; Job 14:4; Ps. 143:3; John 3:6; Rom. 3:9.20.23; Gal. 3:22; and others.

73 Horst Georg Pöhlmann, *Abriss der Dogmatik* (Gütersloh: Gütersloher Verlagshaus, 1985), 190.

74 Philipp Melanchthon, *Apologia Confessionis Augustanae,* AC II: 33, Trans. and ed. Horst Georg Pöhlmann (Gütersloh: Mohn 1967).

75 Ibid.

76 Cf. Christoph Häselbarth, *Befreiung von Vorfahrensschuld und Wachstum im Glauben* (Solingen: Verlag Gottfried Bernhard, 2002).

77 "And so upon you will come all the righteous blood that has been shed on earth, from the blood of righteous Abel to the blood of Zechariah son of Berekiah, whom you murdered between the temple and the altar. Truly I tell you, all this will come upon this generation." (Matt. 23:35-36).

78 Name changed.

79 This event took place on August 5th, 2010.

80   Jobst Bittner, *Die Wahrheit über die Lüge* (Lüdenscheid: Asaph Verlag, 2005).
81   Rose Price, *A Rose from the Ashes: The Rose Price Story* (San Francisco: Purple Pomegranate Productions, 2006), 1.
82   www.rosepriceministries.org.
83   Matth. 6:12-15.
84   Cf. Peter Loth's story by Peter Schmid, *Hass und Misshandlung überlebt,* Jan 22, 2007 and *Schatten des Holocaust: "Es ist Zeit für Vergebung",* Jan 26, 2007, in www.jesus.ch. The transcript of Peter Loth's testimony is taken from here.
85   Tekla Szymanski, "Notizen aus den USA," *Tribüne – Zeitschrift zum Verständnis des Judentums,* (Frankfurt, June 2004).
86   'Amcha' is Hebrew and means "Your People". It was used during and following the Holocaust by persecuted Jews to recognize fellow sufferers. Currently, AMCHA supports approx. 11,000 people in 16 locations all over Israel. About 300 psychologists, therapists, and social workers, as well as more than 600 volunteers answer the needs of the survivors.
87   Natan P.F. Kellermann, "The Long-term Psychological Effects and Treatment of Holocaust Trauma," *Journal of Loss and Trauma,* (2001), 6:197-218.
88   Ibid.
89   Interview by Anne-Ev Ustorf with Dan Bar-On: "Es ist wichtig, Verluste abzuarbeiten," EMOTION, (Hamburg, April 2007), 101.
90   Natan P.F. Kellermann: *Die Zeit heilt nicht alle Wunden,* Dec 2, 2009; www.its-arolsen.org.
91   Kellermann, "Long-term Effects," 197-218.
92   Ibid.
93   Ibid.
94   Ibid.
95   Jeffrey Seif, "Bad Moon Rising," http://www.levitt.tv/media/series/DBMR.
96   Simon Gottschalk, "Reli(e)ving The Past: Emotion Work in The Holocaust's Second Generation" (Las Vegas: University of Nevada, 2000), quoted in Natan P.F. Kellermann, *Die Kinder der Child Survivors,* http://peterfelix.tripod.com/home/Kinder.htm.
97   Kellermann, *Kinder der Child Survivors.*
98   Edith S. Weigand and Eliezer Urbach, *Out of the Fury: The Incredible Odyssey of Eliezer Urbach* (Denver: Zhera Publications, 1987).
99   Chaim Urbach kindly allowed me to use the notes of his presentation. Chaim Urbach, "Redemption for the Wounds of the Next Generation: Children of the Holocaust" (Denver, CO), Feb 10, 2011.
100 Opher-Cohn, et al., eds., *Das Ende der Sprachlosigkeit? Auswirkungen traumatischer Holocausterfahrungen über mehrere Generationen* (Giessen: Psychosozial-Verlag, 2007).
101 Weigand and Urbach, 1987.
102 New York, Penguin, 1979.
103 Kellermann, *Kinder der Child Survivors.*
104 Ibid.
105 Abbye Silverstein, "Methods for healing the collective psychic wounds of the Holocaust," *Intermountain Jewish News,* April 16, 2010.
106 Norbert Lossau, "German Angst in den Genen," *Die Welt,* June 11, 2011.
107 Urbach, "Redemption", 2010.
108 The second generation became visible with the publication of Helen Epstein's watershed New York Times Magazine article, „Heirs of the Holocaust" on June 19, 1977. This article was read by more than 2,000,000 people, cf.: Eva Fogelman, *Religion & Beliefs:*

Third Generation Descendents of Holocaust Survivors and the Future of Remembering, http://www.jewcy.com/religion-and-beliefs/third_generation_descendents_holocaust_survivors_and_future_remembering (May 1, 2008).

109 Ibid.

110 C. Zimmermann, "Enkel des Holocaust" http://www.schoah.org/auschwitz/enkel.htm.

111 "of the Holocaust" is my addition for a better understanding.

112 Zimmermann, "Enkel des Holocaust" l.c.

113 Natalie Krasnostein: Third Generation Holocaust Workshops and Theatrical Play (3GH), http://www.3gh.com.au/articles_natalie.asp.

114 Fogelmann, Religion & Beliefs.

115 Ibid.

116 Cf. his dissertation, Mark Yoslow, *The pride and price of remembrance: An empirical view of transgenerational post-Holocaust trauma and associated transpersonal elements in the third generation* (Palo Alto: Institute of Transpersonal Psychology, 2007), 454 pages. It contains a study of transgenerational post-Holocaust trauma in the generation of grandchildren of Holocaust survivors. One of the instruments used in the study is the Heartland Forgiveness Scale, measuring forgiveness in respect to self, others and in situations outside of personal control.

117 Peter Lossau, "German Angst" *Welt Online*, June 10, 2011, http://www.welt.de/wissenschaft/article13424062/German-Angst-stammt-womoeglich-aus-der-Nazi-Zeit.html.

118 See also: Claudia Brunner and Uwe von Seltmann, *Schweigen die Täter, reden die Enkel*, (Frankfurt: Fischer, 2006), 176.

119 Ibid.

120 Tilman Jens, "Vaters Vergessen" *Frankfurter Allgemeine Zeitung*, March 4, 2008, 37.

121 Ibid.

122 Eckart Conze et al., *Das Amt und die Vergangenheit, Deutsche Diplomaten im Dritten Reich und in der Bundesrepublik* (München: Karl Blessing Verlag, 2010).

123 Ulrike Demmer, "Wie Kriegskinder ihr Trauma vererben," *Spiegel Online*, January 27, 2009.

124 Michael Ermann, "Wir Kriegskinder" (lecture, Suedwestrundfunk, Stuttgart, Germany, November 2003), www.poolalarm.de/kinderschutz/kriegskinder/Wir_Kriegskinder_SWR-Vortrag.pdf.

125 Demmer, "Kriegskinder".

126 Ermann, "Kriegskinder" 5f.

127 Sabine Bode, *Die vergessene Generation: Die Kriegskinder brechen ihr Schweigen* (Stuttgart: Klett-Cotta, 2004), 14ff.

128 Ermann, "Kriegskinder" 5f. For a better understanding, I have slightly adapted the quotation.

129 Bode, *Die vergessene Generation*, 14ff.

130 Ibid.

131 Gabriele v. Arnim, "Eine kleine Preußin erträgt alles," *Die Zeit*, May 19, 2004.

132 Sabine Bode, *Kriegsenkel. Die Erben der vergessenen Generation* (Stuttgart, Klett-Cotta: 2010), 7th edition.

133 Ibid., 21.

134 Ibid., 24.

135 Karl Heinz Brisch, "Bindungsstörungen und Trauma" in *Bindungen und Trauma*, Karl

Heinz Brisch and Theodor Hellbrügge, eds., (Stuttgart: Klett-Cotta, 2003), 130 f.

136 Bode, Kriegsenkel, 23.
137 Brisch, "Bindungsstörungen und Trauma" 130 f.
138 This March of Life took place in 2010. For more information, see Chapter 8.
139 The "Deutsche Dienststelle" (WASt) is an institution in Berlin where direct descendants of members of the Wehrmacht can obtain information on their ancestors' involvement during the war.
140 Bode, Kriegsenkel 107 ff.
141 Ibid., 199.
142 Ibid., 121.
143 *Zeit Magazin* (Hamburg, Germany), No. 46, November 4, 2010.
144 Ibid., 15.
145 Ibid., 24.
146 Ibid., 26.
147 Ibid., 28.
148 See also: www.philippus-dienst.de.
149 This is what Arni Klein points out in his article "Vision für eine Generation," in *Charisma Online-Archiv*, www.chrisma-magazin.eu.
150 Ibid.
151 *Glasnost* means "openness, liberty of speech and information" and was one of General-Secretary Gorbachev's buzzwords for his policy of openness and transparency after 1985. In 1986, he used the term perestroika to describe the transformation process of the Soviet Union's political and economic system.
152 Marcel Redling asks these questions in *Stellvertretende Buße: Biblisches Konzept oder wiederauflebender Irrtum?*, Theologische Akzente, MBS Texte 6 (Erzhausen: Theologisches Seminar Beröa, Martin Bucer Seminar, 2002), 11.
153 Leading advocates for identificational repentance in America are C. Peter Wagner and John and Paula Sandford; for Germany, Wolfhard Margies and Christoph Häselbarth have to be mentioned. In Germany, this teaching is contested mainly by conservative theologians such as Helge Stadelmann and Marcel Redling.
154 Redling, *Stellvertretende Buße*, 13.
155 "Tätervolk" (People of Perpetrators): http://de.wikipedia.org/wiki/T%C3%A4tervolk.
156 "When Jews speak about Germany's collective guilt, they talk about the responsibility of the German nation as such for the crimes committed by the Nazi regime in its name," according to Benjamin Sagalowitz in Wikipidia: "Kollektivschuld" (Collective Guilt). http://de.wikipedia.org/wiki/Kollektivschuld.
157 Ibid.
158 Jael Geis, Übrig sein – Leben ,danach'; *Juden deutscher Herkunft in der britischen und amerikanischen Zone 1945 – 1949* (Berlin: Philo, 2000), 290.
159 Pöhlmann, *Abriss der Dogmatik*, 190.
160 Ibid.
161 Lothar Coenen, Erich Beyreuther, and Hans Bietenhard, eds. *Theologisches Begriffslexikon zum Neuen Testament,* rev. ed., vol. 1 (Wuppertal: Brockhaus, 1983), 72.
162 Wolfram Kopfermann says this in *Prüfet alles und behaltet das Gute,* in www.wedeward.de/anskar (June 2000).
163 As quoted in *Apologia.*
164 Gen. 8:21; Job 14:4; 1Kings 8:46; Ps. 143:2; John 3:6; Rom. 3:9.20.23; Gal. 3:22;

1John 5:19; et al.

165 This is what the Church patriarch Augustinus said, who had grasped the depth of sin unlike any other. See also Pöhlmann, *Apologia*, 180.

166 Ibid.

167 Kathpedia, *Die freie katholische Enzyklopädie*, www.kathpedia.com.

168 Melanchthon, *Apologia*, 197.

169 I seriously doubt whether the recommended discourse with liberal theology actually has a corrective effect. See also Redling, *Stellvertretende Buße*, 29.

170 Matth. 6:23; 7:11.17-18; 12:34; 15,19; 16:4; 18:32; and others.

171 Mark 7:21-23; Eph. 6:16; Rev. 16:2.

172 Gesenius, *Hebräisches und Aramäisches Handwörterbuch*, 654.

173 See also: John Loren Sandford, *Healing for the Nations* (Grand Rapids: Chosen, 2000), 181.

174 This is what the theologian Stefan Haas pointed out to me, who contributed to the exegesis of Ezekiel 18.

175 Wolfhard Margies points this out in *Deutsches Geschichtsbuch*, 9.

176 Deut .19:10; Ps. 106:38; Ezek. 7:23; Hosea 6:8.

177 This is the conclusion of modern research; see also: *Zeit Geschichte*, Feb 2011, 56.

178 The Simon Wiesenthal Center has published a list of seven countries where Nazi war criminals have not been held responsible to this day. Lithuania, Estonia, and Latvia are also on this list. "Wiesenthal Center lobt Deutschland für Kriegsverbrecher-Prozesse", *Die Internetzeitung*, April 24, 2010. http://www.24pr.de/article/esenthal+Center+lobt+De utschland+fuer+Kriegsverbrecher+Prozesse/51894.htm

179 E-mail dated May 29th, 2011; see also www.tageschau.de on May 29th, 2011, *"Lettlands Präsident will vorgezogene Neuwahlen"*.

180 Lossau, "German Angst".

181 I am talking about the 1980s and 1990s here.

182 Shoah (Hebrew for destruction, calamity) denotes the preparations and implementation of the systematic genocide against approximately two thirds of the Jewish population of Europe (roughly six million deaths) through German National Socialism with the support of some allied regimes. See also: http://en.wikipedia.org/wiki/The_Holocaust.

183 See also: http://en.wikipedia.org/wiki/Kislev

184 Hebrew "shammash".

185 The Hasmoneans are the dynasty that founded an independent Jewish state after the Maccabean Revolt in 165 B.C. The kingdom lost its independence in 63 B.C.

186 Dr. Michael Rosenkranz, *Der Sieg über unsere geistige Auslöschung*, http://www.talmud. de/cms/Chanukah_Der_Sieg_ueber.170.0.html

187 Matth. 4:16; Luke 1:79; 22:53; John 3:19; Acts 26:18; Rom. 13:12; 2Cor. 6:14; Eph. 5:11; 1Thess. 5:4-5; 1Pet. 2:9; 1John 1:6.

188 Wolfhard Margies points this out in: Margies, *Deutsches Geschichtsbuch*, 9.

189 YHWH Tzevaot describes God as the One who is over the army of His people (1Sam. 17:45) and who is the commander over the hosts of angels (Josh. 5:14; Ps. 103:21).

190 Find an elaborate comment in Peter Zimmerling, *Die Charismatischen Bewegungen*, rev. ed. (Göttingen: Vandenhoeck & Ruprecht, 2003), 351ff.

191 Wolfram Kopfermann points this out in Kopfermann, *Prüfet alles*.

192 Cf. Lothar Coenen, and Klaus Hacker, *Theologisches Begriffslexikon zum Neuen Testament* (ThBL), vol. 1 (Wuppertal: Neukirchener, 1983), "skotos", 338.

193 John Mulinde, *Light or Darkness Over Europe: How Our Prayers Change the Nations*

(Seaford, UK: Pillars of Fire Trust, 2000), 36ff.

194 The Greek term "skotos" can mean both, and that has to kept in mind concerning the crucifixion: it is the natural phenomenon of a solar eclipse as well as the outward manifestation of the satanic world; cf. ThBL, "skotos", 338.

195 Joseph Ratzinger, Benedikt XVI., *Jesus von Nazareth* (Freiburg – Basel – Wien: Verlag Herder, 2006), 74.

196 Wladimir Solowjew, *Kurze Erzählung vom Antichrist* (Wewel: Sankt Ulrich Verlag, München, 1986).

197 Ratzinger, *Jesus von Nazareth*, 64.

198 Ibid., 200.

199 Bill Johnson, *When Heaven Invades Earth - A Practical Guide to a Life of Miracles* (Shippensburg, PA: Treasure House, an imprint of Destiny Image Publishers, 2005), 154.

200 Ibid., 155.

201 Cf. Friedrich Hauss, *Väter der Christenheit, Von den apostolischen Vätern bis zur Reformation,* vol. 1 (Wuppertal: Verlag Sonne und Schild, 1956), 75ff.

202 AMCHA is the National Center for Psycho-Social Support of Holocaust Survivors and the Second Generation in Israel.

203 Natan Kellermann, *The Long-term Psychological Effects and Treatment of Holocaust Trauma,* Trans. by Anna Jaitner, Journal of Loss and Trauma, 6:197-218, in http://peterfelix.tripod.com/home/Folgen.htm.

204 *Zeit Geschichte,* No 2, (2011), 55.

205 Hans-Peter Besteck, "Mein Großvater - ein Kriegsverbrecher?," in *Offensiv 22,* (2010), 17.

206 Stefan Haas, „Versöhnung in Bibra," in *Offensiv 21,* (2008).

207 M. Basilea Schlink, *Buße – glückseliges Leben* (Darmstadt/ Eberstadt: Evang. Marienschwesternschaft, 1965), 15.

208 Michael L. Brown, *What Do Jewish People Think About Jesus* (Grand Rapids, MI: Chosen Books, 2007), 258.

209 Ibid., 259-260.

210 Andrew McDonald, *The Turner Diaries* (New York: Barricade Books, 1996).

211 On July 31, 1938.

212 For all sources refer to: Wikipedia: "Henry Ford" http://en.wikipedia.org/wiki/Henry_Ford.

213 Jens Steiner, *Antisemitismus in US-Medien,* www.haGalil.com (August 9, 2005).

214 Maria Luiza Tucci Carneiro, *O Antisemitismo nas Americas* (EDUSP: São Paulo, 2008).

215 Steiner, *Antisemitismus.*

216 Georg Bönisch et al., "Der dunkle Kontinent," *Der Spiegel,* (May 18, 2009): 82.

217 Ibid., 86 f.

218 Daniel Blatman, *The Death Marches: The Final Phase of Nazi Genocide* (Belknap Press of Harvard University Press; Tra edition, 2010).

219 Ibid., 30.

220 Ibid., 421 ff. For anyone interested in a closer perpetrator profile, I recommend Blatman's Chapter 11: "The Murderers: Normal Citizens in Abnormal Situations."

221 Will King, "Tübingen Begs for Forgiveness," *Jerusalem Post,* (May 31, 2007).

222 GDR is the acronym for German Democratic Republic.

223 August 10, 2008.

224 Patrick Desbois, *Der vergessene Holocaust. Die Ermordung der ukrainischen Juden* (Berlin: Berlin Verlag, 2009), 7.

225 These are the words of the German ambassador to the Ukraine, Dietmar Stüdemann, in a foreword to the book *Nur wir haben überlebt - Holocaust in der Ukraine,* by Boris

Zabarko, Margret and Werner Müller eds., (Wittenberg: Dittrich Verlag e.K., 2004).

226 Desbois, *Der vergessene Holocaust*, 103.

227 It is rendered here in a slightly abridged form.